i·n·v·e·n·t·i·n·g
ENGLISH

From fairy tales and fables, poems and plays, comic strips and cartoons . . . fictional people, places, and concepts have left their mark on the English language. With this lively alphabetical reference, you can learn the origins of such words and expressions as...

- Everyman
- Faustian bargain
- Pickwickian
- Podsnappery
- the road less traveled
- sad sack
- salad days
- *and many more*

i·n·v·e·n·t·i·n·g
ENGLISH

*The Imaginative Origins of
Everyday Expressions*

DALE COREY

BERKLEY BOOKS, NEW YORK

"The Road Not Taken" and "Stopping By Woods on A Snowy Evening" From THE POETRY OF ROBERT FROST, edited by Edward Connery Lathem. Copyright 1944, 1951 by Robert Frost, copyright 1916, 1923, © 1969 by Henry Holt & Co., Inc. Reprinted by permission of Henry Holt & Co., Inc.

INVENTING ENGLISH

A Berkley Book / published by arrangement with the author

PRINTING HISTORY
Berkley edition / October 1997

All rights reserved.
Copyright © 1997 by Dale Corey.
Cover art copyright © by Tim Grajek/SIS.
Book design by Casey Hampton.
This book may not be reproduced in whole or in part, by mimeograph or any other means, without permission. For information address: The Berkley Publishing Group, a member of Penguin Putnam Inc., 200 Madison Avenue, New York, New York 10016.

The Putnam Berkley World Wide Web site address is http://www.berkley.com

ISBN: 0-425-15228-6

BERKLEY®
Berkley Books are published by The Berkley Publishing Group, a member of Penguin Putnam Inc., 200 Madison Avenue, New York, New York 10016. BERKLEY and the "B" design are trademarks belonging to Berkley Publishing Corporation.

PRINTED IN THE UNITED STATES OF AMERICA

10 9 8 7 6 5 4 3 2 1

In memory of
Jessica Johnson and Frank Melville,
who will live forever within my heart

ACKNOWLEDGMENTS

First, I would like to thank my agent, Regula Noetzli, and my editors at Berkley Books for their patience during a project that took much longer than expected to complete.

Thanks also to Lorri Bond and Charles Carney of Warner Bros. The information and direction provided to me by Mr. Carney proved to be invaluable for the preparation of the entry on Looney Tunes.

The staff of the Jervis Public Library in Rome, New York, provided me with invaluable help in locating many of the works required to write this book. Also, for sharing their professional expertise so willingly and cheerfully, my sincere thanks go to the staff of the Utica, New York, Public Library, particularly Bob Quist and Bob Lalli.

Most of all, I am grateful for the interest and moral support shown by all my coworkers and friends, especially Szilvia Szmuk and Toni and Andy Verkruysse. And, to Szilvia, an added thanks for her help with the entries from Spanish literature.

Finally, I would like to express my gratitude to Mr. Milton Novak, who, thirty-five years ago, directed me to the road less traveled by, and that really has made all the difference.

INTRODUCTION

We often call a mischievous child a *Dennis the Menace,* while one who never does anything wrong receives the epithet *Goody Two-shoes.* For centuries men who are in constant pursuit of the opposite sex have been referred to as *Don Juans, Lotharios,* or *Romeos.* American tabloids had a field day with the story of a promiscuous teenager they dubbed the *Long Island Lolita.* We refer to our long-lost youth as our *salad days,* say of intrusive governments that *Big Brother is watching,* and call social climbing *keeping up with the Joneses.* All of these are allusions to the products of man's imagination, which were first transferred to paper, and which now live on in our language.

From the Elizabethan stage to the Sunday funny papers, fictional people, places, and concepts have left their mark on the English language. Many of the words and expressions we use in everyday English were born in writers' imaginations. They first appeared in literary works: novels, short stories, poems, plays, essays, etc. Quite a few come from popular literature: fairy tales, fables, comic strips, and cartoons. During the twentieth century, as new communications media came into being, Hollywood screenwriters, as well as radio and television scriptwriters, came up with their own linguistic inventions, which have also been made a part of our language. In addition, many authors have been commemorated for their unique literary contributions by having new words formed from their names.

From all these sources, literary allusions abound. Fictional characters come to life over and over again in everyday speech. They have become archetypes or personifications of positive and negative character traits: We call the miser a *Scrooge,* the eternal child a *Peter Pan,* the mediocre man a *Babbitt,* and the hard taskmaster a *Simon Legree.* Someone who is perennially confused by the world around him or her is an *Alice in Wonderland;* one who possesses an active fantasy life is likened to *Walter Mitty.*

Many fictional places have also become linguistic symbols. Thomas More's *Utopia* and James Hilton's *Shangri-La* were imaginary lands of eternal harmony and pleasure; in modern English both have become metaphors for idyllic locales. Grace Metalious set her steamy novel of scandal and adultery in a small New England town called *Peyton Place,* now a synonym for a hotbed of covert sexual intrigue. Charles Dickens's fictional *Circumlocution Office* has lent its name to many real-life government bureaucracies, where the average citizen is thwarted by endless red tape and evasiveness.

Just as a picture is often worth a thousand words, so may be one literary reference. Very complex ideas can be conveyed by alluding to one image that is familiar to us from the printed page. Anyone who has read Aesop's fable, "The Fox and the Grapes," understands how the term *sour grapes* came to be a metaphor for a person's need to denigrate that which is denied him. In *The Merchant of Venice,* Shakespeare made *a pound of flesh* the guarantee for a loan; the literary image was so powerful, it was transformed into a figure of speech for the excessively high price often exacted in return for a favor. The feeling we get when we are overwhelmed by multiple, rapid changes is succinctly summed up in the term *Future Shock,* which is the title of Alvin Toffler's 1970 bestseller.

Authors occasionally invent their own words. Some of these have had so much appeal, or have been so colorful, that they caught on and are now in widespread use. Some examples of made-up words are: *robot,* created by Karel Čapek in his play *R.U.R.*; *chortle,* first used by Lewis Carroll in *Through the Looking-Glass*; and *blurb,* a word Gelett Burgess used on the jacket of his book *Are You a Bromide?* after he had introduced a new, figurative sense of the term *bromide* in that work.

Often, the creators of literary works have been immortalized by having words made out of their names. The political policies advocated by Niccolò Machiavelli in *The Prince* and other writings gave rise to the adjective *Machiavellian,* meaning manipulative and deceitful. In a lighter vein, readers of François Rabelais's lusty tales of *Gargantua and Pantagruel* created the adjective *Rabelaisian* to describe coarse, broad humor or satire. Franz Kafka wrote several novels, including *The Trial,* in which the hero was trapped in a nightmare of blind, inhuman bureaucracy; such an atmosphere is now routinely referred to as *Kafkaesque,* even by those who have never read the Austrian author's works.

Inventing English defines and tells the stories behind all these and many other words and phrases that were coined from the names of writers or from their literary creations. While it does not include every literary allusion in our language—that would require several volumes—it does cover the best-known and most interesting. You will recognize people, places, and objects from your favorite novels, comic strips, and television shows. Those of you who have only a vague memory of *Romeo and Juliet* or *David Copperfield,* having read them way back in high school or college, will have an opportunity to refresh your memory and broaden your knowledge of literary classics while expanding your vocabulary. Most of all, you will be amazed to learn how many of the expressions you use in everyday conversation come from works of fiction.

—DALE COREY

inventing ENGLISH

Aladdin's lamp: any source of instant wealth and good fortune

Something that brings unexpected wealth or good fortune to its owner, such as a lottery ticket that contains winning numbers or a stock that doubles in value overnight, may be referred to as an *Aladdin's lamp*. The allusion is, of course, to one of the stories that is found in *The Arabian Nights' Entertainments*.

"Aladdin and the Wonderful Lamp" begins when an evil magician tricks a poor young man named Aladdin into going into a cave to get a magic lamp for him. When Aladdin refuses to hand the lamp to the magician until he is out of the cave, the trickster becomes furious and slams a stone down on the entrance. Aladdin has no idea how he is going to get out until he accidentally rubs a ring that was given to him by the magician. A genie appears, saying, "I am the slave of the ring and will obey thee in all things."

The genie grants Aladdin's request that he deliver him from the cave.

Back home, Aladdin is making plans to sell the lamp when his mother begins rubbing it to get the dirt off. Another genie appears and asks her what she would like. From that moment on, Aladdin and his mother want for nothing. Whenever they desire food, the genie serves it to them on silver plates, which they then sell. All goes well until Aladdin falls in love with the daughter of the sultan and, with the help of the genie, marries her. When the evil magician finds out that Aladdin did not perish in the cave, he goes to his palace and tricks Aladdin's wife into giving him the lamp. He then transports the palace and the princess to Africa.

The genie of the ring helps Aladdin to find his palace and his wife, and Aladdin avenges himself, killing the magician and taking possession of the lamp once again. Aladdin is then warned by the genie that the brother of the magician intends to kill him, and he stabs the man while he is impersonating a holy woman. Aladdin, his princess, and the genies live happily ever after.

The Arabian Nights' Entertainments or *A Thousand and One Nights*, as it is also called, is a collection of ancient Persian-Indian-Arabian tales. No one can say for sure when the tales originated, but it was around 1450 that they were arranged and written down in the form in which we have come to know them. At that time they were unified by the introduction of the supposed storyteller, Scheherazade. Married to the cruel

Schahriah, who kills each of his wives after one night of marriage, she manages to postpone her execution by beginning a new tale each night and only telling her husband the ending the following night. After a thousand and one nights, Schahriah rescinds his execution order and the two live happily ever after.

Antoine Galland was the first to bring the tales to Europe, translating them into French between 1704 and 1717. His twelve-volume work was based on the oldest known manuscript, which dates from 1548, but he omitted the verse portions and those details he didn't feel would be of interest to European readers. Edward William Lane published a three-volume English translation in 1840; this was followed by John Payne's nine volumes (1882–84) and Sir Richard Burton's scholarly ten-volume annotated edition (1885–86).

In 1898, Scottish scholar Andrew Lang selected those stories in Galland's French version that he felt would appeal most to children and translated them into English with the younger audience in mind. Lang's work introduced generations of English and American youngsters to the magical world of *Arabian Nights*.

alarums and excursions: skirmishing, confused fighting; sudden rushing to and fro

In several of Shakespeare's plays, including *Richard III* and *Henry VI*, fighting occurs offstage. This was indicated in the playwright's stage directions by the phrase *alarums and excursions.*

The word *alarum* is an archaic form of our modern *alarm,* which originally meant a call to arms. An *excursion* was a military term meaning a sortie or sally against an enemy. Where these stage directions appeared, actors behind the scenes simulated the noise of battle, including the sound of trumpets and the clash of arms. The resulting din gave the impression of a surprise attack, with sudden, confused fighting starting up out of nowhere.

We borrowed the stage directions alarums and excursions from Shakespeare, and now apply them to any scene of skirmishing or confused activity, where people are rushing around helter-skelter, as though they had just been victims of a surprise attack.

Alice in Wonderland: someone who is perpetually confused/amazed by the world around them; someone newly arrived in strange surroundings

Alice was spending an ordinary afternoon with her sister, sitting on a riverbank and thinking about making a daisy chain, when a white rabbit ran past her. She didn't think it "so very much out of the way" when she heard it talking to itself, but seeing it take a watch out of its waistcoat pocket piqued her curiosity. She followed it down a rabbit hole and thus began her adventures in Wonderland.

It wasn't long before "so many out-of-the-way things had happened . . . that Alice had begun to think that very few things indeed were really impossible." In fact, Wonderland turned out to be a place where all kinds of irregular things happened with regularity; "curioser and curioser" was the only way in which Alice could describe her experiences in this topsy-turvy world.

First, she found that by eating, drinking, or simply fanning herself she alternately grew and shrank alarmingly. She then discovered that the rabbit was not the only creature that talked to itself: All the birds and animals in Wonderland had the power of speech—one mouse even understood French! Unfortunately, most of what they had to say made little or no sense. Time after time, Alice found herself talking at cross-purposes or going around in circles, trying to make herself understood.

Those of us who read *Alice's Adventures in Wonderland* as children have never forgotten the hookah-smoking caterpillar, the grinning Cheshire-Cat, the Duchess and her pig-baby, the tea party of the Mad Hatter and the March Hare, and the Queen who played croquet using flamingos and hedgehogs. The outlandish cast of characters and the absurdity of the situations in Wonderland are what make Lewis Carroll's story so memorable to readers of all ages. And Alice's reactions—amazement, disbelief, frustration, confusion—are what made the term *Alice in Wonder-*

land a popular way of referring to a person who always seems confused and baffled by the world. We also use the term to describe a person who suddenly finds himself or herself in new surroundings and has trouble adjusting.

Reverend Charles Lutwidge Dodgson was a mathematician and logician as well as an ordained deacon of the Church of England. Under his real name he published works such as *A Syllabus of Plane Algebraical Geometry* and *Euclid and His Modern Rivals*. On July 4, 1862, he went boating with his friend Canon Duckworth and the three daughters of Dean Liddell of Christ Church. To amuse ten-year-old Alice Liddell during the excursion, Dodgson invented the story of *Alice's Adventures Under Ground*. He later wrote it down for her and illustrated it himself. Convinced by friends to publish the story, he revised and enlarged the manuscript and engaged Sir John Tenniel to do the illustrations. *Alice in Wonderland* was published by Macmillan in 1865, and Dodgson employed the pseudonym Lewis Carroll. Carroll's second children's classic, *Through the Looking-Glass*, was also written for Alice Liddell and was published in 1872.

See also: **(grin like a) Cheshire cat, mad as a hatter/mad as a March Hare, mad tea party.**

All quiet on the Western Front: everything's okay, there are no problems

He fell in October 1918, on a day that was so quiet and still on the whole front, that the army report confined itself to the single sentence: All quiet on the Western Front.

The fact that the death of Erich Maria Remarque's young hero took place only weeks before World War I came to an end is not what makes *All Quiet on the Western Front* a tragedy. The tragedy is that he had to die at all. Remarque's novel is a powerful condemnation of a war that took the lives of many of the young men who were sent to fight it. Those who escaped death had to live with an even greater tragedy: the fact that they had left their youth and their souls on the Western Front, never to be found again.

From Germany's point of view, the Western Front was its border with France. It was there that Remarque's hero arrived at the tender age of twenty, and it was there that he wrote of the effect the war had on him and his young friends:

The war swept us away.... We ... have been gripped by it and do not know what the end may be. We know only that in some strange and melancholy way we have become a waste land.

The young soldier goes on to explain that it wasn't always so; when he and his friends enlisted they were enthusiastic, fired by the idea of defending their country. Then, after ten weeks of boot camp, the reality of war replaced their vague ideas. They learned to live with cold, hunger, fatigue and—most of all—death. You can never be the same after you spend a night in a trench, watching the man next to you die in agony. And, when your best friend is blown into a hundred pieces in front of your eyes, something inside you dies, even though you survive the battle.

The extent of his loss and isolation are most apparent to the young soldier when he goes home on leave for the last time. He had imagined that returning home would be comforting. But he has changed. Once home, he finds that he does not belong there any more. Home feels like a foreign world.

Back at the front, the fighting intensifies and the number of dead and wounded keeps rising. Remarque speaks, through his hero, of the injustice of the war: The factory owners in Germany have gotten rich, while the soldiers at the front are dying of starvation and dysentery. The barrels of their guns are so worn out that the shells they fire—when they have shells—fall on them instead of the enemy. They haven't got enough horses. The troops that come to back them up are poorly trained, tired, and ill.

Shortly before his death the young soldier thinks about the future. He knows the armistice is coming soon, and he will go home at last. But to what?

Had we returned home in 1916 . . . we might have unleashed a storm. Now if we go back we will . . . not be able to find our way anymore.

It is obvious that Remarque believed that his hero was one of the lucky ones. He tells us that when the young man's body was turned over the expression on his face was calm, as though he were glad that his ordeal had ended. For others, like Remarque himself, there would never be an end to the war and the devastation it caused.

Erich Maria Remarque was born in 1898 and was nearly the same age as his hero when he fought in World War I. He wrote the semiautobiographical *All Quiet on the Western Front* in 1929 and was widely criticized in Germany for his "unpatriotic" depiction of World War I. He left Nazi Germany in 1932, moving first to Switzerland and then to the United States. After World War II he returned to Switzerland, where he lived until his death in 1970. Ironically, the title of his best-known novel is now another way of saying "everything's okay, there are no problems."

Archie Bunker: a bigot

In America, if you called someone an Alf Garnett, no one would have any idea what you meant. If, however, you said the person was an *Archie Bunker*, it would be readily understood that you were calling him a bigot.

Both Alf and Archie were white, Anglo-Saxon Protestants who blamed most of society's ills on minority groups. Alf came first, when British writer

Johnny Speight created the situation comedy *Till Death Us Do Part*. A tremendous hit in the United Kingdom, it ran on the BBC from 1964 to 1974. In 1971, American producer Norman Lear brought the series to American television: Alf moved from London, England, to Queens, New York, where he became Archie. His long-suffering wife Else was renamed Edith, and the rest is television—and linguistic—history.

Played by Carroll O'Connor, Archie Bunker was a loudmouthed bigot who spent much of each episode hurling racial and religious insults. He was prejudiced against anyone who was not a fellow WASP: Hispanics were "spics," Orientals "gooks," and Italians "wops." Naturally, he had a wide variety of derogatory epithets that he used to refer to Blacks. Giving equal time to all, he often railed against money-hungry "kikes," and he had absolutely no use for those who believed in the infallibility of the Pope. His own son-in-law, who was of Polish extraction, was always called "the meathead" by Archie and was the butt of many Polish jokes. "Queers" and "fairies" were a group to be feared and avoided; women, unfortunately, were a necessary evil; if the "dingbats" stayed in their place they could be tolerated.

After *All in the Family* was canceled in 1979, Archie continued to deliver his weekly diatribes as the owner of a bar called Archie Bunker's Place. That series ended in 1983, but Archie lives on as the stereotype of an ignorant, bigoted person who hates and fears anyone who is not exactly like him.

artful dodger: a thief or con artist

Oliver Twist was written by Charles Dickens in 1838. It is the story of a boy whose mother dies after giving birth to him in one of the workhouses that were common in England during the nineteenth century. At an early age Oliver is apprenticed to an undertaker, in whose service he is abused and taunted. He runs away, headed for London, and on the road he meets a boy who is about the same age as he, but

> *one of the queerest looking boys that Oliver had ever seen. He was a snub-nosed, flat-browed, common-faced boy enough, and as dirty a juvenile as one would wish to see, but he had about him all the airs and manners of a man. He was short of his age, with rather bow-legs, and little, sharp, ugly eyes. His hat was stuck on the top of his head so lightly that it threatened to fall off every moment. . . . He wore a man's coat, which reached nearly to his heels. He had turned the cuffs back, half-way up his arm, to get his hands out of the sleeves. . . . He was, alto-gether, as roystering and swaggering a young gen-tleman as ever stood four feet six, or something less. . . .*

The boy's name is Jack Dawkins, and he provides Oliver with his first meal in a week. He also tells Oliver that his nickname is "the artful Dodger" and offers him lodging with an elderly gentleman who lives in London.

Oliver follows Dawkins to a run-down house, where a group of young boys are sitting, smoking and drinking, in the company of an old, dirty man named Fagin. Oliver soon learns that the children are a gang of pickpockets, and Fagin is their leader. He also learns that Jack Dawkins earned his nickname from his ability to hit and run: picking the pocket of an unsuspecting mark, then getting lost in the crowd before the theft is even noticed. As a result of the popularity of *Oliver Twist*, the name *artful dodger* became a synonym for a street thief or a con artist.

After many adventures among London's criminal elements, including his arrest and his kidnapping by Fagin's gang, Oliver is revealed to be the illegitimate son of one Edward Leeford, a well-to-do gentleman. Leeford's legitimate son has been behind a plot to keep Oliver under the influence of Fagin and away from his rightful inheritance. At the end of the novel Oliver receives his share, is adopted by a professional man, and continues his education.

Despite its happy ending, *Oliver Twist* is a grim tale. In it Dickens accurately depicts the life of the poor in nineteenth-century England. The book was written shortly after the enactment of the new Poor Law of 1834 and is an open indictment of it. The law ended the supplemental dole to the poor and forced husbands, wives, and children into separate workhouses, where they slowly starved to death. Many of those who managed to evade the workhouses were

forced into a life of crime in order to survive. Like
the pickpockets in Fagin's gang, with no place else
to turn, many youngsters were victimized by hardened
criminals.

See also: **Dickensian.**

(have an) ax to grind: have a selfish motive
or a personal interest

There is an old story about a man who wanted to get
his ax ground, or sharpened, but was too lazy to do
it himself. Seeing a young boy near a grindstone, the
man approached and asked the boy to show him how
it worked, giving him his own ax on which to dem-
onstrate. As the boy proudly showed off his skill, the
man continued to praise him until the ax was as sharp
as could be. He then took the sharpened ax, laughing
at the boy for his gullibility, and disappeared.

This story gave rise to the popular expression *have
an ax to grind,* meaning have some selfish motive or
personal interest in a situation. Someone with an ax
to grind is determined to pursue his or her own
agenda and isn't going to let anyone else's interests
get in the way.

Nineteenth-century journalist Charles Miner, who
used the alias Poor Robert, was the author of the
story. It first appeared in the Luzerne, Pennsylvania,
Federalist on September 7, 1810, with the title
"Who'll Turn Grindstones?" In 1815, it was repub-

lished in *Essays from the Desk of Poor Robert the Scribe*. Because of the similarity between the names Poor Robert and Poor Richard, Benjamin Franklin, who went by the latter, has often been given credit for the story.

Babbitt: a smug, middle-class conformist

Babbitt, Sinclair Lewis's award-winning 1922 novel, takes place in 1920, in the mythical American city of Zenith. The title character, George Follansbee Babbitt, is a forty-six-year-old, middle-class man who sells real estate for a living. Everything about him seems materialistic, dull, and unromantic. But often, when he sleeps, he dreams of "the fairy child": a beautiful young girl who tells him he is handsome and gallant and is willing to sail away with him wherever he chooses to go.

These recurring dreams are not the only indication that George F. Babbitt is less than satisfied with his life. He realizes that he hates selling real estate, he dislikes his family, and he dislikes himself for disliking them. He is often cranky, irritable, and tired. Sometimes he'd like to quit what he views as nothing but a game.

Babbitt confesses to one of his friends, Paul Riesling, that he isn't entirely satisfied with his life. Riesling tells Babbitt that he's not satisfied either, and he doesn't believe many men are:

Take all these fellows we know . . . one-third of 'em are miserable and know it. . . . Why do you suppose there's so many "mysterious" suicides?

Babbitt argues with Riesling that it isn't so, but deep inside he knows it is.

When Babbitt meets Mrs. Tanis Judique, an attractive widow, the die is cast. He enters into a clandestine affair with her and becomes part of her social set, the Bunch. When his wife goes out of town for a few weeks, he spends the time carousing with Tanis and his liberal neighbors, the Doppelbraus. Babbitt throws himself into an orgy of dancing and drinking, and throws discretion to the wind. At the same time, he begins voicing liberal opinions in the company of his conservative friends. Before long the whole town is talking about the change that has come over George Babbitt.

George begins to feel the ostracism of his former friends, when they stop including him in their activities and begin whispering about him behind his back. When they form a Good Citizens' League and don't invite him to join, Babbitt knows his foolish fling has been his undoing. He gives up Tanis Judique, swears fidelity to his wife, and stops espousing his liberal views. He knows he is back in favor when he is finally made a member of the Good Citizens' League.

His brief flirtation with freedom and liberalism over, Babbitt returns to the security of conformity and conservatism. The success of Lewis's satirical portrait of a middle-class conformist led to the common use of the name *Babbitt* as a sobriquet for a certain type of American who continues to exist today.

But Sinclair Lewis added a twist to the ending of *Babbitt*, which reveals to the reader that, while he may have suppressed his urge to break out of the bonds of conformity, there is still something of the rebel in George Follansbee Babbitt.

When Babbitt's son, Ted, elopes with his girlfriend, everyone in both families is irate and wants the marriage annulled. Everyone but George, that is. To Ted's surprise, his father takes him aside and tells him:

I've never done a single thing I've wanted to in my whole life! . . . Maybe you'll carry things on further . . . those folks in there will try to bully you, and tame you down. Tell 'em to go to the devil! I'll back you. . . . Don't be scared of the family. No, nor all of Zenith. Nor of yourself, the way I've been. Go ahead, old man! The world is yours!

bad seed: an incorrigible child, a delinquent

We use the expression *bad seed* when we are talking about a child who is simply incorrigible. Getting him or her to behave is such an impossible task that we can't help but think there is something congenitally wrong. The epithet was first applied by William March to a little girl named Rhoda Penmark, in his 1954 novel *The Bad Seed*. The book was turned into a play by Maxwell Anderson, and it was the long, successful run of that play that made the expression *bad seed* a popular phrase in the American lexicon.

Playwright Maxwell Anderson was born in 1888 and reached the height of his fame during the 1930s and 1940s, when many regarded his work as superior to that of Eugene O'Neill. Anderson wrote a series of successful historical dramas: *Elizabeth the Queen, Mary of Scotland*, and *Valley Forge*. These were followed by *Night Over Taos, Both Your Houses, High Tor, Knickerbocker Holiday*, and *Key Largo*, all of which were written during the thirties.

After concentrating on political themes during World War II, Anderson resumed his historical writing with *Joan of Lorraine, Anne of the Thousand Days*, and *Barefoot in Athens*. These were about Joan of Arc, Henry VIII and Anne Boleyn, and Socrates, respectively, and all three were well received by the critics and public alike.

By 1954 Maxwell Anderson was experiencing serious problems with his health. He was suffering from a diaphragmatic hernia, which was pressing against his heart and causing frightening symptoms. His kidneys were also beginning to fail due to prostate trouble. Before the hernia could be repaired Anderson had to undergo prostate surgery, and he checked into Cedars of Lebanon Hospital on July 8. After the operation Maxwell became despondent, fearing that he would never again write a successful play.

In order to lift her husband's spirits, Gilda Anderson brought a copy of March's novel to her husband in the hospital. Anderson read the story of an eight-year-old girl who, while appearing to be a model child, has inherited a genetic propensity for evil that leads her to kill three people. At the end of the story she gets away with the murders, and the reader is left wondering whether or not she will kill again.

Anderson found the novel fascinating, and a few days after his release from the hospital he began to turn it into a screenplay. By August 15 he had completed his final draft. *The Bad Seed* was cast soon after, with young Patty McCormack in the starring role. The other actors included Nancy Kelly, Henry Jones, and Eileen Heckart. *The Bad Seed* opened on Broadway on December 8, 1954, and enjoyed a long and profitable run.

Maxwell Anderson died in 1959. *The Bad Seed* was his last commercially successful play and the only one of his works to make a lasting contribution to our language.

Banquo's Ghost: someone who seems to appear out of thin air

At the beginning of William Shakespeare's *Macbeth*, Macbeth and his friend Banquo encounter the three witches and listen to their prophecies. They tell Macbeth that he will be king; they tell Banquo that he will be lesser than Macbeth, and greater, for he will not be king himself, but he will beget kings.

Macbeth makes the first part of the prophecy reality by murdering King Duncan. The king's son flees the country, and Macbeth is crowned king. Then, in order to prevent the rest of the witches' words from ever becoming reality, he arranges to have Banquo and his son murdered.

It is right after Macbeth receives the news that Banquo has been killed and his son has escaped, that his conscience begins to get the better of him. When the hired assassin departs and Macbeth tries to take his seat in the banquet hall, he sees the ghost of Banquo sitting in his place. No one else can see it, of course, and Lady Macbeth tries to explain away her husband's hysteria by saying that he has suffered from a nervous ailment since his youth. When the ghost disappears as suddenly as it came, Macbeth recovers his wits and begins to make a toast to the dead Banquo. As he raises his glass the ghost reappears, and he begins shouting at it until it vanishes once again.

Banquo's ghost appears to Macbeth once more during the play, in Act IV, when the three witches conjure up his image and those of eight of his de-

scendants who will one day become kings of Scotland. But it is Shakespeare's banquet scene, in which
the ghost materializes and dematerializes twice in
rapid succession, which made *Banquo's Ghost* a synonym for someone who seems to appear out of thin
air.

Bates Motel: a seedy, run-down hotel or motel

"Oh, no. It's the Bates Motel!" If you've ever arrived
at a hotel or motel where you made reservations sight
unseen, you may have uttered these words of dismay.
Since the success of Alfred Hitchcock's 1960 movie,
Psycho, the *Bates Motel* has become a common synonym for a seedy, run-down resting place that gets
very little business.

The original Bates Motel was run by Norman
Bates, a disturbed young man who believed he was
his own mother. Bates and the out-of-the-way motel
that he operated were the literary creations of Robert
Bloch in his 1959 novel, *Psycho*. The novel is all but
forgotten today, but the movie has become a horror
classic and continues to be shown on television and
in theaters.

In Hitchcock's production, the role of Norman
Bates was played by Anthony Perkins. The young
woman who has the misfortune to register at the Bates
Motel and is stabbed by Norman in the famous
shower scene was played by Janet Leigh.

In 1982, Robert Bloch wrote a sequel entitled *Psycho 2*, in which, twenty years after being committed to a hospital for the criminally insane, Norman Bates escapes and begins killing again. Anthony Perkins reprised the role in the 1983 film of *Psycho 2*, which was directed by Richard Franklin, and in *Psycho 3*, which he himself directed in 1986.

beatniks/beat generation: unconventional young people of the 1950s and 1960s, given to radical social criticism

Jack Kerouac saw only good in the works of the generation of artists and writers that came of age in the 1950s: He was so convinced of the purity of their message that he called them *beatific:* blessed, holy, saintly. The epithet, shortened to *beat,* was soon being applied to all who rejected middle-class life and values in favor of a freer, more tolerant, and less materialistic lifestyle.

The term *beat generation* first appeared in John Clellon Holmes's novel *GO*, where the author used it to describe a group of American writers that included, on the East Coast, Kerouac, Allen Ginsberg, Gregory Corso, and William Burroughs and, on the West Coast, Gary Snyder, Lawrence Ferlinghetti, Kenneth Rexroth, and Michael McClure. All of these rebels wrote openly of their experiments with drugs and sex and their iconoclastic views of religion and politics. Their three most sensational and best-known works were Kerouac's *On the Road*, Ginsberg's *Howl*, and Burroughs's *Naked Lunch*.

By the beginning of the 1960s, self-proclaimed beatniks were to be found in both the U.S. and the U.K. They were mostly young people, although the movement did attract a fair number of disillusioned middle-agers. They espoused the doctrines of pacifism, free love, and communal living. Interestingly enough, by the end of the 1970s much of what they preached was no longer considered way out. Today, respected theologians, scientists, and politicians have taken up the causes of the beats: the preservation of the environment, the elimination of the threat of nuclear war, and the movement away from materialism and technology and toward spirituality.

Beatrice and Benedick: *See* Benedick.

Beauty and the Beast: an attractive woman in the company of a homely or uncouth man

The theme of a beautiful woman romantically involved with a beast or monster is found in the folk literature of many countries. As far back as 1550, the *Piacevoli Notti* of Straparola included the story of a pig prince: a king's son who had to marry three women in order to break the spell that kept him in the body of a swine. Another collection of stories from Italy, the *Pentamerone* of 1634, contains the tale of a monster who insists on marrying a beautiful princess. But the best-known of these horrifying tales is that of "Beauty and the Beast," which was popularized by Madame Leprince de Beaumont. She published the story in 1756, as part of her *Magasin des enfants, ou dialogues entre une sage Gouvernante et plusieurs de ses Élèves*. The work was translated into English in 1761, with the title *The Young Misses Magazine*.

It is this version that is familiar to nearly all English and American children. In it, Beauty is the youngest daughter of a merchant who loses his fortune. Her spiritual aspect is as lovely as her physical person, and she quickly adapts to life without riches. When her father makes a journey into town, her sisters ask him to bring them gowns, hats, and all kinds of expensive adornments. Beauty is so disinterested in material things that all she asks for is a rose.

On the way home the merchant becomes lost and seeks shelter in an empty home. There he finds oats for his horse, food for himself, and a warm bed in which he spends the night. Just as he is about to depart for home, he sees some lovely roses and picks one for Beauty. Suddenly a frightful Beast appears and berates him for stealing the rose. The merchant tries to explain that he meant no harm, but the Beast will not be placated and declares that he must die for his offense, unless he is willing to give one of his daughters to the Beast instead. Hoping to see his children once more before he dies, the merchant lies, agreeing to send back one of his daughters, and sets forth for home.

When Beauty hears his story, she insists on exchanging her life for her father's and goes to the Beast's home, expecting to be killed. To her surprise, the Beast does not kill her, but treats her with kindness and respect and asks her to be his wife. For months the Beast repeats his request each night and each night she refuses, although she has grown quite fond of him.

After several months, the Beast consents to allow Beauty to visit her family, and she promises to return within one week. But her evil sisters convince her to stay longer, hoping that the Beast will become enraged and kill her. By the tenth day Beauty is consumed with guilt; moreover, she realizes that she loves the Beast and misses him: "It is neither wit, nor a fine person, in a husband, that makes a woman happy, but virtue, sweetness of temper, and complaisance, and Beast has all these valuable qualifications."

Returning to his palace just in time to save him from dying of a broken heart, Beauty tells the Beast she loves him and wants to be his wife. The Beast disappears and in his place Beauty sees "one of the loveliest princes that eye ever beheld." The prince explains that a wicked fairy had put a spell on him; it could not be broken until a beautiful virgin consented to marry him. And, of course, Beauty and her prince live happily ever after.

The fairy tale became so well-known in English-speaking countries that to this day when we see an attractive woman with a homely or uncouth man, we are apt to refer to them as *Beauty and the Beast*.

The story has also been the inspiration for several poems, pantomimes, and theatrical productions. In the 1980s it was adapted for television and became a hit series: Beauty was a young woman living in New York City, and the Beast—a lionlike creature named Vincent—lived in the tunnels that ran beneath the concrete jungle. An animated version of the tale was filmed by Walt Disney Productions and it, too, enjoyed immense popularity.

belling the cat: risking oneself for the good of others

The Vision of William Concerning Piers Plowman is a moral and social satire that uses an allegorical vision to make its points. Commonly referred to simply as *Piers Plowman*, the poem is written in Middle English and attributed to a contemporary of Chaucer, William Langland or Langley. Three different versions of the poem, all dating from the second half of the fourteenth century, have been found, and the consensus among scholars is that they are the work of several different writers.

Although they differ in their details, all of the versions begin with a dream that the poet has after falling asleep in the countryside. He sees the dwelling places of God and the Devil, and the world of the living that exists between them. He sees all kinds of people, from all social and economic classes, with all their vices and virtues. Some of them would like to find the way to salvation but do not know how to do so. A young plowman named Piers arrives and offers to show them the way if they will help him plow his field. Their varying reactions show who is willing to work for salvation and who expects it to be handed to him on a silver platter.

During the poet's vision, a fable is told: An old mouse suggests to his fellow mice that the best way to warn them all of approaching danger would be to hang a bell around the neck of the cat who stalks them. All agree that the idea is an excellent one, but one young mouse is intelligent enough to see the drawback. "Who," asks the youngster, "is going to undertake the job?"

Since then, the question, "Who'll bell the cat?" has been a popular way of asking, "Who'll be the one to take the risk for everyone else?" And *belling the cat* refers to taking great personal risk to benefit one's friends or neighbors.

Benedick: a confirmed bachelor; a newly married man who has long been a bachelor

In Act I, Scene I of William Shakespeare's *Much Ado About Nothing*, a character named Benedick laments his friend Claudio's desire to marry:

> *Is't come to this? In faith, hath not the world one*
> *man but he will wear his cap with suspicion? Shall*
> *I never see a bachelor of three score again? Go to,*
> *i'faith; an thou wilt needs thrust thy neck into a yoke,*
> *wear the print of it, and sign away Sundays . . .*

In Scene II, Benedick delivers another impassioned speech against marriage and declares that he will live his life to the end as a bachelor. It is chiefly due to these scenes, and to the verbal sparring matches in which he engages with Beatrice, that Benedick's name has become a popular term for a confirmed bachelor.

The second meaning that the name Benedick now carries in English is that of a newly married man who has long been a bachelor. This seemingly contradictory sense comes from Benedick's complete change of heart, which causes him to fall in love with, and marry, Beatrice at the end of the play.

When they first appear on stage together, we are immediately aware that Beatrice and Benedick love each other, in spite of their protestations to the contrary. There is too much passion in their mutual taunting and they are far too preoccupied with one another to be uninvolved emotionally. Knowing this, their friends contrive to trick them into falling in love or, rather, admitting their love for one another. The plot succeeds, and Benedick cheerfully admits he was wrong:

> *. . . since I purpose to marry, I will think nothing to*
> *any purpose that the world can say against it; and*

*therefore never flout at me for what I have said
against it, for man is a giddy thing, and this is my
conclusion.*

For many years *Much Ado About Nothing* was better known by the title *Beatrice and Benedick*, and the
fictional couple became so popular that we still in-
voke their names when referring to a couple who
show their affection for one another by trading quips
and insults.
See also: **much ado about nothing.**

beware of Greeks bearing gifts: watch out
for people with hidden motives

"Timeo Danaos et dona ferentes" ("I fear the
Greeks, even when they offer gifts"), warns the Trojan priest Laocoön in Book II of Virgil's *Aeneid.* He
was referring to the huge wooden horse left behind
by the Greeks when they apparently gave up the siege
of Troy. His countrymen, however, refused to be
guided by his forebodings or by those of the prophetess Cassandra.
The Trojans were convinced by Sinon, the one
Greek who remained behind, that the last thing their
enemies wanted them to do was take the horse into
their walled city. The Greek experiment in reverse
psychology succeeded, and the Trojans opened the
gates and rolled the horse inside. Later that night, as

the Trojans slept, armed Greeks crept out of the horse's belly and rushed through the city, delivering their real gift: death.

Virgil's famous phrase has been used for centuries to point out that people are not always what they seem and that behind their good deeds often lie evil motives.

See also: **Trojan horse.**

Big Brother is watching: those in authority are monitoring our actions

As George Orwell's novel *1984* begins, Winston Smith is arriving home from work. In the lobby and on each landing in the stairway of his apartment building there are giant posters on the walls. The posters depict an enormous face, more than a meter wide. The face is that of a man of about forty-five, with a heavy black mustache. Under the face is the caption "BIG BROTHER IS WATCHING YOU."

The posters are everywhere in the country of Oceania, where Smith lives, and they mean what they say. Inside Smith's apartment there is an oblong metal plaque called a telescreen that receives and transmits sounds and images simultaneously. Propagandistic messages are constantly being sent into homes, offices, and all other buildings in the country. At the same time, the Thought Police maintain surveillance through the telescreens:

Any sound that Winston made, above the level of a very low whisper, would be picked up by it; moreover, so long as he remained within the field of vision which the metal plaque commanded, he could be seen as well as heard. There was of course no way of knowing whether you were being watched at any given moment. . . . You had to live, did live, from habit that became instinct—in the assumption that every sound you made was overheard, and, except in darkness, every movement scrutinized.

The depiction of this police state was Orwell's way of warning us, in the middle of the twentieth century, of the dangers of totalitarianism. In fact, Orwell, an independent socialist and staunch anti-Communist, once said that all his writings were directed against totalitarianism in all forms.

Orwell's two best-known novels, *1984* and *Animal Farm*, both depict societies in which the freedom of the individual has been usurped by the state. *Animal Farm* is a satire on the Russian Revolution and the leadership of Stalin. In it, the farm animals decide to revolt against the farmer and declare their freedom. But their leaders, the pigs, soon subject them to far worse servitude than they ever experienced when human beings were running the farm. *1984* tells the story of Winston Smith, who, when his individualistic leanings are discovered, is subjected to a complete brainwashing, or "reintegration," in order to bring him back into the fold with the other docile, sheeplike citizens of Oceania.

Since the publication of *1984* in 1949, the expression *Big Brother is watching* has become another way of saying that government is intruding into our lives, interfering in affairs that ought to be private. By extension, the phrase is sometimes used by employees to describe a work environment in which their actions are closely monitored by their supervisors.

See also: **Orwellian.**

bionic man/woman: someone with superhuman strength or stamina

Two television series of the 1970s, *The Six Million Dollar Man* and *The Bionic Woman*, were so popular that they gave us the terms *bionic man* and *bionic woman* to refer to people who have greater than normal strength or stamina.

The first series, starring Lee Majors as Captain Steve Austin, aired from 1973 to 1978. Austin is a test pilot who suffers massive injuries when his plane crashes. The government proceeds to invest six million dollars in his reconstruction, giving him several new, improved parts. Part man, part machine, Austin possesses incredible physical powers that he and the government use to pursue and capture evildoers.

Lindsay Wagner starred in *The Bionic Woman* from 1976 to 1978. Her series was a spin-off from *The Six Million Dollar Man* and was based on the same premise. Wagner's character, Jaime Sommers, is also re-

built after an accident, and her superhuman powers
are put to use by the U.S. government to capture spies
and other villains.

Bionic man Steve Austin was created by Martin
Caidin in his 1972 novel, *Cyborg*. The concept of
enhancing a person's hearing, sight, speed, strength,
etc. with state-of-the-art mechanical and electronic
devices immediately captured the imagination of television producers and writers, and just one year later,
The Six Million Dollar Man was born. Caidin produced several sequels to his first book—*Operation
Nuke* (1973), *High Crystal* (1974), and *Cyborg IV*
(1975)—but none had the impact of the original.

Bluebeard: a man who plans the death of his spouse(s)

Charles Perrault wrote down the story of "La barbe
bleue," or "Bluebeard" in his *Histoires ou contes du
temps passé*, which was published in 1697. The first
English translation of Perrault's work was Robert
Samber's *Histories, or Tales of Past Times*, which
appeared in 1729.

The title character of "The Blue Beard" had "the
misfortune to have a Blue Beard, which made him so
frightfully ugly that all the women and girls ran away
from him." Adding to their reluctance was the fact
that "he had already been marry'd to several wives,
and no body ever knew what were become of them."

In order to win the hand of a certain young lady, Blue Beard entertained her, her friends, and her family at one of his country estates. After eight days of lavish entertainment and hospitality, the young lady was won over and consented to marry Blue Beard in spite of his appearance. Shortly after their marriage, Blue Beard told his wife that he was going on a trip and was going to leave the keys to all his apartments and treasure chests with her. But she was not to use one key: that which opened the door to a little closet on the ground floor of the house.

Of course, no sooner did Blue Beard set out than his wife opened the closet where, to her horror, she found the bloody bodies of the wives he had married and murdered, one after another. She quickly locked the closet, but some blood fell on the key and would not come off, no matter how hard she scrubbed it. She waited fearfully for her husband's return and the moment when she would be forced to return the keys to him.

Upon seeing the bloodstained key, Blue Beard realized that his wife's curiosity had led her to disobey his orders. "Very well, Madam," he said, "you shall go in, and take your place amongst the ladies you saw there." Blue Beard gave the terrified woman fifteen minutes in which to say her final prayers. Fortunately, in that time her two brothers came to the rescue and killed the murderous husband before he had a chance to dispatch yet another wife.

From Perrault's tale came the practice of calling a man who murders his wife or wives a *Bluebeard*. The term is favored by journalists reporting on sensational stories of domestic violence.

Although Perrault was the first to publish ''La barbe bleue,'' variations of the story existed throughout Europe both before and after 1697. Many attempts have been made to identify a historical model for Blue Beard. Gilles de Rais, a notorious murderer who lived in France from 1404 to 1440, has been suggested as the real-life Blue Beard. But he had only one wife, and his numerous victims were mostly young boys. A more likely candidate seems to be Comorre the Cursed, who lived in Brittany around A.D. 500. An account of his life, published in 1531, recounts how he murdered four wives and attempted to murder the fifth. St. Gildas is said to have intervened to save her, and she, Tryphine, eventually gave birth to Comorre's son, founded a convent, and was canonized.

blurb: a short, usually laudatory publicity notice

Nowadays we see publicity blurbs for products, movies, television shows, concerts, and just about any other event or object that is widely advertised. But the first *blurb* appeared on a book jacket and was nothing more than a paragraph of nonsensical text that was printed beneath the picture of a pretty girl.

American humorist, illustrator, and author Gelett

Burgess designed a comic jacket for his book *Are You a Bromide?* which was first published in 1906. On it he put the picture of a well-endowed female, whom he called Belinda Blurb. The text might as well have been in a foreign language, for all the sense it made, but Burgess's blurb got his readers' attention nevertheless.

In 1914, Burgess used the word *blurb* again, this time to describe the self-praise publishers were in the habit of including on the dust jackets of the books they produced: "On the 'jacket' of the 'latest' fiction, we find the blurb; abounding in agile adjectives and adverbs, attesting that this book is the 'sensation of the year.'"

Before long Burgess's generic use of the word *blurb* caught on in publishing and advertising, although media specialists and publicity departments certainly don't use it with the same levity that Burgess did when he coined it.

See also: **bromide.**

Bobbsey Twins: two people who are very much alike

When we see two people who are dressed alike or are very similar in looks, we often say, "Here come the *Bobbsey Twins*." The allusion is to two sets of fictional fraternal twins: Bert and Nan Bobbsey, and Freddie and Flossie Bobbsey.

The Bobbsey twins first appeared in *The Bobbsey Twins, or, Merry Days Indoors and Out*, which was published in 1904. It was followed by a long series of stories about the family, which were avidly read by generations of young Americans. In the books, Richard and Mary Bobbsey live in a town called Lakeport, in the southern United States. The older set of Bobbsey twins are twelve years old, with dark hair and eyes. The younger pair are blue-eyed blonds, six years of age. The Bobbseys' cook, Dinah, is a good-natured black woman who tends to laugh heartily no matter how much confusion the children cause in her kitchen.

The books, which have titles such as *The Bobbsey Twins and the Talking Fox Mystery, The Mystery of the King's Puppet, At London Tower, On Blueberry Island*, etc., are adventure stories in which the children become embroiled in the schemes and machinations of underhanded villains but always end up safely home with their parents and Dinah.

The creator of the Bobbsey twins was a man named Edward L. Stratemeyer. Stratemeyer wrote over 400 books for young readers, using more than 20 pen names. His first successful series was *The Rover Boys*, which he wrote under the name Arthur M. Winfield. For the books about the Bobbsey twins, he called himself Laura Lee Hope.

Stratemeyer was also the original author of *Tom Swift, The Hardy Boys*, and *Nancy Drew*. Eventually, he formed a syndicate, providing ideas and outlines to a group of ghostwriters who then filled in the plots for him. He personally edited all the books written by the ghostwriters and continued to write, himself.

When Edward Stratemeyer died in 1930, over six million of his books had been sold. The syndicate was taken over by his two daughters. One of them, Harriet S. Adams, continued to write the Nancy Drew series under the pseudonym Carolyn Keane, and as the new Laura Lee Hope, also produced more Bobbsey Twins novels.

Writing in the early 1900s, Stratemeyer had portrayed Dinah the cook as the typical Southern mammy. In 1950, Adams/Hope revised the first book in the Bobbsey Twins series, making it less racist and generally updating the details that had made it outdated for young readers in the second half of the twentieth century. Many of the books in the series were reissued during the 1960s and 1970s.

bohemian/Bohemian: unconventional, artsy

The first gypsies arrived in Europe in the fourteenth or fifteenth century. Although these dark-skinned nomads came originally from India, they were mistakenly believed to be from Egypt. The English referred to them as "lords and earls of little Egypt," which gave rise to the English name *gypsy*.

Gypsies arrived in Germany, Italy, Spain, and France in the first quarter of the fifteenth century. In France they were called *bohémiens,* either from the belief that the former Czech kingdom of Bohemia was their home or because the first groups to arrive in France came by way of Bohemia.

The gypsies led a life completely different from that of most Europeans. They traveled in caravans, making music and telling fortunes to earn a little money. They slept in their wagons, in makeshift huts, or, in Spain, in caves. And they moved on when they tired of a place or when the local people complained about their thievery or loose living.

In time, the French began to apply the term *bohémiens* to social gypsies: artists and writers who abandoned conventional society and lived together in artsy enclaves. There they engaged in behavior that was considered highly irregular: drinking, taking drugs, engaging in free love, and espousing radical philosophical and political ideals. As a young man, English author William Makepeace Thackeray spent three years in Paris studying to be a painter. During that time he learned firsthand about the mores and milieu of the Parisian bohémiens.

Thackeray incorporated his experiences in Paris into his 1848 novel, *Vanity Fair*. Thackeray's main character, Becky Sharp, is a poor girl who is determined to snare a rich husband. At boarding school she becomes friends with Amelia Sedley and insinuates herself into Amelia's family circle. Becky has her sights set on Amelia's brother, Joseph, but he does not respond to her advances. She next finds employment as a governess in the home of Sir Pitt Crawley and secretly marries his son, Rawdon Crawley.

When the man she married for his money is disinherited, Becky stays with him but takes a lover who is able to support her in style. When the truth about Becky's relationship with her benefactor, Lord Steyne, comes out, her husband leaves England, putting their child in the custody of his brother. Becky is completely ostracized by her former friends and loses her place in society. She moves to the Continent, where "Her taste for disrespectability grew more and more remarkable. She became a perfect Bohemian ere long, herding with people whom it would make your hair stand on end to meet."

In Paris, Becky finds lodgings in the Elephant Hotel. Despite the squalor and dirt, she is happy there:

She was at home with everybody in the place, pedlars, punters, tumblers, students and all. She was of a wild, roving nature, inherited from her father and mother, who were both Bohemians, by taste and circumstance. . . .

The appearance of the word *Bohemian* in these passages from *Vanity Fair* mark its first use in English to mean unconventional or artsy. The word is now more frequently used in lower-case form, as is the word *bohemia,* which has become a common term for a community of artists and writers.

Boob McNutt: *See:* **Rube Goldberg device.**

bowdlerize: expurgate a text

Shakespeare was no Puritan. In fact, he was quite critical of the Puritan movement that was growing in
England at the beginning of the 1600s. Nor is it likely
that those who espoused Puritanism found Shakespeare's plays acceptable entertainment. ''Earthy,''
''ribald,'' ''bawdy''—those are some of the adjectives that have been applied to the works of the Bard
of Avon. ''Obscene'' is another: It was, no doubt, the
word the Puritans found most fitting, and Thomas
Bowdler agreed with them.

Bowdler was an English editor who lived from
1754 to 1825. He was a great admirer of Shakespeare's work, but he didn't feel it was appropriate
for everyone:

> *I can hardly imagine a more pleasing occupation for
> a winter's evening in the country, than for a father
> to read one of Shakespeare's plays to his family cir-
> cle. My object is to enable him to do so without in-
> curring the danger of falling unawares among words
> and expressions which are of such a nature as to
> raise a blush on the cheek of modesty, or render it
> necessary for the reader to pause. . . .*

The way in which Bowdler enabled everyone—
women and children included—to enjoy Shake-

speare's works was to expurgate them. In 1818 he
published a ten-volume *Family Shakespeare*, omitting
the words and expressions he deemed unsuitable for
mixed company. In some cases that meant the cutting
of entire passages of dialogue or, in *Henry IV, Part
II* and *Henry V,* the elimination of what he deemed
to be an offensive character (the prostitute Doll Tear-
sheet). Bowdler even changed the expletive "God"
to "Heaven," in accordance with the Ten Command-
ments.

Bowdler's version was immensely popular. Its success encouraged him to produce an expurgated edition
of *The Decline and Fall of the Roman Empire*, which
was published after his death. It also earned him linguistic immortality when the verb *bowdlerize* became
part of the English language. First used in print in
1836, the word is still used to mean to expurgate offensive or vulgar material from a text.

braggadocio: a braggart; pretentious bragging

It took Edmund Spenser a decade to write the first
three books of *The Faerie Queen*. He intended the
work to be made up of twelve books, but when he
died in 1599 he had only completed six. What Spenser did complete of *The Faerie Queen* is an epic
poem, an allegory peopled with myriad figures that
personify mankind's vices and virtues. Some of them

also represent well-known religious and political figures of sixteenth-century England.

The Faerie Queen herself, who is named Gloriana,
represents both the abstract idea of Glory and its embodiment in the Queen of England, Elizabeth I.
Duessa, or Falsehood, represents the Catholic Mary,
Queen of Scots. Elizabeth's archenemy, Emperor
Philip of Spain, is personified by Archimago or Hypocrisy. Another character, Braggadochio (Vain
Boastfulness) is generally thought to be a caricature
of the Duke of Anjou. Evidently this person was a
cause of great annoyance early in 1580, when Spenser
was beginning *The Faerie Queen.*

In Canto 8 of Book III, a wicked witch creates a
double of the beautiful Florimell, who has been kidnapped. As the double walks through the forest, she
sees a knight:

> Yet knight he was not, but a boastfull swaine
> That deedes of armes had ever in despaire,
> Proud Braggadochio, that in vaunting vaine
> His glory did repose, and credit did maintaine.

Braggadochio tries to force himself on the woman
he thinks is Florimell, boasting that he will fight off
anyone who tries to take her from him. At this point
another knight appears and challenges Braggadochio
to a duel. As they prepare to face off, the cowardly
Braggadochio turns tail and flees, showing his boasting to be nothing more than empty words.

As the personification of empty bragging, Braggadochio made a lasting impression on English literature and on the English language. The word *braggadocio* is now a synonym for a braggart. It is also used to denote the pretentious bragging in which some people constantly engage until they are asked to put their money where their mouth is.

brave new world: a sterile, regimented, soulless society

In Shakespeare's play, *The Tempest*, Miranda, a young woman who has been raised in isolation on an island with only her father for company, is delighted when a young man arrives. "O, brave new world," she cries, "that has such people in't."

Aldous Huxley's 1932 novel *Brave New World* takes place in the year 632 A.F. The initials A.F. stand for "After Ford," and the worship of Henry Ford's industrialism is the closest thing to religion that exists in a world where technology reigns supreme. Throughout most of the world, old age, disease, and unhappiness have been wiped out, as have families, love, and, in fact, any and all strong emotions. Embryos are raised in bottles; they are programmed with the physical and mental characteristics they will need in the position they are designated to hold in society.

There are, however, a few places left on Earth that have not been considered worth the expense of "civilizing." These are called "savage reservations," and the people there still marry, mate, and raise families in the old way. When Bernard Marx, a scientist, and Lenina, the woman he is "having" at the time, visit one of these reservations, they meet a savage named John. John has a mother (Bernard and Lenina can barely bring themselves to say the word), who once lived in the civilized world but was inadvertently left behind on the reservation after going there on vacation.

John, who was ostracized because of his mother's origins, has spent most of his time alone, reading a dog-earred volume of Shakespeare's works that he found on the reservation. John accepts the invitation to return to London with Bernard and Lenina, and he quotes Miranda to show just how happy he is: "O brave new world," he repeated. "O brave new world that has such people in it. Let's start at once." But, Bernard, who has some reservations about "civilization," warns John to wait until he actually sees the new world before judging its merits.

John, who is known as "the Savage," soon realizes that civilization is not all he expected it to be. He cannot understand a world in which all human emotions have been expunged and in which people take a drug called "soma" to escape from any unpleasant sensations they may feel. He is sickened by the cloning of hundreds of human beings from one embryo, resulting in a mass of "twins" who are identical in every way and who virtually live life as one entity. Most of all, he is shocked by Lenina's behavior. When he tells her that he is in love with her, she has no idea what he is talking about. She offers herself to him, not because she returns his love, but because they are both physically attracted to each other, and in her "civilized" society that is all couples share.

John confronts Mustapha Mond, the highest official in London, and tells him exactly what he thinks of his uneventful, sterile world—a world in which comfort comes before everything else:

"... I don't want comfort. I want God ... poetry ... real danger ... freedom ... goodness ... sin."

"In fact," said Mustapha Mond, "you're claiming the right to be unhappy."

"All right then," said the Savage defiantly, "I'm claiming the right to be unhappy."

"Not to mention the right to grow old and ugly ... to have syphilis and cancer ... too little to eat ... to live in constant apprehension ... to be tortured by unspeakable pains ..." There was a long silence.

"I claim them all," said the Savage at last.

When Bernard and his friend Helmholtz are exiled for their free-thinking, John is not allowed to go with them because Mustapha Mond wants to continue his exposure to civilization as an experiment. John runs away, but is such an object of curiosity that he cannot find peace anywhere. He eventually commits suicide in the brave new world.

Huxley's ironic use of Miranda's words made the Shakespearian phrase *brave new world* a part of our language. We now use the term to refer to any society that encourages conformity, and discourages individuality, in all aspects of life.

bread and circuses: spectacles or entertainments that pander to the masses, diverting attention from the real issues

Long since, because we can sell our votes to no one,
We have thrown off our cares; those who once bestowed
Rule, the fasces, *legions, everything, now refrain,*
And hunger for only two things:
Bread and circuses.

Little is known of the private life of Decimus Junius Juvenalis, known to us as Juvenal. He is believed to have been born around A.D. 60 and to have died in A.D. 140. Scholars believe that as a young man he served in the Roman military and that toward the end of his life he was exiled after having criticized one of the emperor's friends.

Juvenal authored sixteen *Satires*, which were grouped into five books, published at varying intervals. They are scathing attacks on the politics and morals of the day. Juvenal frequently laments the state of affairs in the city of Rome, lamenting the rise in crime, the condition of the poor, and the corruption of city officials.

The above quotation comes from Juvenal's tenth *Satire*, which is among his most famous. It was imitated by Samuel Johnson in the *Vanity of Human Wishes*, in which Johnson recounts the disasters that have befallen many people after they have achieved the objects of their ambition and desire. It also gave us the frequently used expression *bread and circuses* to describe a common ploy of those in power, which is to provide enough food and entertainment to draw the people's attention away from the real issues. Unfortunately, the Roman way of manipulating the people is often copied in modern society, where shrewd politicians provide superficial distractions to keep their constituents from asking too many questions. And, even more unfortunate is the fact that the vast majority of the citizenry can be bought off by those who give them a full belly and a good laugh.

Brobdingnagian/brobdingnagian: huge, gigantic

After leaving the country of Lilliput, where the inhabitants are one-twelfth the size of human beings, Lemuel Gulliver returns home to England, only to depart on another voyage two months later. *Gulliver's Travels*, written by Jonathan Swift in 1726, tells the story of these and Gulliver's other voyages to fantastic lands.

Gulliver's second journey takes him to the mythical land of Brobdingnag, where the inhabitants are twelve times larger than he. Left behind by his shipmates, Gulliver is captured by a reaper. The reaper brings him to his master, the farmer, who carries him home in his handkerchief. The farmer's daughter soon becomes his *Glumdalclitch*, or little nurse. She takes care of him and protects him from danger, and the two develop a close bond. The farmer, however, decides to exhibit Gulliver throughout the land and before long Gulliver is a mere shadow of his former self: weary from performing before crowds day in and day out. Believing that Gulliver is about to die, the farmer gladly sells him to the king and queen of Brobdingnag. Gulliver takes up residence in the palace, where he has many adventures and close calls due to his small stature. Fortunately, his little nurse has remained with him and snatches him from the jaws of death more than once.

Swift's descriptions of Gulliver being carried around in the mouth of a dog, wedged into a marrow bone by the queen's dwarf, or hanging forty feet in the air from the waistband of a servant's dress emphasize the contrast between him and these giants. They also brought about the use of the adjective *Brobdingnagian* in English to describe something or someone of gigantic proportions.

See also: **lilliputian, yahoo.**

bromide: a trite and unoriginal person; a commonplace remark

Doctors and chemists have long known that bromine, in combination with other elements, has sedative properties. Potassium bromide, in particular, can put one to sleep.

Gelett Burgess, American author and humorist, also knew about the sleep-inducing properties of bromides, and first made the analogy between these drugs and boring people in his 1906 novel *Are You a Bromide?* He followed this work up with the humorous essay, "Are You a Bromide, or the Sulphitic Theory," in 1907. The popularity of these two works resulted in new, nonchemical definitions being added to the dictionary under the entries *bromide* and *sulphite.*

According to Burgess, a *bromide* is a person who "does his thinking by syndicate. He follows the main-traveled roads, he goes with the crowd." A bromide has unoriginal thoughts and makes trite conversation. Polonius and William McKinley were bromides, in Burgess's view. (If bromides speak in platitudes, as Burgess alleged, then what better example than Polonius?) The word *bromide* became a popular expression for a trite, boring person and, by extension, for the trite, boring statements that constitute his or her conversation.

Conversely, a *sulphite* or *sulfite*—a salt or ester of sulfurous acid—has anything but a calming effect. In fact, the adjective *sulphurous* means hellish, or suggesting the fires of hell. That is why Burgess chose the word *sulphite* to refer to someone who is the antithesis of a bromide: someone who is unconventional, an original thinker, a catalyst to those around him or her.

bumbledom: *See* **Dickensian.**

Buster Brown haircut: a pageboy hairstyle
with straight-across bangs

For a large part of the twentieth century, it was common for children to get *Buster Brown haircuts*: Their
bangs were cut straight across their forehead, and the
rest of their hair was cut into a pageboy style. There
is also an American shoe company that carries a popular line of children's shoes called Buster Browns.

The inspiration for both these fashion trends was a
mischievous American schoolboy drawn by cartoonist
Richard F. Outcault. Outcault, who introduced *The
Yellow Kid* in 1895, is considered the founder of the
American comic strip. The cartoon character Outcault
called Buster Brown wore his hair in the style described above and sported lace-up shoes on his feet.
One of the characters in *The Yellow Kid* was a grinning, talking bulldog called Tige. When Outcault began chronicling the adventures of Buster Brown in
1902, he chose to make Tige the boy's pet and constant companion.

Unlike *The Yellow Kid*, which was geared to lower-
class urban audiences, *Buster Brown* was intended for
more affluent suburban readers. The Brown family
lived at Brownhurst on Creek and vacationed at fashionable resorts. Buster, who has been called a thinly-
veiled reference to Little Lord Fauntleroy, was always
dressed in the latest children's fashions. In fact, for

decades he served as a guide to children's haute couture, with American mothers dressing their little boys like Buster just as English mothers had dressed theirs like Little Lord Fauntleroy a generation earlier.

The plot of the *Buster Brown* strips rarely varied. Buster played a childish prank, was punished, and learned a lesson. Nor was the message delivered subtly: The last frame of each strip contained a scroll-like proclamation that summed up the moral of the story.

Buster Brown continued to be drawn by Outcault until his retirement in 1920 and has been revived several times since.

See also: **Little Lord Fauntleroy, yellow journalism.**

byronic: melancholy, brooding, unconventional

The heroes created by Lord Byron epitomize the Romantic ideal of the nineteenth century. They are brooding, melancholy, highly emotional, and constantly defy convention. Handsome, mysterious, and fearless, they perform the most dangerous feats without hesitation.

Although Byron himself was short, chubby, and had a clubfoot, his image of himself conformed exactly to that of his fictional creations. Rumors of his own wild deeds and debauchery spread during his lifetime, and, rather than denying them, he did everything he could to enhance his bad-boy reputation. The result was the creation of the adjective *byronic* to describe both the poet and his heroes.

In 1810 Byron, who was in his early twenties at the time, made a year-long tour of the Mediterranean, from Spain to the Near East, with a friend. When he returned to England in 1811, he wrote the first two cantos of *Childe Harold's Pilgrimage*, a lengthy poem based on his adventures abroad. The work made Byron an overnight success. Another of his early works, a narrative poem entitled *The Corsair*, was written in 1814 and introduced the first truly byronic hero: the pirate Conrad. Byron's description of Conrad makes it clear that his sympathies lie with the outlaw. Conrad has obviously been driven to a life of crime by the suffering he has undergone and is really a noble and romantic soul:

> *Warp'd by the world in Disappointment's school . . .*
> *He knew himself a villain, but he deem'd*
> *The rest no better than the thing he seem'd;*
> *And scorn'd the best as hypocrites who hid*
> *Those deeds the bolder spirit plainly did. . . .*
> *Lone, wild, and strange, he stood alike exempt*
> *From all affection and from all contempt . . .*
> *None are all evil: quickening round his heart,*
> *One softer feeling would not yet depart. . . .*
> *Yet 'gainst that passion vainly still he strove,*
> *And even in him it asks the name of Love!*

Another quintessential byronic hero is Count Manfred, who in the poetic drama *Manfred* sells his soul to the Devil and lives, estranged from all human beings, in solitude in the Alps.

Although he was only thirty-six years old when he died, Lord Byron left behind a large volume of work. His masterpiece, *Don Juan*, which he began in 1819 and added to throughout his life, was still unfinished at the time of his death.

See also: **Don Juan.**

Caliban: a degraded and savage man

One of the strangest characters created by William Shakespeare is Caliban, who appears in *The Tempest*. The play is set on an island that is inhabited by a magician named Prospero and his daughter, Miranda. Prospero was once the duke of Milan, but many years ago he was deposed by his brother and, with Miranda, abandoned at sea.

When father and daughter reached the island, it was occupied by Caliban: "... a freckled whelp, hag-born, not honour'd with a human shape." Caliban's mother, the witch Sycorax, had been abandoned on the island and had died after giving birth to her monstrous son. Prospero took pity on the hideous, wild creature and attempted to educate him and make him part of his household; Caliban rewarded the magician's kindness by attempting to rape Miranda. Henceforth, Prospero treated him like the brute he was, enslaving him and keeping him under control with his magic spells.

Caliban feels no remorse for betraying Prospero; he boldly states that he wishes he had succeeded in his assault on Miranda, "Thou didst prevent me; I had peopled else This isle with Calibans." Caliban still believes he is the rightful owner and ruler of the island and, filled with bitterness and the desire for revenge, is quick to join in a plot against Prospero.

Caliban quickly befriends Stephano, the servant of Prospero's evil brother, Antonio, who has been shipwrecked on the island. He offers to lead Stephano to the sleeping Prospero, so Stephano can kill him, take his magic books, and possess Miranda. Then, says Caliban, they can rule over the island together.

Caliban's name is an anagram of *canibal,* an accepted seventeenth-century spelling of *cannibal.* It has entered the English language as a synonym for a savage and degraded being, someone whose depravity makes him less than human in our eyes.

California: name of a U.S. state

Several of the states in the U.S.A. have names that came from the Spanish language. As the conquistadors discovered new lands, they often gave them names that reflected their climate or topography. Sierra Nevada means snow-covered mountain range, and this was shortened to Nevada when the area became a state. Likewise, what is now the state of Florida was discovered during the Easter season (Pascua), and that, coupled with its many flowering plants, prompted the Spanish to call it Pascua Florida. In time, this too was shortened, becoming simply Florida (flowery). Colorado is the past participle of the Spanish verb *colorar,* which means to redden or blush. The red-colored rocks and terrain of Colorado gave that state its name.

Another state was named by the Spanish, not from their language, but from their literature. *Amadís de Gaula* is the most famous Spanish *libro de cavallería* or book of chivalry. Amadís embodies the chivalric ideals of valor, fidelity, and bravery. He performs many feats of daring, triumphs over giants and monsters, and always remains faithful to his ladylove, Princess Oriana.

Although there are references to the story as early as 1380, it wasn't until 1508 that it became widely known, thanks to the "corrected and amended" edition published by Garci Rodríguez de Montalvo (also known as Garci Gutiérrez Ordóñez de Montalvo). Montalvo edited the first three books, wrote a fourth dealing with the further adventures of Amadís, and in 1510 added a fifth about Esplandián, the son of Amadís. It was in this fifth book, entitled *Sergas de Esplandián (Feats of Esplandián),* that Montalvo created the imaginary realm he called *California*: an island ruled by Black Amazons "at the right hand of the Indies . . . very close to that of the Terrestrial Paradise."

Amadís de Gaula was an instant success, and nu-

merous sequels and imitations followed Montalvo's
edition. By the time the west coast of North America
was discovered, *Amadís* had engendered a whole
genre of literature, in Spain and throughout Europe.
When the first Spaniards arrived in the southern portion of California in the 1530s, they believed it to be
an island or a group of islands. They called it California after Montalvo's exotic, imaginary island. By
extension, the entire Pacific Coast north from Cape
San Lucas soon came to be called Las Californias.

The name of another exotic, imaginary realm was
given by the Spanish explorers to a portion of South
America. In 1511 a romance entitled *Palmerín de
Oliva* was published anonymously in Salamanca,
Spain. Like *Amadís*, it enjoyed enormous popularity
and was followed by many sequels. The Spanish who
discovered the southern region of South America
named it Patagonia, after the country in which *Palmerín de Oliva* was set. Patagonia was colonized by
the Spanish in the seventeenth century and now be-
longs partly to Chile and partly to Argentina.

Candide: *See* **Panglossian.**

Casanova: a great lover, a philanderer

In the preface to his *Memoirs*, Giacomo Casanova de
Seingalt makes the following confession:

The chief business of my life has always been to in-
dulge my senses; I never knew anything of greater
importance. I felt myself born for the fair sex, I have
ever loved it dearly, and I have been loved by it as
often and as much as I could.

When you begin reading Casanova's multivolume
autobiography, you realize that he isn't kidding. It is
hard to say whether Casanova's life, as described in
the *Memoirs*, is one long adventure punctuated by
love affairs or one long love affair interrupted by a
few adventures. After reliving his first amorous experience, which occurred at the age of thirteen, Casanova goes on to describe, every few pages, another
of his love affairs. He tells of his dalliances with Bet-
tina, Thérèse, Nanette, Marton, Angela, Juliette, Lu-
cie—and that only takes him through the first five
chapters of Volume I! The rest of Volume I and Volumes II through XI contain more of the same.

Although he frequently professes to have been in
love, Casanova moves from affair to affair with few,
if any, regrets. For example, he offers to marry his
pregnant mistress, Rosalie, and claims his heart is
broken when she refuses. But even before Rosalie has
moved out of his house, he is planning to seduce her
maid, Véronique, and the maid's sister, Annette. On
another occasion, he goes to rent rooms for one of his
mistresses and is shown around by the landlord's
wife, a beautiful young woman with an infant. He
turns on the Casanova charm and begins kissing her,
"which she took very kindly, but she smelt of nurs-

ing, which I detested, so I did not go any farther despite her radiant beauty.'' On this rare occasion when Casanova doesn't end up in the bedroom, it is of course he who rejects the lady and not vice versa.

Although there is general agreement among historians and scholars that Casanova's accounts of his romantic conquests are greatly exaggerated, they established his reputation as a philanderer. It soon became common to refer to a man who has great success with women and plays the field as a *Casanova*.

Besides telling of his many love affairs, Casanova's *Memoirs* are a wealth of information about eighteenth-century Europe. Casanova was born in Venice, lived in Padua, was expelled from a seminary for scandalous conduct, and entered the service of a cardinal in Rome. He returned to Venice to pursue a career as a violinist, then traveled through France, Germany, and Austria. Back in Venice he was jailed for practicing magic, but made a daring escape from the Doge's prison. He next visited the Netherlands, Germany, Switzerland, France, and several Italian cities, before going on to London. He traveled as far as St. Petersburg in Russia, then sought refuge in Spain after another scandal and a duel. His final years were spent in Bohemia, as the personal librarian of Count von Waldstein. He died in the count's chateau on June 4, 1798.

A complete, unexpurgated text of the *Memoirs* was not available in English until Willard R. Trask produced a six-volume translation based on Casanova's original manuscript (1966–71). Previous English translations had been based on abridged and severely expurgated French and German editions of the nineteenth century.

Catch-22: a predicament in which the solution is the problem and vice versa; therefore, there is no way out

Very often, recent high school or college graduates who go job hunting are faced with a seemingly unresolvable dilemma: All the jobs they apply for require experience, but they can't get experience unless they have a job, and they can't get a job until they have experience. In this type of circuitous situation, where the solution is the problem, and the problem is the solution, there is no way out. We commonly call such a predicament a *Catch-22*, after Joseph Heller's 1961 novel of the same name.

Catch-22 takes place during World War II and is based on Heller's own experience as a bombardier. Its central character, Captain Yossarian, is an antihero: An average guy who just wants to get out of the war alive. In this he is thwarted by the fanaticism of his commander, Colonel Cathcart, and the rule that seems to prevail: Catch-22.

Each time Yossarian completes the required number of bombing missions to qualify for home leave, Cathcart raises the number. Desperate to find a way out, Yossarian eventually hits upon the idea of pleading insanity so that he will be sent home. But when he visits the squadron's doctor, he finds out that it isn't as easy to get out of combat as he thought:

> There was only one catch and that was Catch-22, which specified that a concern for one's own safety in the face of dangers . . . was the process of a rational mind. Orr was crazy and could be grounded. All he had to do was ask; and as soon as he did, he would no longer be crazy and would have to fly more missions. Orr would be crazy to fly more missions and sane if he didn't, but if he was sane he had to fly them. If he flew them he was crazy and didn't have to; but if he didn't want to he was sane and had to.

In this and other matters, Yossarian finds that there is just no way around Catch-22, which epitomizes the irrational thinking on which the military bases its actions.

Catch-22 was made into a film in 1970, with Alan Arkin in the role of Yossarian. Joseph Heller did not publish his second novel, *Something Happened*, until 1974. He also wrote *Good as Gold* (1979) and *God Knows* (1985). The latter received a French literary award for best foreign novel of the year.

Chateaubriand: a thick, expensive cut of beef

We have a considerable number of words in the English language that have come from the names of writers: Kafkaesque, Felliniesque, Dickensian, Shavian, Rabelaisian, to mention just a few. Nearly all of these pertain to elements of the authors' writing styles, subject matter, or philosophy. But one author has been honored not for his writing, but for his appetite.

François René Châteaubriand was a French author and diplomat who lived from 1768 to 1848. He was a Roman Catholic and implored the French people to abandon the atheism of the French Revolution and return to Christianity. In his book, *Human Words*, Robert Hendrickson recounts a popular story about the way the first *Chateaubriand* was prepared and served. To celebrate the 1802 publication of Châteaubriand's famous work, *Le Génie du Christianisme*, the proprietor of the Paris restaurant where the author and his friend Brillat-Savarin were dining chose a thick tenderloin of beef for the two men's dinner. The tenderloin, symbolizing Christ, was encased between two flank steaks that represented the two thieves between whom he hung on the cross. The outer steaks were seared to blackness, then discarded, leaving the Chateaubriand inside rare and juicy.

Hendrickson suggests that Chateaubriand of beef was more likely to have first been prepared at the French embassy in London by Châteaubriand's personal chef, Montmirel, while the author was ambassador to England.

The *Oxford English Dictionary* quotes E. S. Dallas in *Kettner's Book* (1877) as saying that the steak that

was formerly served under the name filet de boeuf
was now always referred to as Chateaubriand.

(grin like a) Cheshire cat: grin from ear to ear; grin enigmatically

When we say someone is grinning like a Cheshire cat,
we mean one of two things: either the person is wearing a wide grin or their grin is mysterious and enig-
matic—indicating that they know something we don't
and are taking great pleasure in their secret. Both
meanings come from Lewis Carroll's descriptions
(and Sir John Tenniel's illustrations) of the Cheshire-
Cat in *Alice in Wonderland*. The two tales that make
up this classic children's story—*Alice's Adventures
in Wonderland* and *Through the Looking-Glass*—
were first told by Charles Lutwidge Dodgson to Alice
Liddell and her sisters on July 4, 1862. The ten-year-
old Alice was so delighted with the story Dodgson
made up to amuse the children during a summer pic-
nic that she begged him to write it down. He did so,
publishing *Alice in Wonderland* under the pen name
of Lewis Carroll in 1865.

In the first part of the story, Alice falls down a
rabbit hole and embarks on a series of adventures in
a topsy-turvy world. After meeting a variety of talking
animals, she enters a house inhabited by a duchess.
The duchess is sitting on a stool, nursing a baby, as
her cook stirs pepper into a huge pot of soup. Lying

on the hearth is a large cat, which is grinning from ear to ear. When Alice asks the duchess why the cat is grinning, she receives the curt answer that "It's a Cheshire-Cat, and that's why." When Alice says she didn't know that Cheshire-Cats—or any cats, for that matter—could grin, the duchess replies that "They all can, and most of 'em do."

Alice next meets the Cheshire-Cat in the woods, where it is sitting in a tree, wearing the same wide grin. Like the other animals in Wonderland, the cat has the power of speech and engages Alice in an absurd dialogue before it suddenly vanishes. After it appears and disappears a few more times, Alice complains to the cat that it comes and goes so quickly it makes her giddy. The cat then takes to making itself disappear slowly, starting with its tail. The last thing to vanish is its grin, which remains visible for some time after the rest of it has gone.

Lewis Carroll's strange, disembodied feline popularized it but, surprising as it may be, the phrase *grin like a Cheshire cat* did not originate with him. The expression is found in the satiric works of Dr. John Wolcot, who lived from 1738 to 1819 and wrote under the pseudonym of Peter Pindar, and seems to have been in use in England several centuries earlier. The county of Cheshire is famous for its cheeses and it has been suggested that some of these were shaped like cats or had grinning cat faces stamped on them, but there is no historical evidence of this. Another theory is that the phrase originated when a forest warden of Cheshire named Caterling—Cat for short—

showed his pleasure at the hanging of poachers by grinning from ear to ear. In their *Dictionary of Word and Phrase Origins*, William and Mary Morris favor the theory that the original Cheshire cat was the lion on a leading family's coat of arms: In rendering the animal's face, inept local sign painters made it look like a grinning housecat, hence the association.

chortle: a snorting, joyful chuckle

When a person chortles or lets out a chortle, the sound he or she makes is something between a chuckle and a snort. In fact, the word *chortle* is a combination, or portmanteau, word that was made up by Lewis Carroll in 1872. In *Through the Looking-Glass*, Carroll composed a nonsense poem called "Jabberwocky," which included the line "He chortled in his joy."

The poem included two other portmanteau words: *slithy,* from lithe and slimy; and *mimsy,* from flimsy and miserable. Neither of these caught on, but chortle soon became a commonly used word in England and, later, in America.

See also: **jabberwocky, portmanteau word.**

Cinderella story: a rags-to-riches story about a female; the story of a woman who finds wealth and happiness with the man of her dreams

It is impossible to say for sure when and where the first *Cinderella story* appeared. The earliest version we know of appeared in a Chinese book around A.D. 850. The book was compiled by Tuan Ch'êng-shih, a collector of folktales, who stated that he heard the tale from a man who came from the caves of South China.

The Chinese Cinderella is a girl named Yeh-hsien, who is ill treated by her stepmother after her father's death. She is forced to wear tattered clothing and do the household chores while her stepsister is pampered. When her stepmother kills her pet fish, a man comes out of the sky and tells her that by praying to the bones of the fish she can obtain anything she wants. She follows his advice and the fish provides her with a cloak of feathers and shoes of gold to wear to the festival. She loses one of her shoes and it falls into the hands of a king. He orders that all the women in the kingdom try it on. The golden shoe is at least an inch too small for even the smallest foot, until it is Yeh-hsien's turn. Her stepmother and stepsister are killed, she marries the king, and, of course, they live happily ever after.

The many European versions of Cinderella are all very similar to the Chinese tale. In the earliest of these, the Italian "La Gatta Cenerentola" or "The Hearth Cat," which is found in Basile's *Pentamerone*

of 1634, the heroine is named Zezolla. She is aided
by a fairy who lives in a date tree that was given to
her by her father. She too loses a shoe, which is found
by a king. There is a magnetic attraction between her
foot and the shoe, which proves she is its rightful
owner, and she becomes the queen.

In all, over 700 tales of Cinderella have been
found. In some of these the heroine is helped by a
supernatural being; in others a friendly animal or bird
grants her wishes. The version with which we are
most familiar is that of Charles Perrault, whose 1697
Histoires ou Contes du temps passé were translated
into English in 1729 by Robert Samber. A similar
story had appeared in English before Samber's translation was published: that of "Finetta the Cinder-
girl," which Madame d'Aulnoy included in her 1721
Collection of Novels and Tales. The two tales obviously sprang from a common source, although they
differ in their details. Finetta is the servant of her own
sisters; Cinderella (or Cinderilla, according to Samber) serves her stepsisters. Finetta finds a golden key
that unlocks a chest containing her finery; Cinderella
is given clothing and accoutrements by her fairy god-
mother. Finetta loses a red velvet slipper braided with
pearls; Cinderella's is made of glass. (It is possible
that earlier French versions referred to a slipper of fur
[vair], rather than one of glass [verre], but Perrault
was either unfamiliar with these or deliberately chose
the latter.)

The one constant in all the Cinderella stories, including those of Madame d'Aulnoy and Perrault/Sam-

ber, is the ending: The heroine is always elevated from her servile position and becomes the consort of the nobleman who has been searching for her. And the two live happily ever after. That is the key element in any Cinderella story, including those real-life situations to which we give the name. The name Cinderella has also become a popular sobriquet for a downtrodden female.

Circumlocution Office: a government department characterized by red tape and evasiveness

The word *circumlocution* comes from the Latin *circum* plus *locutio*, which means speaking around, or, in modern parlance, beating around the bush. By extension, a *Circumlocution Office* is a place where people beat around the bush or give you the runaround when answering your questions. The term was invented by Charles Dickens in his 1857 novel, *Little Dorrit*, and has become a satirical way of referring to a government office where there is so much red tape and evasiveness that no petitioner ever gets an answer to his or her questions.

Dickens devotes Book I, chapter X of *Little Dorrit* to a description of the Circumlocution Office. He begins by telling the reader that it is the most important department of the government: ''Its finger was in the largest public pie, and in the smallest public tart. . . .

Whatever was required to be done, the Circumlocution Office was beforehand with all the public departments in the art of perceiving—HOW NOT TO DO IT.''

The rest of the chapter is a masterpiece of broad, scathing satire of the English government in general and of its bureaucracy in particular. According to Dickens, all public departments and professional politicians, every new premier and government, every elected official, both houses of Parliament, and even Queen Victoria were constantly looking for ways how not to do it. But, he adds, the Circumlocution Office was more effective than any of them. Why?

Because the Circumlocution Office went on mechanically, every day, keeping this wonderful, all-sufficient wheel of statesmanship, How not to do it, in motion. Because the Circumlocution Office was down upon any ill-advised public servant who was going to do it, or who appeared to be by any surprising accident in remote danger of doing it, with a minute, and a memorandum, and a letter of instructions that extinguished him.

People were often lost, says Dickens, in the Circumlocution Office. After making the rounds of other government offices, where they were bullied, ignored, evaded, etc., they were finally referred to the Circumlocution Office, ''and never reappeared in the light of day.''

This Bermuda Triangle of bureaucracy was the private fiefdom of Mr. Tite Barnacle. The Barnacle family had been in charge of the the Circumlocution Office for some time, and all of them excelled at not doing it. When the hero of *Little Dorrit*, Arthur Clennam, goes to Barnacle to inquire about the case of Dorrit, who has been languishing in debtor's prison, the bureaucrat sidesteps all his questions, "it being one of the principles of the Circumlocution Office never, on any account, to give a straight answer."

Like many other works of Charles Dickens, *Little Dorrit* has a happy ending. But it also contains many grim scenes of life in England in the nineteenth century. Dickens used his novels to bring attention to the plight of the lower classes, to lobby against debtor's prisons and workhouses, and to condemn the inhumane bureaucracy that trapped generations of families in lives of disease, poverty, and crime.

See also: **Dickensian.**

clerihew: a humorous quatrain about a person who is generally named in the first line

There are numerous words in the English language that have come from the last names of writers and their fictional creations (Kafkaesque, Shavian, micawberesque, falstaffian, etc.). A few first names, such as those of Oscar Wilde and Trilby O'Ferrall, have also entered our language (*Oscar* being the British term for a homosexual and a *Trilby* being both a soft felt hat and a person who is easily led). The author of this book has encountered only one case, however, where a literary *middle* name has been turned into an English word.

Clerihew was the middle name of British author Edmund Bentley. Bentley was born in 1875, attended Oxford, and had a career as a journalist. He also wrote detective novels; *Trent's Last Case*, published in 1912, has become a classic in its genre. But Edmund Bentley is best remembered for his *clerihews*: comic four-line poems, made up of two couplets. The first line of a clerihew contains the name of the subject, and the following three lines are made up of satirical or ridiculous "biographical" facts. Bentley is said to have composed the following, his first clerihew, at age sixteen:

> *Sir Humphry Davy*
> *Abominated gravy.*
> *He lived in the odium*
> *Of having discovered sodium.*

Some other examples:

> *Sir Christopher Wren*
> *Said "I'm going to dine with some men.*
> *If anybody calls*
> *Say I'm designing St. Paul's."*

> *It was a weakness of Voltaire's*
> *To forget to say his prayers,*

And which, to his shame,
He never overcame.

Bentley introduced his poetic invention in his 1905 *Biography for Beginners*, and eventually published his creations in book form as *Clerihews*. He had several successful imitators during the 1920s, including Sir Francis Meynell and Edmond Kapp.

cloud-cuckoo-land / Cloud-Cuckoo-Land / Cloud-cuckoo-land: a realm of fantasy, a dreamland

People who live in *cloud-cuckoo-land* inhabit a world of dreams. They are totally divorced from reality and have their heads in the clouds. Cloud-cuckoo-land is also a term for an unrealistic, utopian scheme.

The word cloud-cuckoo-land first began to be used in English at the end of the nineteenth century. It is a translation of the Greek *nephelokokkygia,* the name of an imaginary realm created by the great playwright Aristophanes in his comedy *The Birds.*

The Birds dates from 414 B.C. and has often been referred to as Aristophanes' masterpiece. The play begins when two Athenians, Euelpides and Pisthetaerus, decide that they are fed up with the taxes and fines the Athenian government levies on its citizens. They are looking for a better place: a utopian land where they can live free as a bird.

In Aristophanes' comic world, birds can talk, and the two refugees converse with a bird named Hoopoe. They suggest to him that the birds of the world unite and form a bird metropolis somewhere between heaven and earth. By situating their city so that it blocks the smoke coming up to heaven from the sacrifices made by mortals, the birds will be able to demand tribute from the gods for letting the smoke go through. The birds like the idea and get together to choose a name for their new abode. They want "Something fanciful . . . A touch of clouds and airy spaciousness And lightness." The name they decide on is Cloud-Cuckoo-Land, or Cuckoonebulopolis (the city of birds in the clouds) as it is sometimes translated.

The birds present their demands to the gods, after which a brief war ensues. At the end of the play both sides declare a truce: The birds allow the smoke to go up to heaven in return for the promise that henceforth men will worship them instead of the gods. Zeus also promises his daughter Athena in marriage to Pisthetaerus.

Aristophanes lived from 445 to approximately 380 B.C. He began writing plays at the age of eighteen and for more than twenty years was the undisputed master of comic theater. He used his plays to satirize public figures, social and political institutions, and even the gods. Eleven of his plays have survived: *The Acharnians, The Knights, The Clouds, The Wasps, Peace, The Birds, Lysistrata, Thesmophoriazusae, The Frogs, Ecclesiazusae*, and *Plutus*.

comedy of errors: a situation characterized by misunderstandings and miscommunication

We occasionally find ourselves in a situation where, no matter how hard we try, we can't make ourselves understood by others. We find ourselves talking at cross-purposes—failing to connect with the other party or parties. Finding ourselves thus embroiled, we say we are in a *comedy of errors*.

The original *Comedy of Errors*, which gave us the phrase, is a masterpiece of confusion. The first of William Shakespeare's plays, written in the late 1580s or early 1590s, it has often been criticized for its lack of memorable dialogue and poetry. Although generally regarded as an apprentice piece, it is not without merit, as is attested to by its continued popularity, especially in the nineteenth and twentieth centuries.

The Comedy of Errors is the closest thing Shakespeare wrote to a farce; its plot is fast-moving, with one misunderstanding following another in rapid succession. As the chaos escalates, the entire cast finds itself in a complete dither. The audience, on the other hand, can sit back and laugh condescendingly at the players' confusion, since Shakespeare made sure he let them in on the joke during the first act.

The plot of *The Comedy of Errors*, which Shakespeare adapted from a play by the Roman dramatist Plautus, revolves around the oft-used comic device of mistaken identity. In this case, two sets of identical twins are continually mistaken for one another. The action takes place in the city of Ephesus, where an old man named Egeon has come to search for his twin sons: Twenty-three years earlier, a shipwreck separated him from his wife and one of his sons. He raised the remaining boy alone, and when the child became an adult, he went off in search of his brother. When the play opens, Egeon has not seen him for five years. To complicate matters even more, two other twin boys were separated during the shipwreck; they had been chosen as servants for Egeon's twins, and one had disappeared with Egeon's wife and son.

In act I the audience learns that Antipholus and his servant Dromio, who have been living in Ephesus all along, are in fact Egeon's long-lost son and his servant. They also learn that Egeon's other son, Antipholus of Syracuse, and his servant, Dromio of Syracuse, have arrived in Ephesus. What follows is a series of farcical meetings in which Antipholus of Syracuse and Dromio of Ephesus believe they are servant and master; the wife of Antipholus of Ephesus, Adriana, mistakes his brother for her husband; Antipholus of Syracuse falls in love with Adriana's sister, Luciana, who believes he is her brother-in-law; Antipholus of Ephesus is arrested when he refuses to pay for a gold chain that, in fact, the merchant delivered to Antipholus of Syracuse; etc.

When everyone appears on stage together at the end of the play, the confusion is finally cleared up. The pairs of twins are sorted out, and Egeon is reunited with both his sons. Antipholus of Syracuse is free to woo Luciana, and, to make a happy ending even happier, Egeon finds his lost wife, Emilia: She

has been living in a convent on Ephesus, to which
she invites all her family for a feast of celebration.

Comstockery: overzealous censorship

For more than forty years Anthony Comstock was the
foremost crusader against obscenity and for censorship in the United States. Comstock was an organizer
and chief special agent of the New York Society for
the Suppression of Vice. As such, he personally destroyed over 160 tons of "dirty" pictures and books.
He lobbied for the passage of more stringent laws
against sending obscene matter through the mail; the
resulting Comstock laws were passed in 1873.

Most of Comstock's demands for censorship were
directed against commercial pornography, but from
time to time he spoke out against the obscenity of
established artists and writers, on the principle of
"morals, not art or literature."

George Bernard Shaw was born in Ireland in 1856
and, at the time of his death ninety-four years later,
was the most honored man of letters in Great Britain.
His career began slowly, however, and most of his
early plays were either banned by the censors or refused production. When literary fame finally came, it
was resounding and worldwide, and he won the Nobel
Prize in Literature in 1925.

But Shaw was much more than a playwright: He
was a free-thinker; a socialist; a political, social, and

economic reformer. His literary works were merely the vehicle he used to deliver his messages to the world. He frequently referred to himself as "a social reformer and doctrinaire first, last, and all the time."

It is hardly surprising, therefore, that Shaw was outraged by Comstock's efforts to impose censorship on legitimate artists and authors. In 1905 Shaw was quoted as saying, "*Comstockery* is the world's standing joke at the expense of the United States." The noun he coined from Comstock's name has remained in use to this day. It has become an accepted term for overzealous censorship of the kind advocated by Comstock and deplored by Shaw.

cowardly lion: someone with much bravado but little real courage

In L. Frank Baum's classic tale, *The Wonderful Wizard of Oz*, Dorothy and her dog, Toto, set out on the yellow brick road to find the Wizard of Oz. They have been transported from Kansas to the magical Land of Oz during a cyclone, and Dorothy hopes the Wizard will be able to send them back home.

Along the road Dorothy and Toto meet a number of strange characters, one of whom is the Cowardly Lion. The Lion jumps out at them and their newfound friends, the Scarecrow and the Tin Woodman. When the beast tries to bite Toto, Dorothy rushes up to him and hits him on the nose. She berates him, saying he is nothing but a big coward. To her surprise, the Lion agrees, saying he has always known he was a coward, but he doesn't know how to help it.

When Dorothy asks the Lion what makes him a coward, he tells her it's a mystery. He thinks he must have been born that way, because he has always been a coward. He learned early in life, however, that most of the other animals assumed he was brave and fierce, because he was a lion:

> I learned that if I roared very loudly every living thing was frightened and got out of my way. Whenever I've met a man I've been awfully scared; but I just roared at him, and he has always run away as fast as he could go. If the elephants and the tigers and the bears had ever tried to fight me, I should have run myself—I'm such a coward; but just as soon as they hear me roar they all try to get away from me, and of course I let them go.

The name of Baum's *Cowardly Lion* lives on in our language as a term for a person who rants and raves a lot, and seems extremely intimidating, but who, when push comes to shove, is quick to back down. Like the Lion who hid behind his reputation as King of the Beasts, such a person's roar is worse than his bite.

See also: **Land of Oz, munchkin.**

create a Frankenstein/create a monster:
do something that comes back to haunt you

Mary Shelley was only nineteen years old when she wrote *Frankenstein, or the Modern Prometheus*. In the introduction to the 1831 edition of that work, she talked about the summer of 1816, when she, her husband (poet Percy Bysshe Shelley), a friend named Polidori, and Lord Byron were neighbors in Switzerland. After spending several rainy days reading ghost stories, Lord Byron suggested that they each write their own ghost story. Mary Shelley was unable to think up a tale until she listened to a philosophical discussion between her husband and Lord Byron. The subject was the principle of life and whether or not it could ever be discovered and communicated. The two poets spoke about experiments that Darwin was said to have conducted, in which he was able to get a piece of vermicelli to move. This led to other, more intriguing questions. Could a corpse be reanimated? Could scientists make a creature out of disparate body parts and instill it with life?

These were the questions that Mary Shelley kept turning over in her mind as she tried to fall asleep on that summer evening in 1816:

My imagination, unbidden, possessed and guided me. . . . I saw the pale student of unhallowed arts kneeling beside the thing he had put together. I saw the hideous phantasm of a man stretched out, and then, on the working of some powerful engine, show

*signs of life, and stir with an uneasy, half-vital mo-
tion. . . . His success would terrify the artist; he
would rush away from his hideous handiwork horror-
stricken. He would hope that . . . the silence of the
grave would quench forever the transient existence
of the hideous corpse which he had looked upon as
the cradle of life. He sleeps; but he is awakened; he
opens his eyes; behold, the horrid thing stands at his
bedside, opening his curtains and looking on him
with yellow, watery, but speculative eyes.*

Mary Shelley opened her eyes and realized she had
the makings of a horrific tale. She began writing it
the next day, thinking it would only be a few pages
long. But her husband encouraged her to develop the
idea into a full-length book, and the result was the
novel *Frankenstein*. Percy Shelley wrote the preface,
but the rest was written entirely by Mary, based on
what she had imagined that night.

Frankenstein is the story of young Victor Frankenstein, a student of science who becomes obsessed
with the idea of bringing the inanimate to life. Piecing
together body parts from various corpses, he creates
a man, and, to his surprise, his creation comes alive.
At that moment, he realizes the mistake he has made
in tampering with the natural order of the world and
flees. When he returns the creature is gone. From that
moment on, Frankenstein lives in fear of what it will
do. His worst nightmare comes true when he learns
that the creature has killed his brother. In a confrontation with Frankenstein after the murder, the monster

blames him and the rest of the humans who have shunned him for his crime:

> . . . *I was benevolent; my soul glowed with love and humanity; but am I not alone, miserably alone? You, my creator, abhor me; what hope can I gather from your fellow creatures, who owe me nothing? They spurn and hate me. . . .Shall I not then hate them who abhor me? I will keep no terms with my enemies. I am miserable, and they shall share my wretchedness.*

The monster begs Frankenstein to create a female companion for him, so he will not have to live in total isolation. At first Frankenstein refuses, but when the monster threatens the rest of his family unless he complies, Frankenstein gives in. He begins to put together another creature, but his horror keeps him from completing the experiment. In retaliation, the monster kills Frankenstein's best friend. Then, on Frankenstein's wedding night, the creature kills his bride. From then on, Frankenstein devotes his life to finding the creature and destroying it. The story ends with Frankenstein's death from exhaustion and exposure. He has tracked the creature nearly to the North Pole, but has been unable to find and kill it.

After Frankenstein's death, the creature boards the ship that is carrying his remains back to England. The ship's captain describes the creature, as it stands over Frankenstein's dead body:

Over him hung a form which I cannot find words to describe—gigantic in stature, yet uncouth and distorted in its proportions. . . . his face was concealed by long locks of ragged hair; but one vast hand was extended, in colour and apparent texture like that of a mummy . . . Never did I behold a vision so horrible as his face, of such loathsome yet appalling hideousness.

The monster begs forgiveness of the dead Frankenstein, telling the captain that, even as he committed the most horrible crimes against Frankenstein and his loved ones, what he desired most was to be loved and accepted: ". . . while I destroyed his hopes, I did not satisfy my own desires. They were forever ardent and craving; still I desired love and fellowship, and I was still spurned. . . . Am I to be thought the only criminal, when all humankind sinned against me?" Haunted by his crimes, Frankenstein's monster leaps from the ship, declaring his intention to kill himself— for he knows he will find peace only in death.

Within a few years after its publication, stage adaptations of the story became popular entertainment, precursors of the many horror movies that were to follow. Silent film versions of the story were made in 1910 and 1915. Countless sound films have also been made, but the portrayal of Frankenstein's monster that will never be forgotten was in the very first, made in 1931. That *Frankenstein* starred Colin Clive as Victor Frankenstein and Boris Karloff as a monster who was horrific, yet pathetic, in his alienation and suffering.

Over the years, there has been a tendency to confuse the monster and his creator. An exceedingly ugly individual is frequently, though inaccurately, called a *Frankenstein*.

Just as Prometheus was punished for daring to steal fire from the gods, Victor Frankenstein was punished for playing God, and the result of his arrogance literally haunted him for the rest of his life. In the same way, all of us are haunted by things we do and events we set into motion. In a figurative sense, then, we frequently *create a Frankenstein* or *create a monster* of our own. We must live with the consequences of our actions—for better or worse—just as Frankenstein lived, and died, with the monstrous consequences of his.

Dagwood/Dagwood sandwich: a thick sandwich, made with a variety of fillings

How many times have you raided the refrigerator, piling everything you could find—meats, cheeses, lettuce, tomatoes, pickles, etc.—between two slices of bread? The resulting sandwich was probably so thick you could barely fit it into your mouth: a real *Dagwood*.

The first Dagwood sandwich was made in the comic strip *Blondie*, by one Dagwood Bumstead, hence its name. *Blondie* was created by Murat (Chic) Young in 1930. Young had begun his artistic career working in the art department of a Cleveland newspaper for $22 a week. When he was offered $10,000 to go to work for King Features Syndicate, he didn't have to think twice. During his first four months with King, he drew the cartoon *Beautiful Babs*; for the next five years he was the brains behind *Dumb Dora*.

Throughout the 1920s, these and other "girl" comic strips were immensely popular. In keeping with the times, the strip that Chic Young introduced on September 8, 1930, featured a single girl, Blondie Boopadoop. Blondie was a typical flapper, but only for a little while. Soon she met Dagwood Bumstead, fell in love, and got married. The result was a strip that revolved around the everyday life of the Bumsteads. Dagwood and Blondie represented the average American family, living in the suburbs. Dagwood was a regular guy, though somewhat hapless, and Blondie was definitely the boss of the house and the star of the strip. Blondie and Dagwood became the proud parents of their first child, Baby Dumpling, on April 15, 1934. A daughter was born to the Bumsteads in 1941.

The cartoon couple's first film, *Blondie*, was released in 1938 and starred Penny Singleton. Between 1938 and 1950, over twenty sequels were made, including *Blondie Brings Up Baby, Blondie Goes to College*, and *Blondie Knows Best*. Two television series followed: one premiered in 1957, with Pamela Britton as Blondie; the second ran from 1968 to 1969 and starred Patricia Harty.

David Pringle, in his 1987 work, *Imaginary People*, quoted a source who claimed that *Blondie* was probably the most widely circulated comic strip in the world, with hundreds of millions of people having access to it. Mr. Pringle also noted, however, that

Charles Schulz's *Peanuts* has been credited by other
sources with having a wider circulation.

Dantesque: horrific

No one knows exactly when Dante Alighieri began
his *Divine Comedy*, but most of it was written between 1315 and his death in 1321. The work, which
chronicles the poet's allegorical journey through hell,
purgatory, and paradise, is divided into three sections.
The first and best-known, "Inferno," is the source of
the English expression *Dante's Inferno,* which is often used to denote a hellish place. And, from the horrific sights and sounds that are depicted in Dante's
vision of hell, the adjective *Dantesque,* meaning hellish or horrific, was coined.

With the poet Virgil as his guide, Dante approaches
the gate to hell and reads its inscription: "Through
me is the way into the doleful city; through me the
way into the eternal pain. . . ." Passing through the
gate, he hears "strange tongues, horrible outcries,
words of pain, tones of anger, voices deep and
hoarse. . . ." The sounds are so awful that Dante is
moved to tears before he even lays eyes on the tormented souls who reside here. As it turns out, the
outer regions of the Inferno are reserved for those
whose sins have been minor. "Wherewithal a man
sinneth, by the same also shall he be punished," or,
in plain English, "Let the punishment fit the crime,"

is the basic premise behind Dante's notion of hell.

The sinners just inside the gate are those who have done neither good nor evil in life. In the first circle, which is called Limbo, are blameless spirits who have never been baptized. Circles two through five are reserved for those who have committed "sins of incontinence": adulterers, gluttons, misers, spendthrifts, the ill-tempered, etc. Their punishments are mild. For example, the adulterers are constantly buffeted by the wind, as they were in life by their desires.

The sixth circle contains Satan's City of Dis. The city glows with the fires in which heretics are burned. Those who have committed sins of violence—tyrants, murderers, assassins—are steeped in the river of blood that surrounds the seventh circle, and suicides are forced to spend eternity on a plain of burning sand, where showers of fire fall on them.

In the eighth circle are panderers, flatterers, corrupt clergymen and politicians, sorcerers, and alchemists. The soles of their feet are on fire, they are rent by demons, covered with boiling pitch, and suffer all manner of horrors to expiate their sins against God. Hypocrites wear cloaks of lead and evil counselors are wrapped in flame; thieves inhabit dark, serpent-filled chasms and liars are plagued with disease.

While the sinners in the City of Dis spend eternity in a hot, fiery furnace, those in the ninth circle are forever consigned to a frozen wasteland. The ninth circle is reserved for traitors—those who have turned against their family and friends, their country, and their god. The two archtraitors, Judas Iscariot and Satan himself, are trapped here. A frozen stream of guilt keeps flowing back toward Satan, who created it in the first place. Still wearing the wings of an angel, he flaps these furiously in an effort to free himself from the ice, but all his struggles do is produce a frigid wind that adds to his torment.

It is with great relief that Dante follows Virgil along the road that leads away from the darkness and into the bright world, where he once again sees "the beauteous things which Heaven bears."

Dennis the Menace: a mischievous child, a brat

In October 1994, cartoonist Hank Ketcham announced his retirement. Ketcham began drawing *Dennis the Menace* in 1951, using his then-four-year-old son as the model for the title character. At the time of Ketcham's retirement, his daily cartoons and Sunday strips were being carried by more than 1,800 newspapers worldwide, and the name of *Dennis the Menace* had long since become a popular epithet for a mischievous, bratty child.

Dennis the Menace Mitchell has been described as "a towheaded tornado" and "Hans and Fritz [Katzenjammer] rolled into one." Over the years he has been a source of consternation to his parents, and his appearance in the backyard has been enough to strike fear into the heart of his long-suffering neighbor, Mr.

Wilson. (A recent cartoon showed an exasperated Mr. Wilson with pills in his hand, saying, "Aspirin companies should pay that kid a retainer.")

Dennis the Menace was also a popular television series, which aired from 1959 to 1963 and starred Jay North as the little devil.

Ketcham's Dennis is generally accompanied by his dog, Ruff. In an unusual coincidence, a British cartoonist named David Law also created a character named Dennis the Menace in 1951. Law's little monster had black hair, wore a red-striped jersey, and had a dog named Gnasher. He did not, however, have his own comic strip, but was one of the characters in *The Beano*.

There is good news for the millions of *Dennis the Menace* fans around the world: According to Ketcham, the strip will continue, little changed, in the hands of a team of writers and artists. "Keep giving me that ten seconds a day," says Ketcham, "because Dennis is going to be around for a long time."

Dickensian: starkly realistic, grim

The Reader's Encyclopedia says of Charles Dickens that:

> *No other English writer has created a world of characters so distinctively cruel or suffering, comic or repugnant as Dickens has; no other writer has writ-*

> ten so convincingly of the wrongs inflicted on chil-
> dren by adults in the 19th century.... As a social
> critic, he focused sharply on the iniquities and in-
> equities of his environment.

While most of Dickens's novels have happy endings, they are filled with starkly realistic, grim images
of life in England during the Industrial Revolution.
He describes the London slums, the inhuman working
conditions in the mills, the evils of child labor, the
debtors' prisons, and the workhouses. While there are
good and kind people in Dickens's fictional world,
there is also a plethora of villains who prey on the
young, the old, the poor, and the infirm: Fagin, Heep,
Squeers, Merdstone, Bounderby, to name a few.
There are incompetent and uncaring bureaucrats like
the beadle Bumble, a minor official whose arrogance
and sense of self-importance was immortalized when
the word *bumbledom* was created, and Mr. Tite Barnacle, who runs the Circumlocution Office, a place
where no question is ever answered and no action
ever taken.

Much of Dickens's outrage came from seeing the
suffering of those around him, but some of it came
from personal experience. Dickens's father, a navy
clerk, was constantly in debt and, when Charles was
twelve years old, was thrown into prison. Like the
young hero of *David Copperfield*, Dickens was forced
to go out and work in a factory, a humiliating and
painful experience that had a profound and lasting
effect on him.

The adjective *Dickensian* was coined to describe the stark view of life that pervades the works of Charles Dickens, as well as any real or fictional atmosphere that is equally grim and depressing.

See also: **Circumlocution Office, micawberesque.**

Dolly Varden/dolly varden: a style of dress; a hat; a trout; a crab

Barnaby Rudge was the least successful of Charles Dickens's novels due, it has been suggested, to the weakness of its plot. But even if nineteenth-century readers didn't find the story memorable, at least one of its characters made a lasting impression on them and on the English language.

Barnaby Rudge was written in 1841 and set in England at the time of the anti-Catholic Gordon Riots of 1780. Sixty years after the riots, Charles Dickens used the genre of the historical novel to condemn the English government for its neglect of the poor, which he believed to be one of the main causes of the rioting.

The title character is an innocent, simpleminded young man who participates in the riots because he wants to carry a flag and wear a bow. He is mistakenly identified as one of the leaders of the riot and is condemned to death. Fortunately, through the influence of a locksmith named Gabriel Varden, he is reprieved and allowed to return to his mother's home.

Gabriel Varden's daughter, Dolly Varden, is a fashionable young woman whose transformation from coquette to mature, loving woman forms a subplot of the novel. Dickens describes her as "... a pretty, laughing girl; dimpled and fresh, and healthful—the very impersonation of good-humour and blooming beauty." Dolly loves dressing up, and in more than one of the book's illustrations she is shown decked out in a dress with a tight bodice and a sheer, flowered skirt worn over a bright-colored petticoat. Female readers of *Barnaby Rudge* evidently shared Dolly's taste, for this style of dress soon became popular and was advertised as a *Dolly Varden*.

In one scene Dolly also wears "a smart little cherry-coloured mantle, with a hood of the same drawn over her head, and upon the top of that hood, a little straw hat trimmed with cherry-coloured ribbons, and worn the merest trifle on one side—just enough, in short, to make it the wickedest and most provoking head-dress that ever malicious milliner devised." As a result, fashion-conscious women were soon referring to a beflowered or beribboned hat with a large brim, bent down on one side, as a *Dolly Varden*.

Dolly's love of bright colors, particularly red, led to the renaming of a large trout *(Salvelinus malma),* olivaceous in color with round red spots, after her. The fish, which can grow from two to three feet in length, is found in streams in the American Northwest and in Japan.

Another creature whose coloring brings to mind the coquettish dress of Dolly Varden is the Dolly Varden crab, sometimes called the calico crab. This is a shallow-water crab *(Hepatus epheliticus),* brilliantly spotted with red and found along the coast of the United States, from Maryland south to Cuba and west to Texas.

Don Juan: a philanderer

Men who are constantly on the make, courting women for the sole purpose of sexual relationships, are called Romeos, Lotharios, and *Don Juans.* All of these epithets come from literature and are the names of famous characters who, for one reason or another, are best remembered for their pursuit of the opposite sex.

The legend of Don Juan is supposedly based on the life story of the son of a prominent family, who lived in Seville during the fourteenth century. The story was first put into literary form by Tirso de Molina in his 1630 play *El burlador de Sevilla y el convidado de piedra (The Libertine of Seville and the Stone Guest).* The action begins when Don Juan Tenorio murders Don Gonzalo Ulloa, the outraged father of one of the many women Don Juan has seduced. Later, Don Juan jokingly invites a stone statue of the dead

man to dinner. To his shock, the statue comes to life
and accepts. It then invites Don Juan to a party at the
tomb of Don Gonzalo, where it strangles him and
sends his soul to hell.

El burlador de Sevilla and Tirso's other plays were
so popular and so controversial that in 1625 the Council of Castile recommended that he not be allowed to
write any more because of the scandal they were causing. But the scandalous and intriguing figure of Don
Juan created by Tirso inspired many other authors to
write their own versions of the legend of Don Juan.

Several Italian writers attempted to rework Tirso's
story, as did a number of Frenchmen, including the
comic genius Molière, who in his *Dom Juan* created
the character of Elvire, the wife of the unfaithful protagonist. Other French writers who dealt with the
theme include Corneille, Merimée, Dumas père, Mus-
set, Balzac, and Flaubert. The best-known Spanish
successor of Tirso is José Zorrilla y Moral, who as a
nineteenth-century Romantic made his Don Juan Tenorio fall in love with a virtuous woman, Doña Inés,
whose prayers brought about his repentance and salvation.

The legend of Don Juan also fascinated many English writers, including Thomas Shadwell, whose
1676 play, *The Libertine*, pales in comparison with
the Spanish and French versions. On the other hand,
George Bernard Shaw's ''Don Juan in Hell'' scene in
Man and Superman (1905) has become a classic in
its own right and has been performed apart from the
rest of the play and in dramatic readings. Shaw's Don

Juan is a philosopher, a man who debates with the Devil and insists that man's life has meaning because he has the capacity to recognize and carry out God's will.

Shaw's Don Juan is obviously a far cry from Tirso's sexually obsessed, immoral villain, as is the Don Juan created by Lord Byron in his epic satire. Byron's hero is more of an adventurer than a philanderer, and his cavalier attitude toward romance is only one aspect of his generally devil-may-care personality. He does have the ability to attract women wherever he goes, however, and because of this he is constantly in trouble. His problems begin when his mother's best friend seduces him and he is sent abroad to stop the affair. After he is shipwrecked on a Greek island and nursed back to health by a beautiful young girl named Haidée, her father catches him making love to her and sells him into slavery. Bought by the sultana of Constantinople, Don Juan arouses her anger by carrying on with one of the girls in the sultan's harem. He barely escapes with his life and flees to Russia. There he becomes a favorite of Catherine the Great, who sends him on a mission to England, where the unfinished tale ends.

The most famous musical version of the story of the great philanderer is the opera *Don Giovanni*, composed by Mozart in 1787, for a libretto written by Lorenzo Da Ponte. At one point in the opera, Don Juan's valet says that his master had "in Italy 700 mistresses, in Germany 800, in Turkey and France 91, in Spain 1,003." With a record like that, Don Juan

certainly earned his linguistic immortality!
See also: **byronic, Lothario, Romeo.**

(a) Dorian Gray: one who leads a life of sin
behind a facade of innocence

The first time Dorian Gray sees the portrait of himself
that has been painted by Basil Hallward, he has mixed
emotions. He marvels at his own beauty, captured
perfectly by the artist. At the same time, he thinks
ahead to the day when he will no longer be young
and handsome:

> *Yes, there would be a day when his face would be*
> *wrinkled and wizen, his eyes dim and colourless, the*
> *grace of his figure broken and deformed. The scarlet*
> *would pass away from his lips and the gold steal*
> *from his hair. The life that was to make his soul*
> *would mar his body. He would become dreadful, hid-*
> *eous, and uncouth.*

When Dorian realizes that his portrait will remain
young as he grows old, he makes a wish:

> *If it were I who was to be always young, and the*
> *picture that was to grow old! For that—for that—I*
> *would give everything! . . . I would give my soul for*
> *that!*

Before long, Dorian Gray realizes that someone, somewhere, has heard his wish and granted it. As he sinks further and further into a life of debauchery, treating others cruelly and engaging in all sorts of vices, he begins to notice signs of aging on the portrait. As the picture continues to change, reflecting each immoral act that Dorian commits, it is obvious that he can no longer keep it on display. He locks it away where only he can see, on the canvas, the progressive deterioration of his soul.

Finally, Dorian can stand it no more and shows the portrait to Basil Hallward. Hallward cannot believe his eyes, but as the realization of what has happened to the portrait sinks in, he begs Dorian to mend his ways while he still has time. Dorian explodes with anger, stabbing Hallward to death.

After Hallward's murder, the portrait becomes even more hideous, and blood appears on it. Dorian realizes that it might be used as evidence against him and determines to destroy it. Picking up the knife with which he killed Hallward, he stabs the picture. His servants hear a crash and a horrible scream, and when they enter the room they find hanging on the wall a beautiful portrait of Dorian Gray as a young man. Lying on the floor beneath it is an old man, dead, with a knife in his heart. He is "withered, wrinkled, and loathsome of visage." It is not until they examine the rings on his fingers that they are able to identify him as their master, Dorian Gray.

The Picture of Dorian Gray was written by Irish-born author Oscar Wilde in 1891. The name *Dorian*

Gray is used to describe someone who leads a life of sin behind a facade of innocence. Such an individual might do well to take heed of the lesson of Wilde's tale: In the short run such a deception might work, but in the end our evil deeds always have a way of catching up with us.

> **doublespeak:** the use of euphemisms and other obfuscations to avoid making a direct statement of fact

In the totalitarian country of Oceania, created by George Orwell in his satirical masterpiece *1984*, the official language was Newspeak. Newspeak was a terse, vastly limited form of Oldspeak, or standard English, which was designed to make any heretical thoughts impossible by eliminating the words for them.

Another Orwellian concept was that of doublethink, or reality control, as the Party called it. Those in power in Oceania were constantly rewriting history to make it conform to their propagandistic messages. For example, if the official forecasts of the production of a certain item turned out to be incorrect, the magazine or newspaper articles in which they had appeared would be rewritten to reflect the actual production levels, thus sparing the Party any embarrassment. The result was that the people remembered the original forecasts but accepted the revised version nonetheless because that was what they had been indoctrinated to do. Doublethink prevented them from questioning the implications of two contradictory sets of facts. Doublethink was "an unending series of victories over your own memory."

From Orwell's two linguistic inventions—Newspeak and doublethink—a third word was created: *doublespeak*, which refers to the use of euphemisms and other obfuscations to avoid making a direct statement of fact. When politicians, executives, union leaders, and academics beat around the bush and perform linguistic gymnastics in an effort to avoid coming to the point, we call their strategy *doublespeak*.

In their book *Grand Allusions*, Elizabeth Webber and Mike Feinsilber relate how the term *doublespeak* was coined at the annual meeting of the National Council of Teachers held in November 1971. Webber and Feinsilber say of the word that:

> It was defined as "dishonest and inhumane uses of language" and was an outgrowth of concern expressed by delegates about lack of candor by the U.S. government in communicating with Americans about the Vietnam war.

The word *doublespeak* is often mistakenly believed to have been coined by Orwell himself.

See also: **Big Brother is watching, Orwellian.**

Dragon Lady: a tough woman, hard woman; the consort of a powerful man who capitalizes on his position

Terry and the Pirates was a comic strip that was never intended to be funny. Its creator, Milton Caniff, expected the adventures of a handsome young American in China to win readers. The idea paid off for Caniff, and the strip ran from 1934 until 1973. It was also made into a cinema serial in 1940.

Caniff drew *Terry and the Pirates* until 1946, after which a series of artists continued his work. During the strip's first thirteen years, Terry Lee matured from a young boy to a man. His numerous adventures came about when, while looking for treasure, he kept running afoul of a band of pirates. Caniff added an interesting twist when he made the leader of the pirates a woman.

The Dragon Lady was a cold, calculating criminal for whom Terry became a personal nemesis. The popularity of *Terry and the Pirates* led to the introduction into English of the term *Dragon Lady* to mean a cruel, intimidating woman. More recently, the term has attained worldwide popularity as an epithet for a woman who uses her husband's position or influence to achieve her own ends.

The former first lady of the Philippines, Imelda Marcos, was frequently referred to as The Dragon Lady by her critics.

Milton Caniff was one of the few cartoonists who

drew his characters from live models. He was also meticulous when it came to the details he included about the Far East, researching the language, culture, and geography of the region at the public library before writing. In order to attract the greatest number of readers, Caniff adjusted the story line, emphasizing Terry's heartthrob aspect during the week and concentrating on the adventure element on Sundays, when a large number of children read the funnies.

eat one out of house and home: eat huge quantities of food

Parents frequently complain that their teenaged children *eat them out of house and home*. This colorful phrase, which has been used by all of us at one time or another, has a surprising origin. Its first recorded use in English was by none another than the Bard of Avon, William Shakespeare, whom we tend to associate with far more poetic language.

Shakespeare used the somewhat comic figure of speech in *Henry IV, Part II,* which was written in 1597–98 and first produced in 1599. In Act II, Scene I, Hostess Quickly of the Boar's Head Tavern is complaining about Sir John Falstaff, who has been lodging with her, eating huge quantities of food, and avoiding paying his bill: "He hath eaten me out of house and home, he hath put all my substance into that fat belly of his. . . ."

The phrase *out of house and home* was in use in England as early as the thirteenth century, and during the fifteenth century people often said "he hath eaten me out of house" or "out of house and harbor." But it is in the form that Shakespeare put it that the expression came down to us and continues to enliven our everyday conversation.

emperor's new clothes: a sham, something that isn't what it's claimed to be

In a fairy tale written by Hans Christian Andersen, a sovereign is tricked by his tailor into believing that he is wearing a beautiful new set of clothes that has been created especially for him. The emperor is, in fact, stark naked, but is afraid to question the tailor, lest he appear foolish in his eyes. He goes among his people, showing off his new clothes, and they too are afraid to admit that they don't see anything but flesh. Instead, they rave about the exquisite detail, fine workmanship, and perfect fit of the nonexistent apparel. Only one man has the courage of his convictions and announces to all that the emperor is naked: His new clothes are a sham, a fraud that has been perpetrated by the tailor.

Andersen's tales were published in Danish between 1835 and 1872 and translated into English soon after. They became great favorites of English and American children, and the expression *emperor's new clothes*

soon came to be applied to anything that is not worthy
of the praise bestowed on it: in other words, something that is not what's it's cracked up to be.

See also: **ugly duckling.**

Everyman: John Q. Public, the average person

In medieval times, allegorical dramas were called
moral plays or morality plays. Like mystery plays,
they were presented as popular pageants. But their
characters weren't biblical or historical figures; instead, they were personifications of abstract concepts.
The theme of most morality plays was sin and redemption: Man generally led a life of sin and corruption, and only God's mercy could save him from
eternal damnation. Morality plays were basically dramatic sermons. Hence our use in modern parlance of
the term *morality play* to describe a situation or event
that teaches a basic lesson in right and wrong.

Morality plays appeared toward the end of the Middle Ages; no examples of such dramas exist from before the beginning of the fifteenth century. The most
famous English morality play is *Everyman*, which
was printed in England at the beginning of the sixteenth century and was based on a Dutch play of 1495
titled *Elckerlijk*.

Everyman, the central character, is the only human
being in the play and represents mankind. In the
play's prologue we are told that ''. . . ye shall hear

how our heaven's king Calleth Everyman to a general reckoning.'' God then speaks and says that people are living without fear. All they think of is worldly riches and their own pleasure, and they never think of God or what will be in store for them when they meet their maker. He calls Death and says:

> *Go thou to Everyman,*
> *And show him in my name*
> *A pilgrimage he must on him take,*
> *Which he in no wise may escape;*
> *And that he bring with him a sure reckoning*
> *Without delay or any tarrying.*

When Death finally gets Everyman to understand that he must leave this earth and return to his maker, Everyman asks, "Shall I have no company from this vale terrestrial/Of mine acquaintance the way me to lead?" Death allows him time to ask his acquaintances (i.e., all the things that have been a part of his life) if they would like to accompany him.

One by one, Everyman asks Fellowship, Kindred, Cousin, Goods, Beauty, Five-Wits, Strength, Discretion, and Good-Deeds if they wish to come with him to face God. Only Good-Deeds agrees to go with him. But Good-Deeds knows Everyman needs a stronger companion than he when he faces God, so he asks his sister Knowledge to come along. Everyman, accompanied by Good-Deeds and Knowledge, goes to Confession. Confession gives him penance and tells him, "Ask God mercy, and He will grant truly;/When with the scourge of penance man doth him bind,/The oil of forgiveness then shall he find.''

Thus, Everyman is redeemed, as the Church promises every man can be, by the good deeds he does during his life, the knowledge he acquires, and his confession and penance for his sins. Just as the character Everyman represented each and every person who has lived or will ever live, over the centuries the sobriquet *Everyman* came to be used to mean the average person, John Q. Public, the man on the street, and it is still used in this way today.

Falstaffian: jovial, full of life

Near the beginning of Shakespeare's historical play *Henry IV, Part I*, Sir John Falstaff asks the heir to the throne, young Prince Hal, what time it is. The prince responds:

> *What a devil hast thou to do with the time of the day? Unless hours were cups of sack, and minutes capons, and clocks the tongues of bawds, and dials the signs of leaping-houses, and the blessed sun himself a fair hot wench in flame-coloured taffeta, I see no reason why thou shouldst be so superfluous to demand the time of day.*

And, in fact, unless Falstaff is plotting a theft or the extortion of money from one of his acquaintances, all he is interested in is pleasure. Eating, drinking, making love, and partying with his friends in the

Boar's Head Tavern are what he lives for. He is the epitome of excess: an obese, lecherous drunkard who is also a thief, a liar, and a coward. But he remains one of Shakespeare's most memorable creations and one of the most popular characters in all of English literature. His popularity, past and present, is attested to by the fact that the adjective *Falstaffian* has been in use for centuries and continues to be a commonly used term to describe someone who is jovial and full of life. A jolly, lively person is also frequently dubbed a Falstaff.

In *Henry IV, Part I*, Falstaff's antics amuse the young Prince of Wales and provide the latter with some comic relief from his duties as heir to the throne. Prince Hal has no intention of abandoning his royal responsibilities, but he is perfectly willing to escape from them in the company of Falstaff whenever possible.

An older, decidedly more corrupt Falstaff appears in *Henry IV, Part II*, where he seeks to profit from Prince Hal's new position as King Henry V. But Falstaff's old friend Hal no longer exists, and the King bans Falstaff from his court, although he does provide him with a generous pension. Although Falstaff does not have a role in the next play in Shakespeare's historical series, *Henry V*, his death is described there.

Falstaff also plays a major role in one of Shakespeare's comedies, *The Merry Wives of Windsor*. Still possessed of all his vices, including his overlarge ego, Falstaff ends up being the butt of a joke played on him by Mistress Page and Mistress Ford, two well-to-do married ladies of Windsor. Convinced that both are attracted to him, Falstaff decides to pay court to both in the hope that they will give him money. The two women, however, are not only faithful to their husbands but also good friends of one another, and together they plot revenge on Falstaff. Mistress Ford entertains Falstaff in her home and, on cue, Mistress Page arrives and tells the "lovers" that Ford is on his way home. Falstaff is convinced to hide in a basket of laundry, which Mistress Ford tells her servants to dump into the river. Bloodied but unbowed, Falstaff pays another visit to Mistress Ford. When Mistress Page arrives once again, announcing Ford's approach, the two women dress Falstaff up as an old woman who is reputed to be a witch and whom Ford hates. Ford beats the old woman and ejects her from the house, after which his wife and her friend reveal everything to their husbands.

In a final act of revenge, Falstaff is lured to the woods at midnight, where he expects a tryst with the women. He is greeted instead by a group of children dressed as fairies, who pinch and torment him. The Pages and the Fords then appear and reveal their plot to Falstaff. To show that they bear him no ill will, they invite the fat knight to join in the wedding celebration of the Pages' daughter.

Faustian bargain: a bargain with the Devil;
the selling of one's soul for material things

If you believe in an afterlife where good deeds are
rewarded and sins punished, you might say of someone who has given up the promise of eternal happiness for pleasure in the here and now that he or she
has made a *Faustian bargain*, or a bargain with the
Devil. Even if you don't accept the concepts of
heaven and hell, you are likely to use this figure of
speech to describe those who abandon their scruples
in relationships, business, or politics in order to attain
sensual or material gratification.

The original Faustian bargain was made by a character in literature: Faust, or Doctor Faustus, as he is
called in some works. The fictional Faust seems to
have been based on a real person, although there are
several theories as to who he was and when he lived.
There are references to both a Georgius Faustus and
a Johann Faustus in German records of the sixteenth
century. Both men are said to be doctors of theology,
and both are accused, in legal documents, of practicing magic and necromancy and of engaging in sodomy with young boys. It is generally believed that the
historical Faust died in 1540.

Faust was immortalized in an anonymous work
called the *Faustbuch*, which was published by Johann
Spies in Frankfurt-on-Main in 1587. The book detailed various magical feats said to have been carried
out by the historical Dr. Faustus, but which had been
described in earlier works, where they had been at-

tributed to other magicians. The popularity of the *Faustbuch* lay not so much in the depiction of Faust's magic tricks as in its author's evocative descriptions of hell, the devils who reside there, and Dr. Faustus's rejection of good in favor of evil. The book was quickly translated and was soon being read throughout Europe.

In 1592 an English translation appeared, and it was this version that inspired Christopher Marlowe to write his magnificent drama, *The Tragicall History of Dr. Faustus*, which was published in 1604. Although Marlowe's play retains some of the comic elements that appear in the original *Faustbuch*, it is a true tragedy. Dr. Faustus, having become adept at the art of conjuring up spirits, calls up the spirit of Mephistophilis, one of Lucifer's minions. He commands Mephistophilis to propose the following Faustian bargain to Lucifer:

Say he surrenders up to him his soul,
So he will spare him four and twenty years,
Letting him live in all voluptuousness;
Having thee ever to attend on me;
To give me whatsoever I shall ask,
To tell me whatsoever I demand,
To slay my enemies, and aid my friends,
And always be obedient to my will.

When Mephistophilis returns, he tells Faustus that Lucifer has agreed to the bargain, ''That I shall wait on Faustus whilst he lives, So he will buy my service with his soul.''

True to his word, Lucifer allows Mephistophilis to remain with Faustus, bestowing riches upon him, supplying him all the knowledge in the universe, even bringing the most beautiful woman in the world—Helen of Troy—up from the underworld for his pleasure. Several times during the twenty-four years that Mephistophilis serves him, Faustus comes face to face with angels and other emissaries of God who beg him to repent. He is tempted, but he always returns to the side of Satan.

As the hour of his death nears, Faustus calls on Lucifer to release him from his bargain and on God to save him from eternal damnation. But Lucifer will not relinquish his soul, and it is too late to ask for mercy from the God he has renounced. Before dying, Faustus realizes that he has no one to blame but himself for the loss of his immortal soul. He proposed the bargain and Lucifer kept his end of it; now it is Faustus's turn.

There have been many other versions of the Faust legend, including that of Johann Wolfgang von Goethe, who was inspired to rework the tale after reading the *Faustbuch* and seeing the story in a puppet show. Goethe's *Faust* consists of two parts. Part I was published in 1808 and Part II appeared in 1832. In the first part, Goethe expands the basic plot, adding the character of Gretchen, a young woman who is seduced and made pregnant by Faust. She drowns their child after it is born and is sentenced to death for her crime. Faust wants to spirit her away from prison but she refuses, throwing herself instead on God's mercy. *Faust, Part II* deviates widely from the original legend and ends with Faust's redemption. The most famous *Faust* musical is that of Charles Gounod, which was based on Goethe's work and written in 1859.

See also: **Mephistophelean.**

Felliniesque: having a surrealistic, overdone quality

In an obituary written for *Time* magazine on November 8, 1993, Richard Corliss defined the word *Felliniesque*:

> *[In Fellini's films], overripe images spilled out of his cornucopia: clowns and courtesans, prelates and zealots, overripe creatures from a fantast's bestiary. At first they looked like outrageous cartoons of sensuality and sacrilege. But long before his death ... it was clear they were previews of a moral system spun wildly off its axis. For thirty years and more, the word Felliniesque has defined not just the director's work but a style at the peacock end of film, photography, fashion, advertising, high life and street life.*

In the films of Italian director Federico Fellini, everything is overblown and overdone. Faces, caked with makeup, are pressed against the camera; the actors talk too fast, too loud, and too much; the camera shifts from scene to scene at a furious pace. Nothing is as we are used to seeing or hearing it; our senses are bombarded from every direction.

Corliss mentions that as a boy Fellini once ran away to join a traveling circus. Although he was discovered and sent home, "his heart stayed there." In fact, the feeling of a Fellini film is not unlike that we get at a three-ring circus: So much is going on that we can hardly take it in, but it is all so exciting that we don't want to miss any of it.

Fellini's most famous films are *La Strada, The Nights of Cabiria, Juliet of the Spirits, La Dolce Vita*, and *8½*. His wife of fifty years, Giulietta Masina, appeared in many of his movies through the years.

In many ways Fellini was a prophet: Life in the late twentieth century has become surreal. From morals, to music, to fashion, to leisure activities, it seems that anything goes. The rich are becoming richer, and their excesses are becoming more excessive. The poor are becoming poorer, but within their limited means, they too are seeking more dramatic ways to make themselves seen and heard. Things are done on a grand scale; they change at lightning speed; they don't always make sense. As Corliss says, "If you've been very lucky or very naughty, then life for you is like a Fellini movie."

Fibber McGee closet: a closet that is so full, when you open it everything falls out

In a nonvisual entertainment medium, the only way to represent action is through the use of sound effects. So, from 1935 to 1957, whenever the radio audience heard things falling, clattering, and banging, they knew someone had opened Fibber McGee's closet.

The *Fibber McGee and Molly* radio show was a favorite of Americans for over twenty years. It revolved around the life of a married couple who lived at 79 Wistful Vista, somewhere in the U.S. The husband, Fibber, had a habit of stretching the truth, which is how he earned his nickname. Two McGee films, starring Jim and Marian Jordan, were made in 1941 and 1942.

For two television seasons—from 1959 to 1960—viewers were able to see the contents fall out of Fibber McGee's closet whenever the door was opened, but most Americans remember the closet by the earth-shattering sounds that emanated from their radios. To this day, people are wont to refer to a closet that is crammed full of junk as a *Fibber McGee closet*, and many of us have firsthand knowledge of Fibber McGee–style storage.

Frankenstein: *See* **create a Frankenstein/ create a monster.**

(man/gal) Friday: a right-hand man or woman, an indispensable helper

English writer Daniel Defoe created the character of Robinson Crusoe in his 1719 novel, the full title of which was *The Life and Strange Surprising Adventures of Robinson Crusoe, of York, Mariner: Who Lived Eight and Twenty Years all Alone in an Uninhabited Island on the Coast of AMERICA, Near the Mouth of the Great River of ORINOCO; Having Been Cast on Shore by Shipwreck, Wherein all the Men Perished but Himself. With an Account How He Was at Last as Strangely Delivered by Pirates.*

Despite the title, Robinson Crusoe did not spend the entire eight and twenty years alone: After living by himself for nearly twenty-five years, he finally established contact with another human being. This person, whom he called his Man Friday, remained his faithful servant and boon companion for many years afterward.

During his years of solitude, Crusoe had observed cannibals landing on the shore of his otherwise private domain and feasting on other natives. One day Crusoe saw, from his hiding place, the escape of one of their prisoners. He tells the reader that as he watched the man and the cannibals who pursued him, "It came now very warmly upon my thoughts, and indeed irresistibly, that now was the time to get me a servant, and perhaps a companion or assistant, and that I was called plainly by Providence to save this poor creature's life."

After killing the cannibals, Crusoe reassured the frightened native by gestures and signs. "He came nearer and nearer, kneeling down every ten or twelve steps, in token of acknowledgment for saving his life . . . at length he came close to me; and then he kneeled down again . . . and taking me by the foot, set my foot upon his head; this, it seems, was in token of swearing to be my slave for ever."

Taking the native into his compound, Crusoe began to teach him English. He let him know that his new name was to be Friday, which was the day of the week on which Crusoe had saved his life, and that he was to call Crusoe Master. Before long, Crusoe was able to say that "never man had a more faithful, loving, sincere servant than Friday was to me . . . he would have sacrificed his life for the saving mine upon any occasion whatsoever."

Crusoe and his Man Friday lived alone together on the island for three more years. They were finally brought back to civilization by an English ship, but before long they set sail again. After a brief stop on the island where they had shared so much, they arrived in Brazil and were immediately set upon by a large band of savages. Friday was killed in the skirmish and deeply mourned by Crusoe, "and so ended the life of the most grateful, faithful, honest, and most affectionate servant, that man ever had."

Today's newspapers are full of ads for *man or gal Fridays*: men or women who are hired to work closely with their employer and carry out a wide variety of duties, acting, the way Crusoe's man did, as general factotums.

Fu Manchu mustache: a long, thin mustache that hangs down the sides of the mouth

In one of the novels of Sax Rohmer (pen name of Arthur S. Ward), Dr. Fu Manchu is described as having "a brow like Shakespeare and a face like Satan." Perhaps the most arresting characteristic of his Satanic countenance was his long, thin mustache, which trailed down on either side of his mouth. The style is so closely associated with Rohmer's villain that to this day it is called a *Fu Manchu mustache*.

The "Devil Doctor" was created by Rohmer for *Story-Teller* magazine, where he appeared in a series of short stories that were published during 1912. These were so popular that the following year they were put together and re-released as novels, which soon became bestsellers: *The Mystery of Dr. Fu Manchu* (1913), *The Devil Doctor* (1916), and *The Si-Fan Mysteries* (1917). After this, Rohmer stopped writing about Fu Manchu for several years, but Fu's successful portrayal by Harry Agar Lyons in the silent films of the 1920s created a new interest in the series. Rohmer took up his pen once more and produced nearly a dozen more novels before his death.

Several Fu Manchu films have been made since the era of the talkies began: *The Mysterious Dr. Fu Manchu* (1929) and two others starring Warner Oland; *The Mask of Fu Manchu* (1932) starring Boris Karloff; *Drums of Fu Manchu* (a serial made in 1939) starring Henry Brandon; and, in the 1960s, five movies starring Christopher Lee.

In the 1930s and 1940s Fu Manchu made the transition to radio and comic strips. During the 1950s he was portrayed on American television by Glen Gordon.

Si-Fan was the name of the secret society that Fu Manchu headed, and its goal was to take over the world. Fortunately for those who wished to remain free, Fu's dastardly schemes continued to be thwarted by Rohmer's hero, Dennis Nayland Smith. However, as is so often the case when good and evil are personified, the wholesome character of Smith wasn't nearly as compelling as that of the evil Fu Manchu.

future shock: the disorientation we feel as a result of too much change

In 1970, Alvin Toffler described a new disease that he believed was ravaging twentieth-century man:

> *Future shock will not be found in* Index Medicus *or in any listing of psychological abnormalities. Yet, unless intelligent steps are taken to combat it, millions*

of human beings will find themselves increasingly disoriented, progressively incompetent to deal rationally with their environments. The malaise, mass neurosis, irrationality, and free-floating violence already apparent in contemporary life are merely a foretaste of what may lie ahead unless we come to understand and treat this disease.

Toffler first coined the term *future shock* in a 1965 article for *Horizon*. He used it to describe the shattering stress and disorientation that are induced in individuals when they are subjected to too much change in too short a time. Fascinated by this concept, Toffler spent the next five years at universities, research centers, laboratories, and government agencies probing the subject of change in twentieth-century society. He read all the material he could find on the topic and interviewed experts on change, coping behavior, and the future. In 1970 he published his findings in *Future Shock*, a book that became a bestseller and made future shock a widely used phrase in America.

His conclusion, as the above quotation reflects, was that the greatly accelerated rate of change that has taken place in the twentieth century has left mankind in a state of shock: future shock. Future shock is actually culture shock in one's own society, where things are so ephemeral that just as soon as they become familiar they are swept away on the tide of change.

At the beginning of *Future Shock*, Toffler puts the changes that have occurred in the last century into a new and startling perspective. He states that if the last 50,000 years of man's existence were divided into lifetimes of sixty-two years each, that would make 800 lifetimes. Man spent 650 of those lifetimes living in caves. Only in the last six of those lifetimes did the masses have access to printed material; only in the last two was electricity discovered. And only in this lifetime have most of the goods we use been developed.

The result of the tremendous strides that man has made in the last lifetime is a surfeit of novelty. Things are changing so rapidly that the vast majority of people simply can't keep up with what is transpiring around them. Some feel so threatened by change that they try to deny its existence. Others are worn out trying to keep abreast of all that is new. Toffler examines the many facets of modern-day life that overwhelm us: the replacement of durable goods, passed down from generation to generation, by throwaway items such as paper wedding gowns; the increasingly nomadic existence of young professionals that results in continual job changes and moves; the growing number of fractured families, in which divorce, remarriage, and redivorce occur at an astonishing rate; the ever-increasing number of choices available to us, which make decision making so complicated that we are often paralyzed by inaction; the constant advances in science, medicine, and technology, which make theories obsolete before they have even been proven.

Unfortunately, Toffler's observations are as valid today as they were when his book was first published.

We continue to be bombarded by changes in every area of our lives. We buy a state-of-the-art computer, printer, and software; six months later they have become technological dinosaurs. We enjoy a meal at a Mexican restaurant; when we go back two months later, the new owners are serving sushi and tempura. We're bursting with pride when we finally figure out how to compute our income tax; the following year we get a completely different form in the mail and it's back to square one.

In any one of these cases we are likely to comment that we are suffering from future shock, for in spite of all the advances that have occurred in medicine, no one has yet found a cure for the disease that Alvin Toffler so accurately diagnosed twenty-seven years ago.

gargantuan/Gargantuan: gigantic, colossal

Just before the giantess Gargamelle gave birth to Gargantua, she consumed sixteen hogsheads, two barrels, and six jugs full of tripe. She had been pregnant with her firstborn son for eleven months—a fact that her creator, François Rabelais, didn't consider at all odd, "For women may carry their big bellies as long, and even longer, especially when it is some masterpiece of a personage that is to be born, and one who is to do great deeds in his time."

The legend of a giant named Gargantua had existed in French folklore for at least a century before François Rabelais wrote his masterpiece, *Gargantua and Pantagruel*. The legend seems to have taken on a new life at the beginning of the sixteenth century, and several new lives of Gargantua appeared in France. By the time Rabelais began writing his version, Gargantua was already possessed of gigantic stature, strength, and appetites.

Rabelais's Gargantua showed signs of being a "masterpiece of a personage" from the moment he entered the world. Emerging from his mother's left ear, he proceeded to cry, "Give me a drink! a drink! a drink!" The newborn was given a good stiff drink, taken to the font, and baptized immediately.

Rabelais goes on to describe the infant's diet: ". . . they set aside seventeen-thousand-nine-hundred-thirteen cows of Pontille and Brehemont for his ordinary milk-diet . . . until he was a year and ten months old." He then developed a taste for wine, and whenever he cried or stamped his feet his parents brought him something to drink, which immediately restored his good humor.

The construction of Gargantua's first set of clothing was a major undertaking. With an ell measuring forty-five inches, his shirt was made of 900 ells of cloth, with 900 for the gussets; his doublet took 813 ells of white, with 1509½ dog skins for the laces; his breeches required 1105⅓ ells of white broadcloth. The soles of the boy giant's shoes were made of eleven hundred brown cowhides, shaped like a codfish's tail, and his purse was fashioned from an elephant's penis. The jewelry that completed Gargantua's outfit was exceedingly impressive—and heavy. The gold chain that hung from his neck weighed 166,708⅔ pounds; on the index finger of his left hand he wore a carbuncle as big as an ostrich's egg.

Given the enormous size of Gargantua and everything that surrounds him, it is no wonder that from his name an adjective meaning gigantic or colossal was formed.

Gargantua and Pantagruel consists of four books that were written by Rabelais between 1532 and 1552. A fifth book, published posthumously in 1564, is believed by most scholars to be the work of an imitator. Book II, which deals with the life of Gargantua's son, Pantagruel, was actually the first to be written, in 1532. Two years later Rabelais produced *The Most Horrific Life of the Great Gargantua*, which concentrates on the adventures of Pantagruel's father and which, through its popularity in the original French and in many translations, provided the impetus for the formation of the English word *gargantuan*.

See also: **Rabelaisian.**

Godzilla: a big, strong, oafish person

In October 1994, a gala fortieth birthday party was held at the Toho Company's No. 9 Studio in Tokyo, Japan. The guest of honor was a giant fire-belching lizard named Gojira who beat his chest and announced to the 500 fans in attendance that he was young for a monster and had no plans to retire.

In the United States we know Gojira as *Godzilla*, and, along with the Japanese, we have been following his movie career for the past forty years. *Godzilla, King of the Monsters* was released in America in 1955. Directed by Inoshiro Honda, the film tells the story of a prehistoric, dinosaur-like monster who is awakened from centuries of sleep by an H-bomb test.

The creature then goes on a rampage, trampling over cities and villages and threatening to destroy Tokyo. The film was such a hit that the expression *a real Godzilla* soon became a popular way of referring to a big, strong person, particularly one who is oafish and doesn't know his own strength.

In his first forty years, Godzilla appeared in many Japanese films and cartoons. Twenty-one Godzilla films were made at Toho's No. 9 Studio, including *King Kong vs. Godzilla* (1962), *Godzilla vs. the Thing* (1964), *Destroy All Monsters* (1969), and *Space Godzilla* (1979). *Godzilla vs. Space-Godzilla* opened in Japan in 1995, just after its hero celebrated his fortieth birthday.

Goody Two-shoes: a person who always obeys the rules and never does anything wrong

Often, when a child refuses to join his or her playmates in a mischievous deed, they respond with taunts of *Goody Two-shoes*. They, of course, have no idea that they are using a literary allusion—one that originated over two hundred years ago, in an English nursery story.

John Newbery was a notable publisher of children's books. In 1765 his firm put out a story titled *The History of Little Goody Two-Shoes; Otherwise Called Mrs. Margery Two-Shoes, With the Means by Which She Acquired Her Learning and Wisdom, and in Consequence Thereof Her Estate*. The story may have been written by Oliver Goldsmith, who worked for Newbery, but his authorship has not been proved. *Goody Two-shoes*, as the title is usually abbreviated, is a morality tale, extolling the virtues of hard work and education as the means to upward mobility.

At the beginning of the book Margery is an orphan who only has one shoe. When a kindly benefactor gives her a pair of shoes, she is so thrilled that she shows them to everyone she meets, saying, "two shoes." By dint of hard work, Margery teaches herself to read, becomes a schoolmistress, and marries a well-to-do man.

Goody Two-shoes was an enormous success and was imitated in several subsequent children's stories. A "sequel" was written in 1818 by Mary Elliott. *The Adventures of Thomas Two-Shoes* featured Goody's brother, a sailor. He did not, however, leave his linguistic mark on our language, and it is his sister to whom we allude when we call a person who never breaks the rules or does anything wrong a Goody Two-shoes.

Gotham: *See* knickerbockers

(the) green-eyed monster: jealousy

Colors have long been associated with emotions and character traits: red with anger, yellow with cowardice, blue with sadness, white with purity, etc. We often say a person is green with envy. Jealousy, therefore, was most likely personified as a green-eyed being before William Shakespeare began his writing career, but his works are the first place in which the characterization is found in print.

In *The Merchant of Venice*, which was written from 1596 to 1598, Portia remarks that in the face of love "... all the other passions fleet to air, / As doubtful thoughts, and rash-embraced despair, / And shuddering fear, and green-eyed jealousy!"

By the time he wrote *Othello*, in 1603 or 1604, Shakespeare had embellished on his earlier imagery. Iago warns Othello "O! beware, my lord, of jealousy; / It is the *green-eyed monster* which doth mock / The meat it feeds on. . . ."

Shakespeare's personification has remained an active figure of speech, adding color to our language in more ways than one.

(patient) Griselda: a long-suffering, patient woman (particularly a married one)

A person who has the patience of Job is able to keep a stiff upper lip through all of life's vicissitudes, as did the sufferer of the Bible. Similarly, a *Griselda* or a *patient Griselda*, is a woman who maintains her strength and dignity through many trials. The epithet is most often given to a woman whose husband is the cause of her tribulations. For, while Job's sufferings were sent from God, Griselda's came from her husband.

The best-known version of Griselda's story is told by the clerk in Chaucer's *Canterbury Tales*: Walter, the marquis of Saluzzo, married the beautiful and virtuous peasant girl, Griselda. After the birth of their daughter, "... the marquis so longed in his heart to test his wife in order to know her stability that he could not expel from his heart this remarkable desire to prove his wife. Needlessly, God knows, he decided to alarm her." The marquis ordered the baby to be taken from Griselda and, as far as she knew, killed. Griselda submitted meekly to her husband's will, never showing a sign of sorrow or anger.

After the birth of the couple's second child, a son, the marquis did the same thing, telling Griselda, "I warn you of this, so that you will not suddenly lose control of yourself because of your grief. Be patient, I beg you." And Griselda was nothing if not patient. She replied, "I do not want anything, nor ever shall, unless it pleases you. I am not grieved at all even though my daughter and my son be slain—at your command, that is."

At this point in the story, the narrator breaks in, saying, "But, now, I would like to ask of women whether these tests should not suffice. What more could a stern husband devise to test her wifeliness and her steadfastness. . . . But there are people who, when they have taken a certain purpose, cannot desist from their intention. . . . Just so, the marquis fully intended to test his wife as he had first decided.''

So more trials were in store for Griselda. Her husband expelled her from his house, saying he was going to take another wife, and she was forced to return to her father's home with only the clothes on her back. Still, she showed no rancor: ''Since it pleases you, my lord, in whom all my heart's ease once rested, that I shall go, I will go when you wish.'' Adding insult to injury, the marquis commanded Griselda to prepare his house for the arrival of his new bride and their wedding festivities.

It was not until all the guests were assembled at the wedding feast that the marquis ended Griselda's suffering. He revealed that the young girl he had brought to Saluzzo to be his bride was in fact his daughter and presented her and her brother to Griselda. He told the assembly that Griselda would always be his one and only wife, since she had proved her steadfastness through all his tests.

Lest his readers think the tale is to be taken at face value, Chaucer has the clerk deliver a caveat at the end:

> This story is told, not in order that wives should follow Griselda in humility, for that would be intolerable even if they were willing, but that everyone, whatever his rank, should be as constant in adversity as Griselda. . . . For, since a woman was so patient to a mortal man, we should so much the more receive submissively whatever God sends us. . . . Let us then live in virtuous submission.

Between 1351 and 1353 Giovanni Boccaccio compiled one hundred tales in *The Decameron*. The stories came from popular anecdotes, folklore, fairy tales, fabliaux, and many other ancient sources. The last tale in *The Decameron* is that of "The Patient Griselda," which Boccaccio took from a French source. Boccaccio's tale was translated into Latin by his close friend Petrarch, with the title "De Obidentia ac Fide uxoria Mythologia." It was from the Latin version that Chaucer wrote his tale in the closing years of the fourteenth century. Petrarch's translation was also used by Dekker, Chattle, and Haughton in 1603 for their "Patient Grissil."

Griselda, Grisilda, Grissil, Grisel, and Grazel are a few of the variations used for the heroine's name.

Hamlet: a tortured, indecisive person

The night that the ghost of his father appears to Hamlet and asks him to avenge his murder, Hamlet's first reaction is to take action immediately. He asks the ghost to reveal the name of the murderer: "Haste me to know't, that I, with wings as swift / As meditation or the thoughts of love, / May sweep to my revenge."

The ghost tells Hamlet that he was murdered by his own brother, Hamlet's uncle Claudius, who has now married Hamlet's mother. Hamlet vows to kill Claudius to bring peace to his father's spirit.

But as soon as the ghost vanishes Hamlet begins to have trepidations: "The time is out of joint: O cursed spite, / That ever I was born to set it right!"

From this moment on, Prince Hamlet of Denmark is a changed man: a tormented, tortured soul who cannot bring himself to take action against his father's killer in spite of the solemn vow he made in the presence of the ghost.

Early in Act II of Shakespeare's *Hamlet, Prince of Denmark*, the prince's mother and stepfather/uncle summon Hamlet's friends, Rosencrantz and Guildenstern, because they have noticed such a dramatic change in Hamlet's personality. Neither his looks nor his behavior are the same, and the king and queen hope the young men will be able to draw Hamlet out and learn what is troubling him. But Hamlet claims he doesn't know why he is distressed, telling Rosencrantz and Guildenstern only that he has lost all his interest in life and receives no delight from men or women.

Later, after seeing the emotion an actor puts into the role he plays, Hamlet berates himself for his lack of action:

> *O, what a rogue and peasant slave am I! . . .*
> *A dull and muddy-mettled rascal, peak*
> *Like John-a-dreams, unpregnant of my cause,*
> *And can say nothing; no, not for a king,*
> *Upon whose property and most dear life*
> *A damned defeat was made. . . .*
> *I am pigeon-livered and lack gall. . . .*

Everyone around him is convinced that Hamlet has gone mad, and, in fact, by the third act of the play, he is in such a state of misery that he considers taking his own life. In his famous "To be or not to be" soliloquy, Hamlet expresses his fear of death: the only thing that is keeping him from taking "arms against a sea of troubles" and ending them. Instead, he kills

Polonius, a harmless old busybody who is the father of Ophelia and Laertes. His cruelty toward Ophelia, who has always loved him, drives her to insanity and suicide.

Even after discovering a plot by his stepfather to have him killed, Hamlet does not take revenge. He returns to Denmark, having vowed to have only bloody thoughts, but it is the king who forces his hand. King Claudius plots with Laertes to challenge Hamlet to a duel to avenge the deaths of Polonius and Ophelia. They conspire to put poison on Laertes's sword and to give Hamlet a goblet of poisoned wine.

But things do not go according to plan: Both Hamlet and Laertes are wounded by the poisoned sword; Queen Gertrude drinks from the poisoned cup. It is only after her death, and just before his own, that Hamlet finally takes action, forcing the king to drink the rest of the poison. Hamlet's father is finally avenged, but at the cost of his son's life.

Hamlet's tragic dilemma has captivated audiences since the play was first performed in 1600. Scholars and critics have filled bookshelves with their theories as to the reasons for Hamlet's reluctance to avenge his father's death. But however we interpret the play, Hamlet remains an unforgettable figure—and one who has been immortalized not only on the stage, but also in the English language. To this day we call a person who is tormented by inner demons or who is paralyzed when faced with the need to make a decision a *Hamlet*, in memory of Shakespeare's sweet prince of Denmark.

heebie-jeebies: a bad case of nerves, the jitters

William (Billy) DeBeck was born in 1890. As a young art student, he aspired to be another Rembrandt. At the Chicago Academy of Fine Arts he was told that serious artists never coarsened their style by drawing frivolous or comic subjects. But in life drawing classes DeBeck couldn't refrain from doing caricatures of the models, to the chagrin of his instructors and the delight of his classmates.

The praise he received from the latter convinced him to try to sell his comic work to newspapers in order to finance his serious artistic studies. He soon got a job on the art staff of *Show World*, a Chicago theatrical weekly. This was followed by a stint as a political cartoonist, first in Youngstown, Ohio, and then in Pittsburgh, Pennsylvania.

DeBeck's first comic strip was *Married Life*, which he produced between 1915 and 1919, when King Features Syndicate offered him a contract if he could produce a new and different kind of strip. The result was *Barney Google*, who, with his racehorse Spark Plug, became an overnight sensation. In 1923 there was a song written about ''Barney Google with the goo-goo-googly eyes,'' by Billy Rose and Con Conrad. During the next twenty years, DeBeck added a cast of comic characters that included the hillbilly couple Snuffy and Lowizie Smith and Snuffy's nephew Weaselpuss. The focal point of the strip shifted from Barney to Snuffy. In 1940 Snuffy enlisted in the army, and his adventures provided the nation with comic relief when it was most needed.

Many of the colorful phrases DeBeck introduced in "Barney Google" have been quoted over and over again and have left a lasting impression. Two of these are now commonly used in all English-speaking countries, in the sense given them by DeBeck: *heebie-jeebies*, meaning a bad case of nerves or jitters; and *hotsy-totsy*, meaning high-class or ritzy.

Billy DeBeck died in 1942. Although his career choice cost him artistic fame, more people have read his comic strips and used the phrases he created than have ever seen the works of Rembrandt.

Homeric: larger than life, of epic proportions

The two great epic poems of ancient Greece, the *Iliad* and the *Odyssey*, have traditionally been attributed to a blind poet named Homer. Eight biographies of Homer have survived, but they contain conflicting information and are generally regarded as pure invention. Seven cities have claimed the title "birthplace of Homer," but there is no evidence to support any of their claims. Nor is there any historical evidence that Homer was blind or that he wrote poetry—or that he even existed.

Most scholars believe that the works of Homer are in fact compilations of material that was put together over the centuries by many different storytellers, or bards, as they were called. They suggest that the material in the *Iliad* and *Odyssey* was compiled between the early thirteenth century and the mid-ninth century B.C.—the latter being the date generally given as the time Homer lived—from historical events, legends, and folktales.

Although there are still some unitarians who believe that the Greek epics were the creation of a single man, the most widely accepted opinion today is that an individual named Homer did exist; however, he didn't invent the stories he told, but rather edited and refined the work of earlier poets. This theory is supported by the fact that both the *Iliad* and the *Odyssey* possess a remarkable unity of structure and style, the unmistakable imprint of a single artistic intelligence.

The texts of the *Iliad* and the *Odyssey* that have come down to us date from the sixth century B.C. They were edited at that time for use in Athens, and the *Iliad* in particular was changed substantially by the Athenians to give them a bigger role in the Trojan War. The texts were edited again in the second century B.C., by more impartial scholars: Aristarchus of Samothrace and Aristophanes of Byzantium.

No matter what scholars say, we will probably always refer to the Greek epics as Homer's *Iliad* and Homer's *Odyssey*. The epic nature of the events they chronicle—the ten-year war between Greece and Troy, the battles between both countries' bravest warriors, and the role of the gods in the *Iliad*; the wanderings and adventures of Odysseus through the known world for an entire decade in the *Odyssey*—

brought about the creation of the word *Homeric*. It is now used to describe not only the works of Homer and the scholars who study him, but any event or action of epic proportions and any larger-than-life individual. *Homeric laughter* is like that of the Greek gods who watched the activities of mortals from high on Mount Olympus: lusty and robust, ringing out and echoing through the heavens.

Horatio Alger story: rags-to-riches saga

Ironically, the man whose name has come to be synonymous with going from rags to riches went from riches to rags over the course of his own life.

Horatio Alger was born into a comfortable, conservative family in Brewster, Massachusetts, in 1832. His father was a Unitarian minister who groomed his son to follow in his footsteps from his earliest years. By the time he was nine, the boy was nicknamed Holy Horatio and was reading Plato and trying his hand at theological and philosophical writing. He went on to distinguish himself in classics and French at Harvard University.

But Horatio Alger was a rebel at heart. After graduating from Harvard in 1852, he tried to earn a living as a writer, resisting his father's pressure to enter the ministry. He finally succumbed and enrolled in Harvard Divinity School, graduating in 1860, but it wasn't until 1864 that he was ordained. During the four intervening years, Alger took an unexpected inheritance that he had received and went to London and Paris, where he tried the bohemian life.

Even after his ordination Alger found it difficult to settle down to the conventional life of a small-town minister. He continued to write and actually published several works. Although none achieved success, they inspired the interest of William T. Adams, a New York publisher of children's books. When Adams suggested to Alger that he come to New York and pursue a literary career, Alger resigned his ministry and went.

Alger's first successful work was *Ragged Dick, or Street Life in New York*, which was published in 1867. The book brought him to the attention of social worker Charles O'Conner, who suggested that he visit the Newsboys' Lodging House. This was a home for orphans and runaways, many of whom earned a meager living by selling newspapers on street corners throughout the city. Alger was so affected by the scene that he moved into the home and remained there for the next thirty years. It was there that he wrote over 120 novels, all dealing with poor boys who, by dint of hard work and perseverance, went from rags to riches. Although it has been said that Alger's books are virtually indistinguishable from one another, they made him the most popular and influential author of his time. They also made a lasting contribution to our language, so that when we refer to a real-life *Horatio Alger story*, it is clearly understood that we are talking about someone who has fought his or her way out of poverty and risen to the top of the economic scale.

Among Alger's most popular works were the Ragged Dick, Luck and Pluck, and Tattered Tom series. A typical plot involved a newsboy or a bootblack whose hard work eventually caused fortune to smile on him: The young hero might stop a runaway carriage in the street, thereby saving the life of a young woman whose father just happened to be a millionaire. She, of course, would fall in love with him, and her father—grateful that her life was spared—would give his blessing to their marriage.

At the age of sixty-three, Alger seems to have fallen in love for the first time. The object of his affections was a married woman whose husband learned of her attachment to Alger and took her to Paris. Broke and unable to follow them, Alger wrote two books in twenty-seven days and used the money he earned to book passage to France. When he finally arrived in Paris, the woman he loved told him she had decided to stay with her husband, and Alger suffered a nervous breakdown. He recovered somewhat and lived another four years: at the lodging house until the death of Charles O'Conner and then with his sister until his own death in 1899.

Alger is so closely identified with the rags-to-riches story that we often call a person who has struggled to the top a *Horatio Alger*, although the author himself was anything but.

hotsy-totsy: *See:* **heebie-jeebies.**

Humpty Dumpty: a rotund person

Humpty Dumpty sat on a wall.
Humpty Dumpty had a great fall.
All the King's horses and all the King's men
Couldn't put Humpty together again.

We have no idea where or when the popular nursery rhyme "Humpty Dumpty" originated. According to the *Encyclopedia Brittanica*, parallels to it and several other rhymes/songs, such as "London Bridge Is Falling Down," and "Lady Bird, Lady Bird, Fly Away" exist in the folklore of nearly every country in Europe. Since none of these are direct translations of one another, we can only presume the existence, long ago, of a common source.

We do know, however, that "Humpty Dumpty" was first printed in England in 1810, in a book called *Gammer Gurton's Garland*. The four-line rhyme is really a riddle that asks: What is round and, when it is broken, can't be put back together again? The answer: an egg. And that is just how Humpty Dumpty was depicted in later, illustrated books of nursery rhymes.

It was Lewis Carroll (and his illustrator, Sir John Tenniel) who popularized the figure of Humpty Dumpty in his children's classic, *Through the*

Looking Glass, which was published in England in 1872. Carroll's Humpty is a very ill-tempered egg who seems to be completely unaware of his nursery-rhyme fate. When Alice suggests that he might be safer on the ground than on the narrow wall where he is sitting, he replies, "... If ever I *did* fall off— which there's no chance of—but *if* I did ... *the King has promised me—with his very own mouth*—to— to ..."

"To send all his horses and all his men," Alice interrupts.

Humpty then accuses her of eavesdropping on his private conversations. He wants to know how she found out about the king's promise if she didn't listen in. Alice explains that she read about it in a book, which seems to placate Humpty for a while. But then she makes the mistake of complimenting the egg on his belt, which is, in fact, his tie. ("If only I knew," she thought to herself, "which was neck and which was waist.")

Today, a *Humpty Dumpty* is a rotund person, one who is shaped just like the egg-man who has amused children for centuries.

Incredible Hulk: a huge, strong person

He has the standard body-builder's physique, with two sets of shoulders one on top of the other and wings of lateral muscle that hold his arms out from his sides as if his armpits had piles. He is made remarkable by his avocado complexion [and] eyes like plover's eggs.

That is how Clive James, quoted by David Pringle in *Imaginary People*, once described the Incredible Hulk.

The Hulk originated as the alter ego of one Dr. Bruce Banner, a scientist who was accidentally exposed to gamma rays during a bomb test. Thereafter, every time Dr. Banner experienced anger, he metamorphosed into this strange creature who possessed superhuman strength and engaged in feats of great daring.

Unlike Mr. Hyde, the alter ego of Robert Louis Stevenson's Dr. Jekyll, the Hulk did not represent the evil side of man. Instead, he used his might to conquer villains and wrongdoers. And, while Dr. Jekyll was well aware of the existence of Mr. Hyde and his nefarious acts, Dr. Banner never had any recollection of the time he spent as the Hulk.

The Hulk came out of the imagination of comic book writer Stan Lee and made his first appearance in Marvel Comics in 1962. He was so popular with young readers that the Incredible Hulk became part of the animated television series *Marvel Superheroes*, which aired from 1966 to 1968.

In 1977 a TV movie called *The Incredible Hulk* was made, starring Bill Bixby as Dr. Banner (now renamed David) and Lou Ferrigno as the Hulk. A television series followed and remained on the air until 1982.

The Hulk enjoyed worldwide popularity during the 1970s and '80s. Millions of adventure novels, Hulk dolls, T-shirts, and other trivia were produced and sold. Now, in the '90s, the market for these has waned, but the Hulk lives on in our language. We have come to associate any big, strong man with the comic book character, referring to such a person as an *Incredible Hulk*.

See also: **Jekyll-and-Hyde personality.**

jabberwocky: nonsensical speech or writing that appears to make sense

In 1865 Reverend Charles Lutwidge Dodgson published *Alice's Adventures in Wonderland*, using the pseudonym Lewis Carroll. In 1872 a sequel, *Through the Looking-Glass*, appeared. In the first book Alice fell down a rabbit hole and discovered an absurd world in which animals talked and all sorts of extraordinary events were considered commonplace. The world Carroll's heroine stumbles into in the second book is no less amazing and confusing to her.

This time Alice goes through the looking glass in her living room and finds herself in a world that is the mirror image of her own. One of the first things she finds is a book, but she cannot read it because the writing in looking-glass country is, of course, reversed. When she holds it up to the mirror, she is able to read the words, but they make no sense. As she puts it: " 'It seems very pretty . . . but it's *rather* hard to understand!' (You see she didn't like to confess, even to herself, that she couldn't make it out at all.) 'Somehow it seems to fill my head with ideas—only I don't exactly know what they are!' "

The poem she has found is called "Jabberwocky," and this is its first stanza:

> *'Twas brillig, and the slithy toves*
> *Did gyre and gimble in the wave:*
> *All mimsy were the borogoves,*
> *And the mome raths outgrabe.*

It isn't until Alice meets Humpty Dumpty that she learns the meaning of the unusual words in the poem: *brillig* means four o'clock in the afternoon, the time when you begin broiling things for dinner; *slithy* is a combination of lithe and slimy; *toves* are something like badgers, something like lizards, and something like corkscrews; etc.

However, the poem doesn't make any more sense to Alice—or to us—when she knows what the words mean than when none of them were a part of her vocabulary. The poem is one of Lewis Carroll's masterpieces: complete and utter nonsense that sounds as though it means something. It was such a success that the word *jabberwocky* is now applied to any speech or writing that we listen to or read attentively, think we understand, then say to ourselves, "But what does it mean?"

See also: **chortle, portmanteau word.**

Jekyll-and-Hyde personality: a split personality, with two totally contradictory sides

When we say someone has a *Jekyll-and-Hyde personality*, we are accusing him or her of having two totally different sides: one that is pleasant and sociable and another that is nasty and rude. We are alluding, of course, to Robert Louis Stevenson's memorable novella, *The Strange Case of Dr. Jekyll and Mr. Hyde.*

The story was published in 1886 and concerns the ill-fated attempts of one Dr. Henry Jekyll to separate the two sides of his character. After years of secretly leading a double life—as a scientist dedicated to relieving man's suffering and as a reprobate concerned only with satisfying his own grosser appetites—Jekyll comes to a startling conclusion:

> . . . I learned to recognise the thorough and primitive duality of man; I saw that, of the two natures that contended in the field of my consciousness, even if I could rightly be said to be either, it was only because I was radically both. . . . If each, I told myself, could be housed in separate identities, life would be relieved of all that was unbearable.

In an effort to unbind his two opposite natures, Jekyll begins experimenting with drugs, finally concocting a potion that has the power to transform him into another being: Mr. Edward Hyde. The first time he drinks it, ''The most racking pangs succeeded: a grinding in the bones, deadly nausea, and a horror of the spirit that cannot be exceeded at the hour of birth or death.''

These awful sensations are followed by a feeling of youth and lightness, which Jekyll believes is because ''The evil side of my nature . . . was less robust and less developed than the good. . . . And hence, as I think, it came about that Edward Hyde was so much smaller, slighter and younger than Henry Jekyll.'' The two men differ not only in their physical attributes: ''Even as good shone upon the countenance of the one, evil was written broadly and plainly on the face of the other. . . . When I wore the semblance of Edward Hyde, none could come near to me at first without a visible misgiving of the flesh. This, as I take it, was because all human beings, as we meet them, are commingled out of good and evil: and Edward Hyde, alone in the ranks of mankind, was pure evil.''

Dr. Jekyll begins to live two separate lives, switching back and forth between his two egos by drinking the potion. But, as Mr. Hyde's personality becomes stronger, it begins to reemerge on its own. Eventually, Hyde commits murder, and Jekyll is unable to suppress him. The struggle between the two sides of the doctor ends when, as Hyde, he realizes he is about to be apprehended and commits suicide.

As early as 1888, *The Strange Case of Dr. Jekyll and Mr. Hyde* was adapted for the stage, and several versions of the play were performed in the following decades. Between 1908 and 1921 seven silent films were made of Stevenson's novella. In sound films his tormented doctor was played by screen greats such as Boris Karloff, Spencer Tracy, and Paul Massie.

Kafkaesque: characterized by a nightmarish, surreal feeling of being trapped

Franz Kafka lived from 1883 until 1924. Of Austrian parentage, he grew up in the German-Jewish sector of Prague, Czechoslovakia, and was the victim of both anti-Semitism and anti-German/Austrian sentiment. His relationship with his demanding, domineering father caused him to suffer from an inferiority complex and, in his own words, "a boundless feeling of guilt." It is obvious that Kafka's problems with his father are reflected in many of his works, where young, powerless people are tormented by their fathers or other authority figures.

Franz Kafka was also given to lifelong introspection on the nature of God and on the existence of man. A sense of absurdity and unreality pervades the fictional world he created in *The Metamorphosis*, *Amerika*, *The Trial*, and *The Castle*. Like Alice in

Wonderland, his characters struggle to remain rational in a world where nothing makes sense. But Kafka's world is a far more dangerous place than Carroll's Wonderland: In it helpless victims are mowed down by a relentless, unstoppable juggernaut.

It is in *The Trial* that Kafka paints the most frightening picture of a world in which man's reason is powerless against unknown and unyielding forces. *The Trial* begins with a simple, unemotional statement of fact: "Someone must have traduced Joseph K., for without having done anything wrong he was arrested one fine morning."

K., an innocuous bank employee, wakes up to a knock at his door. Two men enter his room and tell him that he cannot go out because he has been arrested. When he asks why, he is told that they have not been authorized to tell him. "Proceedings have been instituted against you," one of them tells him, "and you will be informed of everything in due course."

From this moment forth, K. is embroiled in a case. It seems that there are many cases pending against citizens like K., and he is told that no one can predict how long it will be before his case is resolved. He is told to go about his usual business, including his work at the bank, but to make himself available for interrogations whenever the authorities schedule them.

The circumstances surrounding the first interrogation are bizarre, to say the least. K. is told to go to a certain address, which turns out to be a tenement. Not knowing where the interrogation is to be held, he goes from door to door. At one door he is greeted by a young washerwoman who tells him to go through to the next room. This turns out to be a large meeting room, which is filled to the rafters with people. The examining magistrate is sitting at one end of the room, and K. is escorted up to him. K. begins to harangue the court, accusing the government of harassing innocent citizens. In the middle of his impassioned address, the washerwoman and an unknown man begin making love in the back of the room and the crowd shifts its attention from K. to the spectacle. The people at the front of the room pay no attention, however, and restrain K. physically when he tries to go to the back of the room. It is then that he sees the badges all of them are wearing and realizes they are not spectators, but government agents. He stalks out of the room and returns home.

The next time K. goes to the tenement, the washerwoman is alone in what is now a living room. She explains that her husband is an usher and that they have been given this apartment but must clear it out when court is in session. The man with whom she was making love is a law student who is constantly pursuing her, and she must accept his advances so her husband will not lose his job. The student arrives and carries her off, and her husband offers to take K. to the offices that are in the attic of the building. Although it is Sunday, there are officials at work and accused people sitting on benches. The heat and the stifling atmosphere get the better of K., and he flees from the attic as soon as he can.

Eventually, K.'s entire life is devoted to his case. On the advice of his uncle he retains an attorney, but the man does nothing to further his case. K. considers drawing up a written defense and submitting it to the court, but he is afraid it will just be filed, unread. Eventually, K. realizes that his innocence will have no bearing on the outcome of the case: "I have to fight against countless subtleties in which the Court indulges. And in the end, out of nothing at all, an enormous fabric of guilt will be conjured up."

Joseph K. is not surprised, therefore, when one year after his arrest, he is taken from his house by two men and led to a deserted quarry. Just before he is stabbed to death, K. wonders, "Where was the Judge whom he had never seen? Where was the High Court, to which he had never penetrated?"

Kafka once said that his books reflected his "own dreamlike inner life." In fact, the life he depicts in his works is nothing less than nightmarish. And the adjective *Kafkaesque* is frequently applied to situations in which an individual is trapped in a nightmarish world, manipulated and eventually destroyed by forces that he cannot see or understand.

keeping up with the Joneses: trying to amass as much material wealth as your neighbors

Your neighbor may be named Rivera, Rourke, or Rockefeller, but if he buys himself a Cadillac, and you go out and get one too, you are said to be *keeping up with the Joneses*. The expression, which was in common use in the U.S. before 1920 and in England by World War II, is used to describe the struggle to match the lifestyle and spending patterns of one's neighbors: to have as big a home and as expensive an automobile, to go on vacation to the same in places, to send one's children to the same prestigious schools, etc.

Keeping up with the Joneses was the name of a comic strip created by Arthur "Pop" Momand and introduced in several U.S. newpapers in 1913. Momand claimed to have based the strip on his own experiences living beyond his means in a prosperous neighborhood, where he and his neighbors were engaged in a never-ending contest to outdo one another's conspicuous consumption.

Incidentally, Momand's first choice for the title of his comic strip was *Keeping up with the Smiths*, which was vetoed by his publisher, who felt that *the Joneses* had a more harmonious sound.

Keystone Cops/Kops: incompetent, bumbling enforcers of the law

Mack Sennett began his career, around 1908, as an actor at Biograph Studios, where D. W. Griffith was chief director. Even then he was constantly offering Griffith ideas for scenarios—the main one being that policemen were a perfect source for comedy. Griffith was not convinced, and Sennett spent several years in front of the cameras before anyone took his ideas seriously.

In 1912 Sennett left Biograph to form the Keystone Company, and within a year the slapstick comedies put out by Keystone were famous. By 1914 Sennett owned his own studio, where he could finally put his favorite theory—that policemen could be funny—to the test.

The result was the creation of the Keystone Cops (or Kops), a group of bumbling, incompetent policemen who spent more time getting into each other's way than enforcing the law. They were led by Ford Sterling, who supposedly began the pie-throwing craze that soon overtook silent films. A comedy made on the Keystone lot usually included at least one wild chase scene, in which a carful of the zany men in blue careened through the streets on a wild-goose chase. Some of the actors who played the cops were Fatty Arbuckle, Rube Miller, Hank Mann, Al St. John, Mack Swain, and George Jesky.

When Ford Sterling's contract with Keystone ended, Mack Sennett began looking for someone to replace him. He soon found his new star, playing in vaudeville: The young man was named Charles Chaplin, and Sennett offered him the then-tremendous sum of $150 a week to join the Keystone Company. Chaplin only remained with Keystone for one year, moving to Essanay Studios when they offered him $1,250 a week.

Then Sennett hit upon another idea to increase the
popularity of the cops: He teamed them up with a
bevy of beautiful girls, who were christened the Bathing Beauty Brigade. Naturally, much of the action in
these films took place near the water. At first the entire troupe was transported to the ocean, some sixteen
miles from Hollywood, but Sennett soon tired of making the trip and had a swimming pool built on the
Keystone lot. The rest of the Bathing Beauty series
was shot there.

The popularity of the Keystone Cops reached its
height prior to 1920, but their name continues to be
used with regularity. It is a common courtroom tactic
of defense lawyers who are attempting to discredit
police officers to call them *Keystone Cops*. The judge,
jury, and spectators understand, with no further explanation, that the lawmen are being compared to the
bungling, inept figures that brought laughs to millions
of Americans in the early twentieth century.

King Kong: a big, strong man, an ape of a
fellow

A man who is big and strong has long been called an
ape or apelike. For the past sixty years, however, such
a fellow has been given a more specific name: He is
now commonly referred to as *King Kong*.

A normal ape possesses far greater strength than a
man, but the gigantic ape who made his film debut in

1933 made others of his kind look like ninety-eight-pound weaklings. *King Kong* was the creation of Merian Cooper and Edgar Wallace, in collaboration with screenwriters James Creelman and Ruth Rose. Cooper and Ernest B. Schoedsack directed the film. King Kong was animated by special-effects expert Willis J. O'Brien.

The film begins with the capture of King Kong on the imaginary Skull Island in the Pacific. The huge ape is brought to America as a circus attraction. He escapes from his captors in New York City, where he creates fear and mayhem. In the film's most famous scene, Kong scales the Empire State Building with a beautiful young lady, played by Fay Wray, for whom he has the tenderest of feelings. At the end of the film, King Kong is fired on by fighter planes and is killed.

Kong's death didn't prevent filmmakers from producing several sequels and spinoffs, including *Son of Kong* (1934), *King Kong vs. Godzilla* (1962), and *King Kong Escapes* (1967). The original *King Kong* was remade in 1976, with Jessica Lange in the role made famous by Fay Wray.

knickerbockers: full pants gathered and banded below the knee

Many Americans do not know that the New York Knicks is not the complete name of that city's basketball team. Knicks is short for Knickerbockers, and Knickerbocker is another name for a New Yorker. Knickerbockers are also loose-fitting men's pants, which reach just below the knees, where they are gathered and banded. Knickerbockers were once the garment of choice for bicyclists, golfers, and other sportsmen and were also worn as an undergarment by women. The words *knickerbocker* and *knickerbockers* were the creations of author Washington Irving.

Irving was born in New York City in 1783, and his first book, *A History of New York from the Beginning of the World to the End of the Dutch Dynasty*, began as a parody of a popular travel book of the time. In it Irving created the character of Diedrich Knickerbocker, who was supposedly its author. The book's drawings were done by famous English illustrator George Cruickshank, who depicted Irving's Dutchmen in knee-breeches. From the time *A History of New York* appeared in 1809 until the present, knee-length pants such as those drawn by Cruickshank have been called knickerbockers. (The name *knickerbocker*, translated literally, means a baker of knickers, knickers being clay marbles.)

Washington Irving was also the first to call New York City Gotham, a name that is still in use today. (By extension, New Yorkers are also called Gothamites.) Irving introduced the name in *Salmagundi; or, The Whim-Whams and Opinions of Launcelot Langstaff, Esq. and Others*, a humorous periodical he and his brother, William, produced in collaboration with James Kirk Paulding. The periodical was modeled on Addison and Steele's *Spectator*, which had been a great success in England at the beginning of the eighteenth century. The three young men wrote humorous and satirical essays on a variety of subjects—politics, theater, fashion, manners, etc.—and signed them with fantastic pseudonyms. The publication was an instant success, and the *Salmagundi Papers* were published in book form in 1808.

By the way, the choice of the periodical's title was not at all gratuitous: Salmagundi is a spicy stewlike concoction, whose ingredients are as many and as varied as the subjects covered by Launcelot Langstaff and others.

Lady Bountiful: a kind, benevolent woman

George Farquhar never became a household name, but his plays were popular enough for the name of one of his characters to become a sobriquet for a kind, benevolent woman. When we say a female is a *Lady Bountiful* or is *playing Lady Bountiful*, we mean that she takes care of others physically, emotionally, or financially. She puts their needs before her own and is always ready to lend a helping hand.

Lady Bountiful (or Bountyful, as it was spelled in the eighteenth century) is one of the characters in Farquhar's comedy, *The Beaux' Stratagem*. The beaux are Thomas Aimwell and his friend Archer, two young men who are nearly destitute when they arrive in Litchfield, home of Lady Bountyful and her family. The two are seeking their fortunes, wherever and however they may find them, and are masquerading as master and servant.

They first hear of Lady Bountyful from the landlord of the inn where they are staying:

My Lady Bountyful is one of the best of Women: Her last Husband Sir Charles Bountyful left her worth a Thousand Pounds a Year; and I believe she lays out one half on't in charitable Uses for the Good of her Neighbours; she cures Rheumatisms, Ruptures, and broken Shins in Men, Green Sickness, Obstructions, and Fits of the Mother in Women;—The Kings-Evil, Chin-Cough, and Chilblains in Children; in short, she has cured more People in and about Litchfield within Ten Years than the Doctors have kill'd in Twenty; and that's a bold Word.

When Aimwell learns that Lady Bountyful has a beautiful daughter, Dorinda, he pretends to be deathly ill so that Lady Bountyful will care for him in her home. In spite of his deception, Dorinda falls in love with him, and at the end of the play they marry. Archer, in the meantime, has fallen in love with Mrs. Sullen, the wife of Lady Bountyful's drunken, uncouth son. The lout is persuaded to give her a divorce, and she and Archer make plans for a future together.

George Farquhar was born in 1678, and his plays reflect the movement of the theater away from the lighthearted, witty comedy of the Restoration and toward more simple, sentimental themes. Besides *The Beaux' Strategem*, which was written just before his death in 1707, two of his earlier plays are fairly well known: *The Constant Couple* (1699) and *The Recruiting Officer* (1706).

Lady Macbeth strategy: strategy used by a company involved in a hostile takeover

In twentieth-century business jargon, the expression *Lady Macbeth strategy* refers to the manner in which one company plots the hostile takeover of another. For example, if the ABC Company is faced with a hostile takeover bid by the XYZ Company, the LMNOP Company may offer its support to ABC to combat the takeover. After winning ABC's confidence, LMNOP will suddenly join forces with XYZ, and both will take over ABC. LMNOP has, in fact, engaged in the Lady Macbeth strategy.

The reference is, of course, to Shakespeare's great tragedy, *Macbeth*, which was written between 1603 and 1606, long before there were such things as stock markets and takeover bids. At the beginning of the play Lady Macbeth is determined that her husband will become king of Scotland. She encourages him to kill the legitimate king, Duncan, and usurp the throne. When King Duncan arrives at her home, Lady Macbeth receives him with great deference, all the while plotting to drug his guards and kill him while they are in a stupor. Lulled into a false sense of security, Duncan sleeps soundly and, like ABC, meets his end at the hands of one he trusted.

Lady Macbeth syndrome: an unresolved guilt complex that manifests itself in obsessive hand washing

As Lord and Lady Macbeth plot the murder of King Duncan of Scotland in the first act of Shakespeare's *Macbeth*, Lady Macbeth berates her husband when he begins to lose his nerve:

> *. . . I have given suck, and know*
> *How tender 't is to love the babe that milks me:*
> *I would, while it was smiling in my face,*
> *Have pluck'd my nipple from his boneless gums,*
> *And dash'd the brains out, had I so sworn as you*
> *Have done to this.*

Even before he has killed the king, Macbeth begins to have hallucinations, but he forces himself to commit the murder. He is in a terrible state afterward, and once again his wife takes control, returning the bloody dagger to the scene of the crime.

Lady Macbeth seems to be totally devoid of feeling; as the drama proceeds we continue to be shocked by the cold-blooded, calculating way in which she plots murder after murder to put her husband on the throne. First the king's guards are killed, then Banquo, then the wife and son of Macduff. Through it all, Lady Macbeth never wavers, and we are just about convinced that no greater monster ever lived when Shakespeare suddenly shows us that she is human after all.

In the final act of the play, this woman of steel begins to crumble, and Shakespeare's depiction of her descent into madness is nothing short of brilliant. We learn that this once-fearless woman is now afraid of the dark. She walks in her sleep, rubbing her hands together, as if washing them, for a quarter of an hour at a time. As she does so, she talks to herself: "Yet here's a spot. . . . Out, damned spot! out, I say. . . . What! will these hands ne'er be clean?. . . . Here's the smell of the blood still: all the perfumes of Arabia will not sweeten this little hand . . ." Lady Macbeth eventually succumbs under the weight of her conscience and commits suicide just before Macbeth goes into battle with Macduff.

The famous sleepwalking scene, quoted above, has provided us with a commonly used psychological term. People who suffer from bacteriophobia have an irrational fear of bacteria: They are obsessed with cleanliness, washing themselves—particularly their hands—dozens of times each day. Psychiatrists and psychologists often attribute this odd behavior to unresolved guilt, resulting in their use of the term *Lady Macbeth syndrome* as an alternate name for bacteriophobia.

Land of Oz: a magical place

In L. Frank Baum's children's classic, *The Wonderful Wizard of Oz*, an orphan from Kansas named Dorothy and her dog Toto are transported to a magical land during a cyclone. The country in which their house touches down is called the Land of Oz and is divided into four sectors. Each of these—North, South, East, and West—is ruled by a witch. The witches of the North and South are good witches; those of the East and West are wicked. Dorothy's house lands right on the wicked Witch of the East, crushing her and liberating the Munchkins who had been her slaves.

The Witch of the North tells Dorothy that the only hope she has of returning to Kansas lies with the Wizard of Oz. He lives in the Emerald City, right in the center of Oz. Dorothy and Toto set out along the yellow brick road that leads to the Emerald City.

The Land of Oz is truly a magical place. The first person Dorothy meets on the yellow brick road is a scarecrow who is able to talk. He tells her he has no brains and asks if he can accompany her on her journey and ask the Wizard to give him some. The next individual who crosses their path is the Tin Woodman, whose joints are so rusted he cannot move. He asks Dorothy to oil them, which she does, and now that he can walk he declares his intention to go with them to the Emerald City and ask the Wizard to give him a heart. It seems the Woodman was once made of flesh and blood and had a heart. But the Wicked Witch of the East caused him to accidentally cut off all of his limbs and his head, one after another. A tinsmith replaced them with metal ones, but then the Woodman's ax slipped and cut his torso in two. The

tinsmith made him a metal torso, but he couldn't give
him a heart.

Joined by the Cowardly Lion, who wants nothing
more than some courage, the strange little party proceeds toward the Emerald City. Aided by other talking animals, such as a stork and thousands of field
mice, they weather many perils as they approach the
city of the Great Oz. Once there, they are given special spectacles so they will not be blinded by the
brightness and glory of the city. Even with the spectacles, the group is amazed by the brilliance of the
Emerald City: Its streets are lined with beautiful
homes, all built of green marble and studded with
sparkling emeralds; the pavement is made of blocks
of the same marble, joined together by rows of emeralds. Everything in the city is green, including the
rays of the sun, the clothing of the people, and even
their skin.

One by one the friends are admitted into the presence of the Great Oz, who tells them all that he will
not grant their wishes until the Wicked Witch of the
West is dead. They must return to the Emerald City
with proof that they have killed her if they want him
to help them.

When the wicked Witch of the West learns that the
friends are in her country, she sends wolves, crows,
bees, and winged monkeys to destroy them. The monkeys succeed in disabling the Scarecrow and the Tin
Woodman, and they capture Dorothy, Toto, and the
Cowardly Lion. One day the witch tries to take one
of Dorothy's silver shoes (changed to ruby slippers in

the film version), which belonged to the Witch of the East and which have great magic powers. The angry Dorothy throws a pail of water on the witch, who proceeds to melt away. The Scarecrow and the Tin Woodman are repaired, and Dorothy and her friends return to the Emerald City to claim their rewards from the Wizard.

The Wizard tells them he cannot grant their wishes after all. He confesses that he has no magic powers: He is just a ventriloquist from Omaha, Nebraska, whose balloon went off course and ended up in Oz. He has been fooling the people of the Emerald City— which only looks green because of the green glasses he makes everyone wear—into thinking he is a wizard. He does, however, know how to use his imagination to provide the Scarecrow with brains, the Tin Woodman with a heart, and the Cowardly Lion with courage. Then Dorothy helps him build a balloon in which the two plan to set off, with Toto, for their homes in the Midwest.

But at the last minute Dorothy can't find Toto, and the Wizard takes off without her. The only way she can get home now is by enlisting the aid of the good Witch of the South, Glinda. Accompanied by her friends, she makes the journey to Glinda's realm, where the witch tells her she already possesses all she needs to get her home: the silver shoes. Glinda promises to help her friends get back to their new homes: The Scarecrow will rule the Winkies, the former slaves of the Wicked Witch of the West; the Tin

Woodman will rule over the Emerald City; and the once-Cowardly Lion has been asked by the beasts of the forest to be their leader. Dorothy bids them all good-bye and returns to Kansas, where her aunt and uncle welcome her but have no idea what she means when she says she's come from the Land of Oz.

Today, however, when we refer to a place as the Land of Oz, there are very few people who don't understand the allusion. A *Land of Oz* is a magical place, a place where anything and everything is possible. Those who live in a Land of Oz don't see the world the way it is, but the way they'd like it to be.

See also: **cowardly lion, munchkin.**

Larry, Curly, and Moe: *See* **(the) Three Stooges**

last of the Mohicans: the last member of any group with a certain identity or certain beliefs

James Fenimore Cooper wrote his first book in 1820, at the age of thirty-one. From then until his death in 1851 he published more than fifty books, the most popular of which were the five novels that made up his Leatherstocking Tales. These followed the life and adventures of Natty Bumppo, also referred to throughout the stories as Leatherstocking, Hawkeye, Deerslayer, Pathfinder, and La Longue Carabine (Long Rifle).

Bumppo was a white man who respected American Indian customs and beliefs more than those of his own race. He chose to live close to nature, as a guide and scout in the rugged, sparsely inhabited wilderness of New York State.

When taken in chronological order, the Leather-stocking tales span sixty-five years of the life of Natty Bumppo. *The Deerslayer*, which was written in 1841, takes place in 1740, when Bumppo is only 20 years old. Written in 1826, *The Last of the Mohicans: A Narrative of 1757* features Bumppo, then thirty-seven, at the height of his physical and mental powers. *The Pathfinder* (1840) takes place in 1760, when the forty-year-old Bumppo fights in the French and Indian Wars on Lake Erie. The next book in the series, *The Pioneers*, was the first one written (1823). In it, Bumppo and his Mohican friend, Chingachgook, are old men living in a frontier village in the West, where Chingachgook dies. Finally, *The Prairie*, written in 1827 but set on the Great Plains in 1804, deals with the old age and death of Bumppo among the Pawnee Indians.

The Last of the Mohicans takes its title from one of the characters: Uncas, son of Chingachgook. At the beginning of the tale, Natty Bumppo asks Chingach-gook where the rest of his tribe are to be found, and the Indian replies:

> . . . all of my family departed, each in his turn, to the
> land of the spirits. I am on the hill-top, and must go
> down into the valley; and when Uncas follows in my
> footsteps, there will no longer be any of the blood of
> the sagamores, for my boy is the last of the Mohi-
> cans.

Ironically, it is Chingachgook himself who turns
out to be the last of the Mohicans. He, Bumppo, and
Uncas attempt to lead a party of English travelers
from Albany to Fort William Henry. During the trip
they run into Magua, the evil leader of a group of
Hurons who have taken the side of the French against
the British. At the end of the novel Uncas is killed
trying to save the life of one of the travelers, and
Chingachgook becomes the only survivor of his once-
powerful tribe.

In actuality, two related Algonkian tribes—the Mahicans and the Mohegans—existed in North America.
The Mahicans were found in New York's Hudson
Valley north of the Catskill Mountains. The Mohegans lived in the Thames Valley in Connecticut. The
names Mahican, Mohegan, Mohican, and several
other variations come from the Algonkian word for
wolf. According to the Encyclopedia Brittanica, Cooper's work is mistitled, for descendents of both the
Mahicans and Mohegans were still to be found in
Connecticut, Massachusetts, and Wisconsin in the
1960s.

Even though Cooper took liberty with the history
of the Mohicans, it was he who gave them a perma-
nent place in the English language. The immense pop-

ularity of his Leather-stocking Tales brought about
the use of the phrase *last of the Mohicans* to denote
the last member of any group: the holdout who continues to represent the group's identity or uphold its
beliefs.

lesbian/Lesbian: a female homosexual; relating to female homosexuality

Originally, a Lesbian was an inhabitant of Lesbos, an
island in the Aegean Sea. Lesbian civilization reached
its peak around 600 B.C., under the rule of Pittacus,
whose wise administration earned him a place among
the Seven Sages of Greece. Art flourished on the island, in particular, the art of lyric poetry. The musician Terpander, the dithyrambist Arion, and the poet
Alcaeus were among the Lesbian artists who had a
great influence on Greek music and poetry. But it is
the poetess Sappho who is most often associated
with the island of Lesbos, and it was her poetry
that made the word *lesbian* synonymous with female homosexuality.

Sappho lived on Lesbos from around 610 to 580
B.C. She was a native of the island and apparently
came from one of its upper-class families. Surpris-
ingly, given her reputation, she was married to a certain Cercolas, a wealthy man from Andros, and had
at least one child by him.

It was the fashion in Lesbos during this period for

women of means to spend their days together in sa-
lons, conversing and dabbling in the arts and, in particular, composing and reciting poetry. Sappho was
the leader of one of these coteries and, as such, attracted a great number of followers on Lesbos and
abroad. Most of Sappho's poetry dealt with personal
themes, in particular her relationships with her followers and with members of rival coteries. Jealousy
and hatred are expressed toward women who
switched their alliance from Sappho to another poetess; artistic rivals are attacked and ridiculed.

In many of her poems, Sappho expounded on her
feelings for her female friends, which ranged from
mild affection to passionate love. Although there are
no references to physical intimacy in the large body
of verse that is extant, the strong emotions she expressed were sufficient to convince ancient writers
that she and her entourage were practicing homosex-
uals. As a result, the terms *lesbianism* and *sapphism*
are now commonly used to refer to homosexual relations between women, and *lesbian* has become the
accepted term for a female homosexual.

Sappho left another, less sensational mark on our
language in the word *Sapphic* or *sapphic*. This is the
name given to the verse form invented and used by
the poetess. The Sapphic is a four-line stanza, the first
three lines of which are each eleven syllables long
and divisible into five poetic feet; the fourth line is
five syllables long, consisting of a dactyl followed by
a spondee. After Sappho, the Sapphic was used with
great success in Latin by Catullus and Horace.

(the) life of Riley: a carefree, easy life

James Whitcomb Riley was born in Greenfield, Indiana, in 1849. As a young man he traveled throughout rural Indiana as an itinerant sign painter, entertainer, and assistant in medicine shows. In his travels he gained intimate knowledge of life and customs in the rural areas of the state.

Life in Indiana at that time was simple, slow paced, and free of stress, particularly for the young. Without radio, television, and video games, children devised their own entertainment after they finished their daily chores. During the summer, a great deal of time was spent outdoors, swimming, fishing, or just lolling in the sun.

Riley's observations of this idyllic life led to the publication of his first series of poems, in Hoosier dialect. The poems, which first appeared for the *Indianapolis Daily Journal*, were ostensibly written by a farmer, Benj. F. Johnson, of Boone. In 1883 they were published, under Riley's name, as *The Old Swimmin' Hole and 'Leven More Poems*. Riley's literary reputation was established, and the phrase *the life of Riley* entered the English language. Ever since, it has been used to denote an easy, carefree life, such as the one enjoyed by the youngsters who frequented the old swimmin' hole.

Hailed as "the poet of the common people" and "the Hoosier poet," Riley soon became the wealthiest American writer of his time. His lectures and humorous sketches brought him substantial additional income. Among the later volumes of poetry he published are: *Pipes o' Pan at Zekesbury* (1888), *Old-Fashioned Roses* (1888), *The Flying Islands of the Night* (1891), *A Child-World* (1896), and *Home Folks* (1900). After his death in 1916, a ten-volume memorial edition of his *Complete Works* was released.

See also: **Little Orphan Annie.**

lilliputian/Lilliputian: small in stature; small-minded, petty

Gulliver's Travels was written in 1726 by Jonathan Swift and has rarely been rivaled as a satiric work. Some of the satire in the book was directed at clerics and politicians of the time and has, therefore, lost its edge for the modern reader. But the majority of Swift's satire was directed toward human follies that transcend time. As such, it is as relevant today as it was in the eighteenth century.

One of the most entertaining portions of *Gulliver's Travels* deals with Lemuel Gulliver's arrival in the land of Lilliput. After he is shipwrecked, Gulliver swims to an island, lies down on the beach, and falls asleep. He awakes to find himself tied firmly to the ground, with little men crawling over his body. The tiny creatures are the Lilliputians, and although Gulliver has no trouble breaking his bonds, he is not impervious to the sting of the hundreds of tiny arrows they proceed to launch at him. He gives them his

word of honor that he will not try to escape, if they
will cease their shooting.

The Lilliputians take themselves quite seriously.
They have the audacity to tell their captive that he
must be searched, and they confiscate his sword and
pistols. They seem to be completely unaware that
Gulliver has no need of these; he could crush them
in his hands or step on them if he cared to do so. The
situation becomes more absurd as the Lilliputians
give Gulliver his freedom, contingent on several conditions that they lay down.

The Lilliputians are divided into two political factions: the High-Heels and the Low-Heels. They dis-
agree on the height of the heels that should be worn
throughout the kingdom and "the animosities between these two parties run so high, that they will
neither eat nor drink, nor talk with each other." They
are also at odds with the neighboring kingdom of Ble-
fuscu over the issue of how to break an egg. At one
time everyone broke their eggs on the larger end, until
the heir to the throne cut his finger doing so. The
reigning emperor then commanded everyone to break
the smaller end of their eggs. Gulliver is told that
"The people so highly resented this law, that our histories tell us there have been six rebellions raised on
that account."

It is obvious to the reader that the Lilliputians are
small in stature and even smaller in mind. Swift's
portrait of these fussy little people was so compelling
that to this day we use the adjective *lilliputian* to refer
to people or objects that are smaller than normal. We

also apply it to individuals who, like Gulliver's captors, have a tendency to make mountains out of molehills.

See also: **Brobdingnagian, yahoo.**

Little Lord Fauntleroy: a sissy; a style of clothing popular during the Victorian era

Although the term *Little Lord Fauntleroy* is not as popular today as it was at the turn of the century, it is still a readily recognized term for a boy who looks and acts like a sissy.

Little Lord Fauntleroy is the title of an 1886 children's book written by Frances Hodgson Burnett and illustrated by Reginald Birch. The sentimental story was immensely popular and was adapted as a play, *The Real Lord Fauntleroy*, in 1888. At the beginning of the tale, seven-year-old Cedric Errol is living with his parents in poverty in New York City. His mother is an American, and his father is an English nobleman whose family disinherited him when he married her. When Cedric's father dies, the boy is summoned to England, where he meets his noble relatives and wins them over with his polite, charming ways. His mother is welcomed back into the family and joins him in England, where he assumes the title Lord, which he has inherited from his grandfather.

Burnett's descriptions and Birch's illustrations depict a very pretty little boy, with long golden curls, who dresses in a black velvet suit with a lace collar. Mothers in late Victorian and Edwardian England were so taken with the portrait of this doll-like creature that they began dressing their sons in the same costume. The *Little Lord Fauntleroy* style in children's clothing lasted at least a generation, to the dismay of many little boys.

Little Orphan Annie: someone who gives the impression of being alone and pathetic

Very few people are aware that the popular comic strip waif, Little Orphan Annie, began life as a character in a poem by John Whitcomb Riley, the acclaimed nineteenth-century "Hoosier poet." "Little Orphan Annie" was written by Riley in 1885. His heroine was a brave little girl, who worked hard for her keep and believed in goblins.

Like Riley, cartoonist Harold Gray was born and raised in the midwest. He grew up on a farm in Illinois and went to Indiana's Purdue University. In 1924 Gray was working in the *Chicago Tribune*'s art department as an assistant on the comic strip *The Gumps*. When his boss, Joseph Patterson, requested a new strip featuring a little girl, Gray remembered the heroine of Riley's poem, and *Little Orphan Annie* was reborn on August 5, 1924.

Gray reprised the character of the plucky foundling living in an orphanage, where she is constantly running afoul of the heartless Miss Asthma Dickens. In 1925, he arranged for Annie to be adopted by Mrs. Oliver Warbucks, but the adoption didn't work out, and Annie returned to the orphanage, where she continued to have all sorts of adventures. She left the orphanage again, this time for good, when billionaire munitions magnate Daddy Warbucks adopted her. While her new father was away on business, Annie and her dog, Sandy, managed to get into—and out of—as much trouble as ever. Gray once summed up his formula for a successful comic strip: "Keep your characters in hot water all the time, but don't have it hot enough to scald their courage."

During the 1930s two films were made about the adventures of Little Orphan Annie, and a long-running radio show was developed from the comic strip. Gray's heroine soon became so popular that calling someone a *Little Orphan Annie* was a readily understood way of saying that a person looked alone, lost, and pathetic—like an orphaned child with nowhere to turn. The expression remains in use today, due in part to the resurgence of interest in the character when her story was turned into the award-winning Broadway musical *Annie* in 1977 and an equally acclaimed film in 1982.

See also: **life of Riley.**

Lolita: a sexually precocious young girl

In the early 1990s, American newspapers from coast to coast carried headlines about the *Long Island Lolita*, a sixteen-year-old girl who had tried to kill the wife of her much-older, married lover. It was proven in court that the Long Island Lolita had a lot more in common with the fictional character after whom she was nicknamed than anyone would ever have imagined.

After four American publishers turned down Vladimir Nabokov's twelfth novel, *Lolita*, it was published in Paris by Olympia Press in September 1955. Unbeknownst to Nabokov, Olympia's owner, Maurice Girodias, had a reputation for printing obscene works, and *Lolita* was unfairly stigmatized as a result. The English-speaking world took little notice of the novel until the following year, when respected author Graham Greene hailed it as one of the best books of 1955. Greene's comments set off a battle among critics and newspaper columnists, with some defending its value as a work of literature and others refusing to consider it anything other than a dirty book. *Lolita* caused great controversy in Italy as well, and in France it was banned on three separate occasions.

The first American edition of *Lolita* was published by G. P. Putnam's Sons in 1958, by which time the storm had already blown over. Despite protests from conservatives, the novel quickly climbed to the top of the bestseller list. Americans were fascinated by the story of middle-aged Humbert Humbert's fatal pas-

sion for twelve-year-old Dolores Haze, whom he calls
Lolita.

At the beginning of the novel, Humbert is in jail
after having killed Clare Quilty, a debauched playwright for whom Lolita left him. In flashbacks, Humbert tells the reader about his nearly lifelong
obsession with girls between the ages of nine and
fourteen and how he became enamored of Dolores
Haze, his landlady's daughter. In order to be close to
the girl he married her mother, but shortly after their
marriage, the woman read his diary and discovered
his secret passion for her daughter. After confronting
Humbert and swearing he would never see Lolita
again, she ran from the house and was hit by a car.

Humbert was finally free to pursue his real love.
He and Lolita began traveling around the country,
sharing motel rooms as father and daughter. After a
few tentative overtures, Humbert slipped into Lolita's
bed one night and slept beside her. The next morning,
"... by six she was wide awake, and by six fifteen
we were technically lovers ... it was she who seduced me."

Humbert goes on to relate how, upon waking up,
Lolita kissed him in a very unchildlike way. To his
shock, she then suggested they play a game she had
learned from her friend Charlie. When Humbert answered that he had never played such a game, she
showed him exactly what to do, and he discovered
just how adult his little nymphet really was:

> ... not a trace of modesty did I perceive in this beau-
> tiful hardly formed young girl whom modern co-

*education, juvenile mores, the campfire racket and so
forth had utterly and hopelessly depraved. She saw
the stark act merely as part of a youngster's furtive
world, unknown to adults . . . My life was handled by
little Lo in an energetic, matter-of-fact manner. . . .*

Before long Lolita was using sex as a way to get
whatever she wanted from Humbert. She began demanding money in return for her sexual favors, and
Humbert began to fear that she was trying to save
enough to leave him. Eventually, she did just that,
with Clare Quilty.

After several years, Humbert found Lolita, married
and pregnant. She told him she had left Quilty soon
after running off with him because he had insisted
she take part in orgies with his friends, something she
could not do because she really loved Quilty. She had
then married Dick Schiller and was planning to move
with him to Alaska. After begging in vain that Lolita
leave Schiller and resume her life with him, Humbert
set out to track down and kill Quilty, the man he
continued to blame for his loss of Lolita's love.

Humbert died in prison of a heart attack while
awaiting trial for Quilty's murder. Lolita, the flirta-
tious and manipulative nymphet, died in childbirth at
the age of seventeen.

Lone Ranger: someone who relies only on him/herself, who prefers to do things alone

When we call someone a *Lone Ranger*, there is little doubt as to what we mean: We are saying that the person prefers to do things on his or her own, to be in control, and not to rely on others. In short, he or she follows the same modus operandi as John Reid, the masked adventurer who called himself the Lone Ranger while several generations of Americans were growing up.

Reid/The Ranger was created by producer George W. Trendle and scriptwriter Fran Striker. The dual character made his radio debut in 1933, and the *Lone Ranger* series continued to run on radio until 1954. Reid was introduced as a former Texas Ranger who had turned to freelance law enforcement, calling himself the Lone Ranger as he rode through the Old West, in disguise, righting wrongs. While he insisted on working outside official law enforcement channels, he did accept the aid of a faithful Indian friend, Tonto. The first actor to provide the radio voice of the Lone Ranger was Jack Deeds. He was followed by George Seaton, Brace Beemer, and Earle W. Graser.

It became even more apparent that the Lone Ranger was the quintessential good guy, when he appeared on the movie screen dressed in white and riding a white stallion named Silver. The first film, titled simply *The Lone Ranger*, was released in 1938 and starred Lee Powell. The following year *The Lone Ranger Rides Again* appeared, with Robert Livingston

in the title role. Clayton Moore played the masked
man on television from 1949 to 1957, with Jay Sil-
verheels in the role of Tonto. Moore also appeared in
two Lone Ranger films.

Add to this seventeen novels written by Fran
Striker between 1936 and 1957, a *Lone Ranger* magazine that was published in 1937, numerous *Lone
Ranger* comic strips and comic books, a cartoon series that ran on television from 1966 to 1969, and a
full-length movie released in 1981. Is it any wonder
we no longer need to ask: "Who was that masked
man?"

Looney Tune: a person who behaves in an eccentric or odd way

When we see a person engaging in eccentric or odd
behavior, we are apt to call him or her a real *Looney
Tune* or say that he or she is *Looney Tunes*. In doing
so, we are alluding to the antics of a group of characters who have delighted film and television audiences for over six decades.

The Looney Tunes theatrical shorts were first created in 1930, by Leon Schlesinger Productions, to
promote Warner Bros.' feature film music and publishing catalog. Each short featured a Warner Bros.
song, and the title Looney Tunes was devised for
them as a response to Walt Disney's animated Silly
Symphonies. In 1931 Schlesinger's staff also began

creating Merrie Melodies, shorts that contained only
a single verse from a Warner Bros. song.

Two of the biggest stars of Looney Tunes first appeared in the Merrie Melodies: Porky Pig and Bugs
Bunny. In 1935 Porky Pig starred in his first Merrie
Melodies cartoon. In the following years more shorts
were made featuring Porky, including *Porky's Hare
Hunt* (1938) and *Hare-Um Scare-Um* (1939). The
hare in these last two films was a hyperactive, frenetic
rabbit drawn by Ben "Bugs" Hardaway. When Hardaway and animator Charlie Thorsen worked together
to further develop the rabbit's character, Thorsen
wrote "Bugs's Bunny" on Hardaway's drawings, and
the name, slightly modified, stuck. In 1940, animator
Tex Avery slowed Bugs down and made him less
physical and more cerebral. The new, improved Bugs
stood upright, ate carrots, and delivered for the first
time his now-trademark line, "What's up, Doc?" in
a voice supplied by the inimitable Mel Blanc.

Leon Schlesinger Productions was sold to Jack
Warner in 1943 and became Warner Bros. Animation.
Looney Tunes eventually became a generic term for
all the theatrical shorts produced by Warner Bros. studios. In the following decades, a series of now-
legendary Warner animators, including Friz Freleng,
Chuck Jones, Bob Clampett, Robert McKimson, and
Tex Avery all contributed to the continuing success of
the ever-expanding Looney Tunes gang: Porky, Bugs,
Daffy Duck, Elmer Fudd, Yosemite Sam, the Tas-
manian Devil, Speedy Gonzales, Sylvester, Tweety,

Tweety, the Road Runner, Wile E. Coyote, etc.

Possessing far more than simple amusement value, the Looney Tunes characters went on to become icons of the American folk hero tradition. For six decades they have embodied our robust national spirit and the character traits we most admire: Bugs Bunny's patriotic, resourceful, and defiant spirit; the self-centered but ever-optimistic and persistent Daffy Duck; the loyalty and determination of Porky Pig; Wile E. Coyote's all-American ingenuity; even Yosemite Sam's old-fashioned orneriness.

Throughout America's many dark hours—the Great Depression, World War II, the Cold War, the Vietnam era—the Looney Tunes could always be counted on to help us forget our troubles, inspiring laughter with their energy and wit. During World War II, Bugs Bunny was awarded a service record by the U.S. Marine Corps, adopted as an official member of the Seabees, and served unofficially for weather squadrons and parachute batallions. His likeness was used as a morale builder on hospital ships and bombers.

In the words of director Chuck Jones, "Variations on the believable—that is the essence of all humor—all great cartoon characters are based on human behavior we recognize in ourselves." The Looney Tunes, in fact, possess all of the intellectual and emotional traits of human beings: Some, like Tweety, Bugs, and the Road Runner, are as sharp as can be—shrewd, cunning, and self-confident. Others, like Elmer Fudd, Sylvester, and Yosemite Sam, are what one might call dim bulbs: No matter how hard they try, they'll never be a match for their cool and wily adversaries. But they just can't stop themselves from trying just one more time to get the upper hand. Their exaggerated reactions when their wacky, oddball schemes fail and their persistence in the face of constant defeat are what make us laugh at their escapades time after time.

Children love the slapstick comedy, funny voices, and quick repartee of the Looney Tunes. But the cartoons are written for adults, who find them all the more amusing because they understand the motivation behind the characters' actions. Grown-ups laugh at the crazy situations the Looney Tunes get into in large part because they ring a personal bell: Fans of the zany group can't help but recognize in them and their behavior their own friends, coworkers, family members—and, yes, even themselves.

Lothario/lothario: a seducer of women, a libertine

A few years ago the press had a field day with the story of the *Long Island Lothario* and his *Lolita*. The man who was given the label was Joey Buttafuoco, owner of an automobile repair shop and lover of sixteen-year-old Amy Fisher. The case hit the headlines when Ms. Fisher tried, unsuccessfully, to murder Buttafuoco's wife.

The reporters who created the term *Long Island Lothario* were alluding to a literary character whose name has become a synonym for a man who makes a habit of seducing women: a love 'em and leave 'em kind of guy.

The original Lothario did just that, in a play called *The Fair Penitent*, which was written by English playwright Nicholas Rowe in 1703. Rowe based his tragic drama on *The Fatal Dowry* by Massinger and Field. He simplified their story and made it into a melancholy tale of private woes, which set the fashion for many later eighteenth-century dramas.

The fair penitent of the play is Calista, a young woman who has been betrothed to Altamont in accordance with her father's wishes. Altamont adores her, but, unfortunately, she does not return his love. She is in love with Lothario, who is an enemy of Altamont and his family. Lothario once asked Calista's father for her hand in marriage but was refused. Partly because of his basic immorality, and partly to get revenge on Altamont, Lothario seduces Calista. Predictably, after taking Calista's virginity, Lothario is no longer interested in her:

> *I found my heart no more beat high with transport,*
> *No more I sighed and languished for enjoyment:*
> *'Twas past, and reason took her turn to reign*
> *While ev'ry weakness fell before her throne.*

Calista is devastated when Lothario tells her that he has no intention of marrying her. He is quite willing to continue their affair, but doesn't intend to "load it with the marriage chain."

When Altamont learns about Lothario's seduction of Calista and her continuing love for the man who dishonored her, he kills Lothario. Calista's father, Sciolto, is outraged and wants to kill his daughter, but Altamont will not permit it. Sciolto is then wounded mortally by the family of Lothario, who blames him for their kinsman's death. Although before he dies Sciolto forgives Calista, she cannot bear to live with the knowledge that she caused his death, and she stabs herself. After her death, Altamont no longer has the will to live. He is carried from the stage in a faint, and his friend Horatio prays he will find the strength to go on.

The Fair Penitent ends as Horatio gives a homily on the tragic consequences of illicit love:

> *By such examples are we taught to prove*
> *The sorrows that attend unlawful love;*
> *Death, or some worse misfortunes, soon divide*
> *The injured bridegroom from his guilty bride:*
> *If you would have the nuptial union last,*
> *Let virtue be the bond that ties it fast.*

Rowe's plays are rarely read today, and he is best known in literary circles as the eighteenth-century editor of Shakespeare's works. But his fictional liber-

tine, the cruel and fickle Lothario, was such a
successful creation that we still can't think of a better
way to describe a cad than to call him by the name
Lothario.

See also: **Lolita.**

Machiavellian: manipulative, cunning

*Every one admits how praiseworthy it is in a prince
to keep faith, and to live with integrity and not with
craft. Nevertheless our experience has been that
those princes who have done great things have held
good faith of little account, and have known how to
circumvent the intellect of men by craft, and in the
end have overcome those who relied on their word.*

It is advice like this, given by Niccolò Machiavelli
to Lorenzo de Medici, that brought about the creation
of the adjective *machiavellian* to describe philosophy
or behavior in which cunning and duplicity are used
to attain power over others.

Machiavelli was born in Florence in 1469 and
served for fourteen years as Florentine secretary or
envoy to the principalities of Italy and to neighboring
European countries. When the Medici family was re-

stored to power in 1512, Machiavelli lost his position and was exiled from Florence for a year. He was imprisoned and tortured for taking part in a conspiracy against the Medicis, when in fact he was completely innocent of the charges.

After his release, Machiavelli retired to a small farm outside Florence, where he actually worked the land. In his spare time, he wrote his political treatises, including the above-quoted work, *Il Principe (The Prince)*. He hoped, of course, that his books would come to the attention of the ruling family and convince them of his value as a political adviser. It was not his serious writings, however, that brought him back into favor; the fame Machiavelli achieved as a result of his dramatic works, particularly the comedy *La Mandragola (The Mandrake)* is what caused the Medicis to make him an adviser in their government.

Some of the other recommendations Machiavelli gave in *The Prince* include the need to adopt the characteristics of both the lion and the fox ". . . because the lion cannot defend himself against snares and the fox cannot defend himself against wolves. Therefore, it is necessary to be a fox to discover the snares and a lion to terrify the wolves."

Machiavelli's cynicism is most apparent when he recommends that a ruler is not obliged to keep his promises to his subjects if circumstances change. "If men were entirely good," he comments, "this precept would not hold, but because they are bad, and will not keep faith with you, you too are not bound to observe it with them."

Machiavelli believed that it is more important for a ruler to be feared than loved, but that it is always in the prince's best interests not to inspire hatred among his subjects. To this end, he recommends exercising a moderate amount of cruelty and planning it well. He gives the example of Cesare Borgia, who, when he became Duke Valentino, selected a swift and cruel man named Messer Ramiro d'Orco (de Lorqua) to maintain order in the areas he occupied. The duke was aware that Ramiro's highly effective but excessively cruel methods had caused some hatred toward him, as the ruler. In order to gain back the goodwill of the people, he announced that any cruelty they might have been subjected to was not countenanced by him but was strictly the doing of Ramiro. Ramiro thus became the scapegoat. He was executed and the people praised the duke for seeing that justice was done.

Machiavelli again fell out of political favor when the Florentine Republic was restored shortly before his death. He applied for his old position of Florentine secretary, but he was too closely associated with the Medicis to be trusted, and his application was denied. He died in 1527, having established a lasting reputation as a proponent of cold, calculating egotism and the abandonment of morality in exchange for power.

mad as a hatter/mad as a March Hare:
completely crazy

Both these phrases were used to describe someone whose behavior was decidedly odd, long before Lewis Carroll published *Alice's Adventures in Wonderland* in 1865. But it was Carroll's story, written for ten-year-old Alice Liddell, that popularized them and still makes us associate these expressions with *his* mad hatter and hare.

The expression *mad as a hatter* most likely has its origins in the effects that mercury, which was used to make felt hats, had on those who worked with it. It is now known that this chemical can cause Saint Vitus' dance and other spastic movements. The use of the phrase *mad as a hatter* was recorded in America in 1836, and it appeared in Thackeray's *Pendennis* in 1849–50.

Hares were generally regarded to be wild and unpredictable during the month of March, which is their mating season: hence the probable origin of the phrase *mad as a March Hare.*

Already well known for their fits of lunacy, a hatter and a hare made perfect hosts for the mad tea party that Alice attended during her stay in Wonderland.

See also: **mad tea party.**

mad tea party: an event characterized by confusion and chaos

As soon as Alice saw the table, which was set out under a tree in front of the March Hare's house, she realized something was amiss. The Mad Hatter and the March Hare were having tea, leaning on a sleeping dormouse.

The table was a large one, but the three were all crowded together at one corner of it. "No room! No room!" they cried out when they saw Alice coming. "There's plenty of room," said Alice indignantly, and she sat down in a large arm-chair at one end of the table.

Thus begins the mad tea party in Lewis Carroll's classic, *Alice's Adventures in Wonderland*, which was published in 1865. Alice is offered wine, then told there is none. The Hatter berates the Hare for putting butter in his watch, and the Hare proceeds to dunk the watch into his teacup. (The watch, by the way, tells the day of the month, not the time.)

Alice is perplexed by the strange goings-on, as any sane person would be, but her attempts to clarify her hosts' statements are ignored. The Hatter poses a riddle, then tells Alice he has no idea what the answer is. He then tells her that Time is a person with whom he quarreled the year before; that's why it's always teatime at his house. As a result, they have no time to wash the cups and saucers between teas, so they just keep moving around the table. When Alice asks what happens when they get back to the beginning, the Hatter changes the subject. The party goes on, with the Dormouse telling a story that Alice doesn't understand and the group moving around the table. When the inane conversation becomes too much for Alice to bear, she gets up and leaves. The Dormouse promptly falls asleep, and the other two try to stuff it into the teapot.

One of the most memorable scenes in English literature, Carroll's *mad tea party* is the epitome of chaos and confusion. As such, it soon became a colorful metaphor for an event that is characterized by meaningless activity and rampant confusion.

See also: **mad as a hatter/mad as a March Hare.**

Madame Bovary: a woman with an inflated, glamorized opinion of herself

Gustave Flaubert's masterpiece, *Madame Bovary*, first appeared in 1856. It is the tragic story of Emma Bovary, a woman for whom real life can never measure up to the idealized picture she has painted of it. Unable to accept her station in life, she tries every avenue of escape, until the only one left is death.

Charles Bovary met his future bride, Emma, when he was called to her father's farm on a medical emergency. When she greeted him at the door, he was surprised to see her wearing "a blue merino dress with three flounces." He noticed that she couldn't sew and kept pricking her fingers with the needle, but

he was more interested in "the whiteness of her fingernails . . . almond-shaped, tapering, as polished and
shining as Dieppe ivories."

Emma was no ordinary farmer's daughter. She had
been sent to convent school and had received a fine
education, including dancing, geography, drawing,
needlework, and piano. She had loved everything
about the school, especially the visits of the old
woman who looked after the linen. Emma and her
friends would slip out of study hall to visit with this
colorful figure, a noblewoman whose family had been
ruined by the Revolution. She sang eighteenth-
century love songs and gave the girls novels about
love affairs, lovers, and mistresses.

Emma also loved the novels of Sir Walter Scott
and spent her adolescence dreaming of knights in
shining armor:

> *She would have liked to live in some old manor, like
> those long-waisted chatelaines who spent their days
> leaning out of fretted Gothic casements, elbow on
> parapet and chin in hand, watching a white-plumed
> knight come galloping out of the distance on a black
> horse.*

Was it any wonder, then, that she was disappointed
in the reality of marriage to a simple country doctor
like Charles Bovary? Even in the first days of her
marriage Emma wished she could be elsewhere. Her
dreary surroundings and the uneventful life she led in
Charles's house made her long for something more:

It seemed to her that certain portions of the earth must produce happiness—as though it were a plant native only to those soils and doomed to languish elsewhere. Why couldn't she be leaning over the balcony of some Swiss chalet? Or nursing her melancholy clad in a long black velvet coat and wearing soft leather shoes, a high-crowned hat and fancy cuffs?

As the years went by, Emma's discontent grew. She became involved in two affairs, but neither of her lovers was as serious as she, and both liaisons ended in disappointment. As a result of her constant need to surround herself with beautiful and expensive things, she found herself with debts she had no way of paying, and she finally killed herself.

Emma Bovary's attempt to be something she was not led to the use of the name *Madame Bovary* to describe a woman who has an inflated, glamorized view of herself—who puts on airs in front of others.

Other, less common English words that were coined from the name of Flaubert's tragic heroine are *bovarism/bovarysm,* meaning a conception of oneself as other than one is; *bovarist,* a person who is subject to bovarism; and the verb *to bovarize,* meaning to develop an inflated image of oneself.

malapropism: the misuse of one word for another

"You will promise to forget this fellow—to illiterate him, I say, quite from your memory."

". . . I hope you will represent her to the captain as an object not altogether illegible."

"I am sorry to say . . . that my affluence over my niece is very small."

". . . as headstrong as an allegory on the banks of the Nile."

The above quotations are some of the first malapropisms to be found in the English language. They come from the mouth of one Mrs. Malaprop, a character who was so skilled in the misuse of language that the word *malaproprism* was coined in her honor: It is still used to describe the incorrect substitution of one word for another.

Mrs. Malaprop is one of the funniest elements of Robert Brinsley Sheridan's 1775 play, *The Rivals*. Her name comes from the French *mal à propros,* which means out of place or inappropriate. And that is exactly what the words she uses are. In trying to impress others, particularly the wealthy Mr. Anthony Absolute, Mrs. Malaprop attempts to show off her large and varied vocabulary.

The only trouble is, she doesn't know the meaning of most of the words that she uses. As a result, she constantly confuses words with similar-sounding ones, inserting them into sentences in which they don't belong. What follows is a series of hilarious statements that make absolutely no sense. Instead of telling her niece to obliterate the young man she loves from her memory, Mrs. Malaprop suggests that she "illiterate" him. *Illegible* is confused with *ineligible, affluence* with *influence, allegory* with *alligator,* and on and on throughout the play. What makes the situation even more humorous is that Mrs. Malaprop is completely unaware of her verbal gaffes: She believes that she excels at making polite conversation.

The Rivals is not as well known as Sheridan's *School for Scandal*, but it is a lively and well-written comedy. The main plot revolves around the romance of Miss Lydia Languish and Captain Jack Absolute. Lydia's aunt, Mrs. Malaprop, and Jack's father, Anthony Absolute, are trying to get the young people together. Unbeknownst to them, or to Lydia herself, Jack has been paying court to the young lady in the person of Ensign Beverly. He assumed the identity of a poor enlisted man to satisfy Lydia's dreams of a romantic elopement in defiance of convention. Lydia is furious when she learns about Jack's masquerade, and she breaks off their engagement. At the end, of course, she forgives him and agrees to marry him even if they can't elope and their elders are not dead set against their union.

masochism: the derivation of sexual pleasure
through pain; the satisfaction some people get
from suffering

The writings of the Marquis de Sade, which contain
graphic scenes in which one partner derives sexual
pleasure from inflicting pain on the other, gave us the
word *sadism*. Sadism is considered to be a deviant psychological condition, and anyone who enjoys seeing
others suffer—whether or not sex is involved—is now
called a sadist. The opposite, and no less aberrant, condition is called *masochism*.

Masochists enjoy pain, either physical or psychological. They received their name from Austrian
writer Leopold von Sacher-Masoch, who suffered
from the condition himself. Sacher-Masoch was born
in Lemburg, Austria, in 1836 and died in 1895. He
studied at the universities of Prague and Graz and
held several teaching positions during his life.

Sacher-Masoch wrote many short stories, novels,
and plays. His novels were reflective of the late-
nineteenth-century trend toward realism, dealing with
peasant life and incorporating Jewish themes. In many
of these fictional works he created characters who
shared his own masochistic tendencies.

Sacher-Masoch's best-known works are a collec-
tion of stories called *Das Vermächtnis Kains (The
Legacy of Cain),* which includes the popular story
"Venus im Pelz" ("Venus in Furs"); *Falscher He-
melion (False Ermine); Die Messalinen Wiens (The
Messalinas of Vienna); Der Don Juan von Kolomea*

(The Don Juan from Kolomea); and *Judengeschichten (Jewish Stories).*

  See also: **sadism.**

Mephistophelean/Mephistophelian: devilish, demonic

The origin of the name Mephistopheles is unknown: It may be Greek (*mephos-phigein,* not loving light) or Hebrew (*mephis-tofel,* destroyer-liar). It is possible that the name was invented by the anonymous author of the first *Faustbuch,* since after its publication in 1587 the name Mephistopheles, which had never been included before, began to be added to the lists of devils in many other books.

Mephistopheles is not the Devil, who is the fallen angel Lucifer. That is made clear in all the existing versions of the Faust legend. He is a servant of Lucifer, one of the many spirits who do his bidding on Earth.

In one Faustian work, the *Magia Naturalis et Innaturalis,* Mephisto is said to be one of the seven planetary spirits or adversaries of the planetary gods. The author associates him with Jupiter, refers to his role as Faust's familiar, and describes him as taking the shape of a chubby little monk.

In Christopher Marlowe's 1604 drama, *Doctor Faustus,* the title character conjures up Mephisto-

philis, as Marlowe refers to him, by uttering these
words:

> Hail spirits of fire, air, and water! Belzebub, Prince
> of the East, monarch of burning hell, and Demogor-
> gon, we call upon you, that Mephistophilis may ap-
> pear and rise.

When Mephistophilis does appear, and Faustus
commands the demon to wait upon him and do whatever he wishes for the rest of his life, Mephistophilis
makes it clear that he has another, more important
master:

> I am a servant to great Lucifer,
> And may not follow thee without his leave:
> No more than he commands must we perform.

When Faustus asks Mephistophilis who he and the
other demons that serve Lucifer are, he replies that
they are all

> Unhappy spirits that fell with Lucifer,
> Conspired against our God with Lucifer,
> And are for ever damned with Lucifer.

Faustus then asks Mephistophilis to go back to hell
and ask his master to allow him to serve Faustus for
the rest of his life in return for Faustus's soul.

In part I of Goethe's *Faust*, which appeared in
1808, Mephistopheles is a more independent, self-

assured demon. He is sophisticated and witty, and does not have to go back to hell to get his orders. In fact, in the prologue, he and God have a conversation in which Mephistopheles asks permission to "guide [Faust] in paths I choose him." God responds, "You shall have leave to do as you prefer, so long as earth remains his mortal dwelling." Mephistopheles thanks the Lord, saying that he'd much rather deal with the living than with the dead:

> *For frankly it's repelling*
> *To have so much to do with the deceased.*
> *For me a glowing cheek is like a feast.*
> *I'm not at home to corpses in my house:*
> *There's something in me of the cat-and-mouse.*

In spite of Goethe's lighthearted portrayal of Mephistopheles, his name has come down to us as a synonym for an evil being, a devil or demon. The adjective *Mephistophelean,* which was created from his name, is now used when describing forces of darkness and those with a demonic nature.

See also: **Faustian bargain.**

micawberesque: characterized by unrealistic and undaunted optimism

When, as a young boy, David Copperfield is sent to work in London, he lodges with Mr. Wilkins Micawber, his wife, and their two small children. Although Micawber is employed as an agent for the firm of Murdstone & Grinbys, the family is always having financial problems, due to Mr. Micawber's habit of spending every penny he gets his hands on. Much of his money is lost in outlandish business ventures that are doomed to fail, but he remains undaunted. "Something will turn up," is his eternal refrain. His undaunted optimism led to the creation of the English adjective *micawberesque,* which is frequently applied to an incurable optimist who never gives up hope, no matter how hopeless the situation may be.

Micawber is a good man at heart—he saves his boss, Mr. Wickfield, from the blackmail of the villainous Uriah Heep—but one can't help thinking that the saying "A fool and his money are soon parted" was coined with him in mind. Eventually, when all his schemes fail, Micawber emigrates to Australia, where he becomes a magistrate.

David Copperfield was written by Charles Dickens in 1849 and 1850, and is in large part autobiographical. Dickens freely admitted that the character of Wilkins Micawber was based on his own father, a navy clerk who was constantly in debt. When Dickens was only twelve years old, his father was thrown into debtors' prison, and, like David Copperfield, Dickens was forced to go to work in a factory. After his father's release Dickens managed to obtain an education, becoming an office boy in a law firm, a reporter, and, finally, the most popular English writer of his time.

Mickey Mouse: trivial; of little consequence
or value

Before Walt Disney became head of a cartoon empire,
he worked out of a garage in Kansas City, Missouri.
The company was called Laugh O'Gram, and Disney
shared the space with several other artists—and with
quite a few mice.

The walls of the garage were a fertile breeding
ground for the creatures, and early in 1923 ten little
mice were born there. Unlike his fellow cartoonists,
who were all for setting mousetraps, Disney liked
having the mice around. He devised a humane trap to
catch them and kept them in cages on his desk. He
often brought an extra lunch to work, just for his little
pets. One mouse, whom he had named Mortimer, became so tame that he allowed it to scurry around his
desk when he was working alone late at night. In
August 1923 Disney left Kansas City for Hollywood.
Before he left he released the mice in a vacant lot.
Nine of them ran off immediately, but Mortimer just
stood and looked at Disney until the man stamped his
foot and shouted.

Disney never forgot his little friend Mortimer. On
March 16, 1928, he had a dream about the mouse,
and the next day he drew it. The cartoon rodent was
dressed in red velvet pants, big yellow shoes, and
white gloves. He had ruffled hair and a tail, neither
of which was included in later portrayals. Of course
Disney wanted to call him Mortimer Mouse, but his

wife convinced him that Mickey Mouse was a better
name for a cartoon character.

Later that year Mickey made his debut in the short
silent film *Plane Crazy*. Soon after, he starred in the
world's first animated sound cartoon, *Steamboat Willie*,
with Disney supplying his voice. The mouse was
an instant sensation, not only in the United States, but
all over the world. During the 1920s and early 1930s
numerous Mickey Mouse films were made. By 1931
there were one million members of Mickey Mouse
clubs. Over 100,000 people saw Mickey on the screen
every day; his cartoons appeared in twenty foreign
newspapers; his likeness was even on display in Madame
Tussaud's Wax Museum.

Since then Mickey Mouse has become one of the
best-loved—and most profitable—fictional characters
of all time. His likeness appears on thousands of commercial
items, including the perennially popular
Mickey Mouse watch. The watches were introduced
in the 1940s and had a picture of the famous rodent
on the dial, his outspread arms functioning as hands.
It was due to these cheap, gimmicky timepieces that
the phrase *Mickey Mouse* came to mean something
that is of little value or consequence. We now speak
of a Mickey Mouse project, Mickey Mouse deals, a
Mickey Mouse car, etc. The name of the most famous
mouse in the history of the world has even been
turned into a verb, as in they mickey-moused the
sound, meaning they made it less powerful, less resonant.

miles to go before I sleep: a lot to do before I can rest/die

Robert Frost lived from 1874 to 1973. He spent most of his life in Massachusetts and New Hampshire. One of his best-known poems is "Stopping by Woods on a Snowy Evening," in which he creates the atmosphere of a lonely, dark wood on a winter's night.

While out riding, the narrator decides to stop at an uninhabited spot, owned by someone who lives in the village, "to watch his woods fill up with snow." It is something he does on the spur of the moment, yielding to a sudden impulse to break out of his familiar routine and experience the beauty that surrounds him. Evidently this indulgence in the impractical is a rare thing for, as he comments, "My little horse must think it queer / To stop without a farmhouse near / . . . He gives his harness bells a shake / To ask if there is some mistake."

Unfortunately, the escape from the mundane into the poetic cannot be of long duration. The wistfulness of the narrator is apparent, as he resigns himself to continuing his journey:

The woods are lovely, dark and deep.
But I have promises to keep,
And miles to go before I sleep,
And miles to go before I sleep.

It has been said that Frost's poetry appeals to a wide variety of readers because it can be enjoyed in so many different ways. To those who appreciate nature, his descriptions of the New England landscape and its inhabitants are reason enough to read his poems. On another, deeper level, the rural imagery of Frost's poems is filled with symbolism. "Stopping by Woods on a Snowy Evening" is a perfect example of this: The narrator finds a moment's respite from the world. He would love to linger a while in this quiet place, but his sense of duty forces him to move on. Taken in this sense, the poem's last line "And *miles to go before I sleep*," has become a popular figure of speech for having a great deal to do before one can rest (i.e., take time out of one's busy life to stop and smell the roses—or watch the snow).

If one chooses to, one can look for an even more metaphysical meaning in the poem: The narrator, traveling through life, is weary and is tempted by the lovely, dark, deep woods—that is to say, by death. What a relief it would be to stay for eternity in a place where he has no duties, no cares. But he does not succumb to the temptation: He must continue on the path of life until he has fulfilled his destiny; only then will he have earned eternal rest.

See also: **(the) road less traveled.**

(the) milk of human kindness: compassion

Today, when we say someone is full of *the milk of human kindness*, we mean it as a compliment: We apply the figure of speech to someone who is compassionate and concerned about his fellow men. However, the literary character who introduced the expression to our language was being anything but complimentary when she used it in reference to her husband.

As Act I, Scene 5 of William Shakespeare's *Macbeth* opens, Lady Macbeth is reading a letter from her husband. In it he recounts his meeting with the three witches and their prophecies that he would be Thane of Cawdor and, eventually, king of Scotland. He also tells his wife that right after this encounter he was, in fact, made Thane of Cawdor by King Duncan. The fact that the witches' first prediction has come true has made him believe a great future lies ahead for him.

But Lady Macbeth knows her husband very well. She says, as if to him, "Yet do I fear thy nature; it is too full o' the milk of human kindness to catch the nearest way . . . Hie thee hither, that I may pour my spirits in thine ear. . . ." She knows that, without her urging, Macbeth's scruples will take precedence over his ambition. So intensely does she wish to suppress any tender feelings in herself, as well as in her husband, that when she hears that King Duncan is in the vicinity she implores the powers that be to ". . . fill me from the crown to the toe top full / Of direst cruelty . . . Stop up the access and passage to remorse / . . . Come to my woman's breasts, / And take my milk for gall. . . ."

Her prayers are answered, at least temporarily,

when her relentless hounding of Macbeth finally cul-
minates in his murder of King Duncan, and she and
Macbeth assume the throne of Scotland.

milquetoast/Milquetoast: a timid, meek person

There are few foods that are more bland than milk
toast: buttered toast that is soaked in hot milk and,
for those who can handle it, sprinkled with a little
sugar. Along with Jell-O, custard, and weak tea, milk
toast has long been a mainstay of people who suffer
from digestive disorders. This bland, inoffensive food
also inspired the creation of a popular cartoon character, who in turn left his mark on the English language.

Cartoonist Harold T. Webster lived from 1885 to
1952. "Webby," as he was affectionately called,
grew up in the Midwest. After high school he worked
until he was able to save $150, then set off for Chi-
cago, where he used the money to study art.

When Webster began to draw a comic strip called
The Timid Soul, Milquetoast seemed to him to be the
perfect name for a man who was unable to assert himself with his family, boss, or coworkers. So he created
the bland, inoffensive Caspar Milquetoast, around
whose life and difficulties the strip revolved.

Webster was once quoted as saying that Caspar
Milquetoast embodied his own view of himself. But

while his hero was never successful at anything he
tried, Webster certainly was. *The Timid Soul* was a
vast success and its hero such a well-recognized figure that it soon became common to call a passive
person a *Caspar Milquetoast* or simply a *milquetoast*.

Moby Dick: an enormous object; an awesome, monstrous object that inspires fear

A neighbor of mine drives an enormous station wagon
that she and everyone else calls *Moby Dick*. She uses
the name in the literal sense, because the car seems
as big as the famous white whale created by Herman
Melville. But those of us who have to pass her on the
road use the term figuratively, as a way of denoting
an awesome, monstrous object that has the power to
destroy anyone or anything that crosses its path. We
dread an encounter with that car as much as sailors
feared meeting the white whale on the open seas.

Moby-Dick, or The Whale was published in 1851.
Although it was almost forgotten by the time of Melville's death in 1891, *Moby-Dick* was rediscovered
during the 1920s and eventually gained its well-
deserved reputation as the greatest American novel of
the nineteenth century.

Moby-Dick is the story of Captain Ahab's mono-
maniacal quest for revenge against the beast that tore
off his leg. Abandoning the pursuit of ordinary whales
for commercial use that is the purpose of his voyage,

Ahab turns his ship toward the area in which the white whale has recently been sighted. Ignoring the appeals of his first mate to give up his ungodly mission, Ahab spurs the crew on with promises of gold and continues to pursue Moby-Dick. When he finally locates the white whale, he orders the crew to kill it, but their harpoons fail to stop the monster. Ahab throws his harpoon into the white whale but gets caught in its line and is shot out of the boat, never to be seen again. Meanwhile, the *Pequod* has been rammed by the whale and sinks into the sea. There is only one survivor of Ahab's fateful voyage. The narrator of the tale, Ishmael, remains afloat on a coffin made by his friend, Queequeg, until he is rescued by a passing ship.

Since the rediscovery of *Moby-Dick*, there have been many interpretations of the meaning of Melville's white whale. To some, Moby-Dick is the embodiment of evil in the world, and Ahab represents man's futile attempts to wipe it from the face of the earth. Others see the whale as a symbol of knowledge and Ahab as a seeker of truth who is willing to sacrifice everything in its pursuit. Moby-Dick has also been identified with the personal demons that torment all human beings and that we spend our lives trying to conquer.

Whatever Melville meant to symbolize in Moby-Dick, the colossal creature remains one of the most powerful creations in literary history. There is no doubt that the white whale is an object of awe: Once glimpsed, it is never forgotten:

> *Moby Dick moved on, still withholding from sight the*
> *full terrors of his submerged trunk, entirely hiding*
> *the wretched hideousness of his jaw. But soon the*
> *fore part of him slowly rose from the water; for an*
> *instant his whole marbleized body formed a high*
> *arch, like Virginia's Natural Bridge, and warningly*
> *waved his bannered flukes in the air, the grand god*
> *revealed himself, sounded, and went out of sight.*

Montagues and Capulets: feuding families

Long before their real-life quarrel made the Hatfields
and McCoys a synonym for feuding families, the
names of a fictional pair of families were used to refer
to two warring clans. We still call families that have
a grudge against one another *Montagues and Capu-*
lets.

William Shakespeare's *Romeo and Juliet* was written in the late 1590s and was preceded by many other
versions of the tale. In fact, some elements of the
story can be found in Latin literature as far back as
the third century A.D. However, the first writer to
name the lovers Romeo and Giulietta and make their
families the feuding Montagues and Capulets of Verona was Luigi Da Porto, who published his work in
1530.

Da Porto believed he was relating a true story, as
did Shakespeare when he wrote his version. Charles
Boyce, in *Shakespeare A to Z*, suggests that Da

Porto's claim may have been based on a line in Dante's *Inferno*, in which the Capelletti and Montecchi families are mentioned as having caused civil disorder. But, as Boyce points out, the Montecchi lived in Verona and the Capelletti in Cremona, and no historical connection has been established between them.

Shakespeare never tells us the cause of the feud between the Montagues and the Capulets, only that it is an ancient quarrel. The Prince of Verona refers to "Three civil brawls, bred of an airy word, / By thee, old Capulet, and Montague . . ." Whatever its origin, the bad blood between the families has incited them to violent acts for many years.

And, tragically, it isn't until each of them has lost one of their children that the old men agree to end their feud:

> *From forth the fatal loins of these two foes*
> *A pair of star-cross'd lovers take their life;*
> *Whose misadventured piteous overthrows*
> *Do with their death bury their parents' strife.*
> *The fearful passage of their death-mark'd love,*
> *And the continuance of their parents' rage,*
> *Which, but their children's end, nought could re-*
> *move . . .*

morality play: *See* **Everyman.**

much ado about nothing: a reaction totally out of proportion to the situation

When we see people making a big fuss over something of very little importance—overreacting, as it were—we are liable to say they are making *much ado about nothing.* The phrase comes, as you may know, from the title of one of William Shakespeare's comedies, which was written in 1598.

The main plot of *Much Ado About Nothing* revolves around the courtship of Hero and Claudio, the attempts of the evil Don John to thwart their love, and their final reconciliation and wedding. Shakespeare took this part of the story from Italian sources, who had, in turn, adapted the storyline from late classical writers. Shakespeare added to the main plot by introducing another pair of lovers—Beatrice and Benedick—who pretend to be enemies at the beginning of the play, but are united at the end through the subterfuge of their friends. Add to this mélange the bumbling characters of Constable Dogberry and his second-in-command, Verges, and you have an action-packed comedy in which emotions run high, tempers flare, schemes abound—and, when it's all over, everyone lives happily ever after.

See also: **Benedick.**

Munchausen/munchausen: wildly improbable; fabricated

When we say someone is telling a *Munchausen* tale or a *Munchausenism*, we are accusing them of making up a wildly improbable story. The reference is to Karl Friedrich Hieronymus, Baron von Münchausen of Bodenwerder in Hanover. Baron von Münchausen was a historical figure who lived from 1720 to 1797. After fighting with the Russians against the Turks, he retired to his estates and became famous for the fabulous stories he told of his exploits as a soldier and hunter. A collection of seventeen stories, all attributed to the baron (although several have been traced to earlier sources), was published in Germany in the early 1780s.

The German collection did not receive widespread attention, however, and it is due to an English edition of his tales that the baron owes his literary—and linguistic—fame. Rudolf Erich Raspe, a German scientist and writer, was living in England when he published a volume of tall tales ostensibly related to him by the baron, whose acquaintance he had made in Germany. The book was titled *Baron Munchausen's Narrative of his Marvelous Travels and Campaigns in Russia*, and it appeared in London in 1785.

In 1786 an enlarged, illustrated edition was published and its title was expanded to *Gulliver Reviv'd: the Singular Travels, Campaigns, Voyages and Sporting Adventures of Baron Munnikhousen, commonly pronounced Munchausen; as he relates them over a bottle when surrounded by his friends.* The book rapidly went into several editions and one of these was translated back into German, with the translator adding thirteen tales of his own. During the nineteenth century, the tales were translated into many languages and illustrated by many well-known artists, including George Cruikshank and Gustave Doré.

The name *Münchausen* soon became synonymous with exaggerations and even outright lies. A Munchausen tale or a Munchausenism is, therefore, to be taken with a very large grain of salt. A person who Munchausenizes should be listened to with the same skepticism.

Through the literary efforts of Raspe, Baron von Munchausen became so well known that his name was applied by the medical community to a syndrome that is characterized by fabricated illness. A person who is afflicted with Munchausen syndrome repeatedly produces symptoms of various diseases in himself or herself, often going so far as to make himself or herself deathly ill. The syndrome appears to be the result of a desperate need for attention and sympathy from doctors, family, and friends. In a bizarre and cruel variant of the syndrome, called *Munchausen by proxy*, a parent will use a child as a surrogate patient, inflicting all kinds of injuries and illnesses on the child and then seeking medical help to rescue the victim. In *Munchausen by adult proxy*, an illness is induced in another adult, so the caregiver receives support and sympathy.

munchkin: a sweet little child; a low-level person

When a cyclone hits the farm in Kansas where a little girl named Dorothy lives with her aunt and uncle, it lifts up their house and carries it away to a magical land. Dorothy and her dog Toto are the only ones in the house at the time, her aunt and uncle having gone down into the cyclone cellar just in time to escape the storm.

While airborne, Dorothy falls asleep and doesn't wake up until the house hits the ground with a bump. Looking outside, she sees a country of marvelous beauty. Green grass is everywhere; there are huge trees filled with ripe fruit; flowers are in bloom; birds flutter through the trees, singing as they fly. As she studies this landscape, which is so different from the gray plains of Kansas, she spots a group of people coming toward her:

They were not as big as the grown folk she had always been used to; but neither were they very small. In fact, they seemed about as tall as Dorothy—who was a well-grown child for her age—although they were, as far as looks go, many years older.

The little people—three men and one woman—are dressed very oddly in Dorothy's view. They are wearing broad-brimmed, pointy hats that are about a foot in height and trimmed in bells. The men are all dressed in blue and wear high boots trimmed in the same color. The woman wears a white hat and a white dress that is sprinkled with little stars that glisten in the sun. The woman, who appears to be much older than the men, approaches Dorothy and addresses her with the following words:

> *You are welcome, most noble Sorceress, to the land of the Munchkins. We are so grateful to you for having killed the wicked Witch of the East, and for setting our people free from bondage.*

Dorothy, of course, has no idea what the woman is talking about. The woman then points to Dorothy's house, which has apparently fallen on the witch and killed her. She tells Dorothy that the witch held the Munchkins, the people of this land, in bondage for many years. Now that she is dead they are no longer slaves. Dorothy asks the woman who she is, and she replies that she is the Witch of the North and a friend of the Munchkins. She further explains that she and the Witch of the South are good witches and that now there is only one bad witch left: the Witch of the West.

Dorothy tells the Witch of the North that she wants to go home to Kansas, and the witch advises her to follow the yellow brick road to the Emerald City, in the center of the Land of Oz. That is the home of the great Wizard of Oz, who is the only one who can help her. Dorothy and Toto set out, walking along the yellow brick road until nightfall, when they are given supper, entertained, and put up for the night in the house of one of the richest Munchkins.

The rest of the story is concerned with Dorothy's journey to the Emerald City, the dangers she runs into, and the characters she meets along the way. Dorothy, the Munchkins, the Witch of the North, and the other fantastic inhabitants of the Land of Oz were created by Lyman Frank Baum. *The Wonderful Wizard of Oz* was the best-selling children's book of the 1900 Christmas season. Baum produced a musical stage version of *The Wizard of Oz* in 1902, and it was on this that the classic 1939 film, starring Judy Garland, was based. He also wrote several sequels to *The Wonderful Wizard of Oz*, but none of them ever attained the popularity of the original.

It is from *The Wonderful Wizard of Oz* that we got the term *munchkin,* which is used to describe a sweet, cute little child. In recent years, the word has been used pejoratively, to denote insignificance or lack of power, as when hourly workers or rookie policemen are referred to as low-level munchkins, because they have no say in what they do and follow whatever orders they are given by their higher-ups.

See also: **cowardly lion, Land of Oz.**

Mutt and Jeff: two people, one of whom is very short and the other very tall

It is not uncommon to refer to two people, one of whom is short and the other tall, as *Mutt and Jeff.*

The original Mutt and Jeff were a pair of buffoons who appeared in the third comic strip to be created in the United States.

Harry Conway Fisher, nicknamed Bud Fisher, was born in 1884 and began his career as a cartoonist while working for the *San Francisco Chronicle*. Beginning in 1907, he created a daily sports cartoon about a horse racing fan named A. Mutt. The cartoon continued to revolve around this one central character until 1910, when Fisher found inspiration for a second character in the much-publicized heavyweight boxing match between James J. Jeffries and Jack Johnson. Fisher wrote a plot line in which the tall, simple-minded Mutt checks into a mental hospital and meets Jeff, a short fellow who, although no Einstein himself, has a slightly higher IQ than Mutt. From then on the interaction between the two characters derived much of its humor from traditional slapstick comedy, including punches in the nose and pies in the face.

Bud Fisher was one of the few cartoonists who had the foresight to copyright his comic strip under his own name. The *San Francisco Chronicle* was part of the Hearst Syndicate, and when Fisher quit the newspaper in 1915, his former employer tried to lay claim to the strip. Fisher sued and won, and *Mutt and Jeff* went with him to the Wheeler Syndicate.

From 1916 to 1920 Mutt and Jeff appeared in a series of short animated films. The cartoon reached its greatest fame in the 1920s but continued to appear for many decades afterward. Bud Fisher died in 1954.

naked ape: man

In *The Origin of Species by Means of Natural Selection* (1859), Charles Darwin set forth his controversial theory that man and other primates are descended from a common ancestor. To prove his point, he discussed in depth the numerous physical similarities between man and the lower primates: apes, monkeys, chimpanzees, etc. He also listed many of the differences between human beings and other mammals, one of which is the absence of hair on a large part of the human body, especially that of the female. Darwin attributed this nakedness to the process of natural selection of sexual traits, a subject that he covered in greater detail in *The Descent of Man and Selection in Relation to Sex* (1871).

One hundred years after Darwin's history-making studies were published, Desmond Morris made the term *naked ape* a synonym for man/woman. Starting with Darwin's view of man as a hairless primate, Morris undertook "A Zoologist's Study of the Human Animal," the findings of which he published as *The Naked Ape* in 1967.

Studying his subjects from an objective, scientific point of view, Morris examines "the typical behavior of typical naked apes" in such areas as mating/sex, child rearing, exploration, fighting, feeding, comfort, and relations with other animals. He notes the similarity of the reactions of young monkeys and human children when they first hear music or are presented with a new toy. He compares the preening and flirting of humans with the mating behavior of monkeys and apes.

In *The Naked Ape* Morris paints a picture of his fellow man that is both laughable and humbling. For, when you strip human beings of the veneer of civilization with which they have covered themselves, what you have are, in fact, nothing more or less than naked apes.

namby-pamby: weak, wishy-washy

Ambrose Philips was a minor English poet who lived from 1674 to 1749. His name has been immortalized in the expression *namby-pamby*, but not, as one might expect, in honor of his contribution to English literature. Nor is it likely that he would be pleased by the way in which he is remembered linguistically.

On the contrary: The name *Namby Pamby* was meant to be disparaging, and was first given to Philips by one of his literary and political rivals, Henry Carey. Carey created the nickname by shortening Ambrose to Amby, putting an N at the beginning, then repeating the same sound, this time preceded by the first initial of Philips's last name. Commenting on some children's poems written by Philips, Carey quipped: "So the Nurses get by Heart Namby Pamby's Little Rhimes."

Like Carey, Jonathan Swift was a Tory, and he too ridiculed the poems of Philips, who was a Whig, calling them "little flams"—fanciful bits of nonsense. But Philips's chief rival and detractor was Alexander Pope. Samuel Johnson referred to the ongoing quarrel between Philips and Pope as a "perpetual reciprocation of malevolence." Thus, in the 1733 edition of Pope's mock epic, *The Dunciad*, where the author satirized one after another of his enemies, Ambrose Philips was once again referred to by the nickname Carey had given him.

The popularity of *The Dunciad* resulted in Namby Pamby becoming a synonym for someone who is weak or sentimental: in short, a sissy. It is also used to indicate that someone or something is insipid or wishy-washy. Over the years a hyphen was added, and the word became both an adjective and a common, rather than proper, noun.

Neverland/Never-Never-Land: a fantasy land, a place where reality never intrudes

Superstar Michael Jackson's penchant for escapism is well known, as is his interest in toys and games that generally appeal only to children. In these tastes, he is a lot like Peter Pan, the fictional boy who wouldn't grow up. Jackson himself must be aware of the similarity, as he named his Florida ranch *Neverland*, after the imaginary realm over which Peter presided.

The Never Land, as described by J. M. Barrie in his 1904 stage play *Peter Pan, or The Boy Who Would Not Grow Up*, is an island. Barrie recommends that you wear spectacles when looking at it, because "the wonders of it might hurt your eyes." The Never Land is the abode of fairies, mermaids, pirates, and Indians. It is also the place where little boys who fall out of their prams and are not claimed in seven days go to live, with Peter Pan as their captain. Barrie says of this magical land:

> *You have often half seen it before, or even three-quarters, after the night-lights were lit, and you might then have beached your coracle on it if you had not always at the great moment fallen asleep. . . . a forest, with a beautiful lagoon beyond but not really far away . . . it is summer time on the trees and on the lagoon but winter on the river, which is not remarkable on Peter's island where all the four seasons may pass while you are filling a jug at the well.*

It is to this magical place that Peter flies with Wendy, John, and Michael Darling. It is there that they fight the evil Captain Hook and his band of pirates. And, when their adventures are over and the Darling children are back home in their nursery, it is to the Never Land that Peter returns. He has no desire to live in the mundane world of reality: He prefers to live on his private island, in the little house that was built for Wendy ". . . high up among the tree-tops where [the fairies] sleep at night."

Barrie's Never Land captured the imagination of English and American theatergoers, who made the name *Neverland* (or *Never-Never-Land*, to which it was corrupted) a synonym for any fantasy world, any place that we create in our mind and escape to when we feel we can no longer stand reality.

See also: **Peter Pan/Peter Pan complex.**

nihilism: a nineteenth-century philosophical movement that advocated utilitarianism and rationalism

"Our actions are governed by utility," Bazarov said. *"In these days, negation is the most useful thing of all—and so we deny."*
   "Everything?"
   "Everything."

*"What? Not only art, poetry . . . but also . . . I am
afraid to say it . . ."*

*"Everything," Bazarov repeated with inexpressi-
ble calm.*

In the above passage Bazarov, a young proponent
of nihilism, is explaining his philosophy to Paul Pe-
trovich Kirsanov, the uncle of his friend Arcady. Bazarov and Arcady belong to the generation of sons,
in Ivan Turgenev's novel *Fathers and Sons*. Their es-
pousal of a philosophy that denies the utility of existing institutions and moral values causes them to
clash violently with their elders.

The word *nihilism* comes from *nihil,* the Latin
word for nothing. It had already been used for other
negative philosophies and was first applied to the
nineteenth-century Russian movement by Nikolai Na-
dezhdin. But it was the publication of Turgenev's
work, in 1862, that popularized the term throughout
Russia.

The novel created a storm, and Turgenev was attacked by both radicals and reactionaries. The former
group claimed he had made Bazarov into a caricature;
the latter accused him of glamorizing Bazarov and the
ideas he stood for. Soon after *Fathers and Sons* was
published, fires broke out all over St. Petersburg, and
the followers of Bazarov were blamed. Turgenev
wrote at the time, "I returned to St. Petersburg on the
very day when Apraxyn Market was set ablaze and
the word 'nihilism' was on everybody's lips. A friend
. . . said to me—'Look what your nihilists are doing!

There is arson all over St. Petersburg!' ''

In fact, Russian nihilism began as a mainly philosophical and literary movement. The original nihilists
advocated utilitarianism and rationalism. They were
greatly influenced by the works of scientists such as
Charles Darwin, and fundamental to their philosophy
was the belief that all evil stems from ignorance. Only
scientific truth could provide man with the means to
overcome his ignorance. While it is true that the nihilists denied the utility of existing institutions such
as government, church, and family, they did not ad-
vocate revolution to overthrow the existing order. Denial rather than destruction was their modus operandi.

By 1862, however, this original ideology had
evolved into something completely different. University students and other dissenters had begun demon-
strating, advocating wholesale nationalization and
bloody, ruthless revolution. Before long the nihilists
were outnumbered by the anarchists. These extremists
sought the complete overthrow of the state, law, and
order. The violence perpetrated by them continued to
escalate, culminating in the assassination of Tsar Alexander II in 1881.

odd couple: two people who are completely mismatched

Imagine the frustration a compulsively neat and clean individual would feel if he or she were forced to live with a total slob. That is exactly what Neil Simon did in his Broadway play, *The Odd Couple*. The hit show, which made its debut in 1965, revolved around the relationship of two male friends. Oscar Madison is a divorced sportswriter who lives in filth and chaos. Felix Unger is a photographer whose wife throws him out because she can no longer stand his constant cleaning and organizing of their home. Feeling sorry for Felix, Oscar invites him to move in. The resulting conflicts keep the audience laughing throughout.

The play was made into a film in 1968, with Jack Lemmon taking the role of the compulsive Felix and Walter Matthau playing the slovenly Oscar. But the two actors whom most of us identify with Felix and

Oscar are Tony Randall and Jack Klugman, who played them with resounding success on television from 1970 to 1975.

Simon's memorable duo have left their mark on our language, together and separately. We now commonly refer to two people who are completely mismatched as *the odd couple* or as *Felix and Oscar*. We also call a compulsively neat person a *Felix Unger*, and an out-and-out slob is dubbed an *Oscar Madison*.

odyssey: a long journey; a spiritual quest

An *odyssey* is a long journey, either real or symbolic. In modern English, we often refer to a person's quest for spiritual enlightenment or inner peace as an odyssey. The word *odyssey* comes from ancient Greek and means *Odysseus's tale*. And quite a tale it was! As told by Homer in his epic poem, *The Odyssey*, it spans ten years of wandering and adventures.

Odysseus was a mythical king of Ithaca, who fought with the Greeks in the Trojan War. After the sacking of Troy, he sailed homeward but was blown off course and encountered the Lotus-Eaters, the Cyclops Polyphemus, the cannibal Laestrygonians, and the wicked Circe. He then journeyed to the Underworld and was told that he would find his way home only if he was able to control himself and his men. More adventures followed: their escape from the Sirens' songs, the Wandering Rocks, the monsters

Scylla and Charybdis. When his men refused to obey
him and insisted on slaughtering the Cattle of the Sun,
they were killed for their sacrilege. Odysseus, alone,
fells into the clutches of the enchantress Calypso.

It was not until the gods finally decided that the
hero had suffered enough that they freed him from
Calypso's spell, and he found his way home. His long
journey over, he asserted his authority in Ithaca and
was reunited with his wife, the patient Penelope, and
his by-then-adult son, Telemachus.

ogre: a mean person, one who is feared

The word *ogre* first appeared in French in 1697, in
Charles Perrault's *Contes de ma mère l'oye*. Translated into English as *Mother Goose Tales*, the stories
were an immense success and before long ogres—
giants who fed on human flesh—were feared by English-speaking children as well as by French ones.

Perrault is generally acknowledged as the creator
of the word *ogre,* although he never revealed its origin. Most etymologists believe Perrault borrowed a
word from Italian dialect—*ogro*—and gave it a
French form. *Ogro,* in turn, came from the standard
Italian word *orco,* which means ''fiend'' or ''demon.'' Orcus was the name of the Roman god of the
Underworld, the precursor of the grim reaper who

walked the earth in search of subjects for his kingdom. It was also the name of his realm.

The ogres of Perrault's tales have given their name
to any person whom we perceive as cruel or who
inspires fear in others. A child would probably award
the title to his or her teacher; adults usually reserve
it for the boss. If the dreaded person is a woman, she
would more correctly be called an ogress. The adjective *ogreish* or *ogrish* is applied to a person whose
character traits remind one of Perrault's bloodthirsty
giants.

(An alternate, nonliterary etymology has been suggested for the word *ogre*, but it has never been widely
accepted. During the tenth century, the German people were terrorized by raiders they called Magyars or
Uigurs; the memory of their raids may have remained
linguistically, when Uigur was transformed to ogre
and became a word for a cruel killer.)

O. Henry ending: an ironic, unexpected end-
ing

When asked where he found his plots, William Sidney Porter, who wrote under the pen name O. Henry,
answered, "Oh, everywhere. There are stories in
everything."

Judging by his literary output, O. Henry must have
been correct in his observation. Once he began writing, he never stopped. His first twelve short stories

were written while he was serving a prison sentence for embezzlement. He submitted two of them to magazines, and they were published while he was still behind bars. After his release, O. Henry moved to Pittsburgh, where he rented a small room and continued writing and sending his manuscripts to publishers. In the spring of 1902 he was offered a job in New York City, and eight years later O. Henry was the most widely read author in the country.

From December 1903 to January 1906, O. Henry wrote one story each week for the *New York World*. He also wrote continuously for syndicated magazines. His first book of collected stories was *Cabbages and Kings*, which appeared in 1904 and contained tales about South America that he had written after escaping to Honduras to avoid prosecution. His second book, *The Four Million*, was a collection of stories about New York, the city with which O. Henry is most often associated. Other tales—many of which were based on the adventures of his fellow inmates at the Columbus, Ohio, penitentiary—continued to be published until O. Henry's death in 1910 and in three books published after he passed away. *The Complete Works of O. Henry*, published in two volumes in 1953, contains close to three hundred stories and poems.

Many of O. Henry's stories were quite short—only a page or two—but the author managed to pack a great deal into a few words. His stories deal, for the most part, with people from the lower classes: men and women who are struggling to make a living and

who are often forced by circumstances to bend their
moral code a little bit. They are often the forgotten
people: the nameless faces one sees while walking in
the poorer parts of our cities, those in whose drab,
uneventful lives only O. Henry could find something
worth writing about.

O. Henry is famous for the unusual endings he gave
to many of his stories: An *O. Henry ending* is unexpected and often ironic. Two of O. Henry's most famous stories are "The Gift of the Magi" and "The
Last Leaf." Both have typical O. Henry endings.

"The Gift of the Magi" takes place during the
Christmas season and revolves around a young couple's attempt to please one another with the gifts they
exchange. On the day before Christmas the wife,
Della, has only $1.87 with which to buy her beloved
husband, Jim, a present. But she does possess one
thing that is worth a substantial amount of money:
her hair. Reaching below her knees, it is her pride
and joy, but she decides to sacrifice it for her husband.
She receives $20 for the hair, which she immediately
spends on a platinum fob chain for Jim's treasured
pocket watch.

When Jim arrives home and sees Della's hair, he
is in a state of shock. He hands her the gift he bought
for her: a set of tortoiseshell combs, with jeweled
rims, that she had seen in a shop window and wanted
for her hair. It's all right, she tells him, "my hair
grows so fast," and she gives him the platinum chain.

But Jim no longer has a watch to attach the chain
to; he sold it to buy the combs for Della's hair, which

she sold to buy him the chain for which he no longer has a watch.

"The Last Leaf" is the tale of a young woman who catches pneumonia and is convinced she is going to die as soon as the last leaf of ivy falls from the vine on the wall opposite her window. But as the days go by, the leaf remains on the vine, and she begins to recover. It is only then that she learns the truth about the leaf: It was painted on the wall by an old artist who lived in her apartment building. As soon as the real last leaf fell, the man rushed out to the yard, despite the cold and rain, and hastily painted a replacement. He died two days later from the pneumonia he contracted while striving to save her life.

one for Ripley: any strange, unbelievable happening

When we say that a fact or an event is *one for Ripley*, we mean that it is so out of the ordinary or so unbelievable that it would make a good subject for Robert Leroy Ripley's cartoon, *Believe It or Not*.

Ripley lived from 1893 to 1949 and began his career as a cartoonist. When at the age of fourteen, he sold his first cartoon to *Life* magazine. The drawing, titled "The Village Belle Was Slowly Ringing," depicted a girl putting clothes through the wringer of an old-fashioned washing machine. At sixteen, Ripley went to work for *The San Francisco Bulletin*, and before long was hired by *The San Francisco Chron-*

icle. He then decided to try his luck in New York, where he was hired as a sports cartoonist by the *Evening Globe*

In 1921, while he was working for the *Globe*, Ripley created his first *Believe It or Not* cartoon. The idea came to him accidentally: One night he was illustrating odd facts in sports and decided to title his drawings *Believe It or Not*. Readers of the paper loved the notion, and *Believe It or Not* quickly went from a once-a-week feature to a daily cartoon. Ripley also expanded the subject matter to deal with strange happenings in all areas of life. After drawing the cartoon for several other newspapers, Ripley joined the Hearst chain in 1929 and *Believe It or Not* began to be distributed to hundreds of papers all over the world by the King Features Syndicate.

Robert Ripley began traveling all over the world in search of strange stories and facts. In one year—1932—he went on five separate trips, covering a total of more than 60,000 miles—to find material for the feature. He received more than one million letters a year, some questioning the veracity of items he had published and others providing him with leads on new stories. Ripley always maintained that all the information that appeared in his column was true and that he checked each story out himself.

Ripley's *Believe It or Not* has been made into radio and television series, Jack Palance being the most recent star to host the show on TV. There is also a *Believe It or Not* museum that is a popular tourist attraction in Niagara Falls, New York.

Orwellian: characterized by totalitarian oppression and dehumanization

Under the pen name George Orwell, Eric Arthur Blair wrote a variety of fictional and nonfictional works, all of which, he said, were directed against totalitarianism in all forms.

Orwell was born in India, where his father was a civil servant. After studying at Eton on a scholarship, he spent five years with the Imperial Police in Burma, then used what little money he had to travel around Europe. His first novel, *Burmese Days*, was written in 1934 and is an attack on British imperialism. *The Road to Wigan Pier* (1937) is a condemnation of the conditions under which the coal miners in Northern England were forced to live and work.

Orwell considered himself an independent socialist. After fighting on the Republican side in the Spanish Civil War, he developed a hatred of Communism that is reflected in the nonfictional *Homage to Catalonia* (1938) and in one of his best-known works of fiction, *Animal Farm* (1945). *Animal Farm* is, in fact, a satirical portrait of the Soviet Union: The farm animals (the Russian people) revolted against the farmer (the Tsar) only to find themselves even more oppressed by their new leaders, the pigs (the Communists).

Orwell's other popular novel, *1984*, is equally condemnatory of totalitarian government and the methods it uses to keep its citizens in line. Under constant surveillance by the Thought Police, the novel's hero is found to be less than totally committed to his government. In order to bring him back into line, he is subjected to intense brainwashing, until he reaches the point where he believes whatever he is told, including that he loves Big Brother.

The grim, freedomless societies portrayed by Orwell in his works have resulted in the formation of the adjective *Orwellian* to describe systems, governments, organizations, or societies in which there is no room for individuality. An Orwellian institution is one in which people are oppressed and dehumanized by those who, under the pretense of acting in their best interests, exercise complete power over them.

See also: **Big Brother is watching.**

Ozymandian: huge, grandiose

One of the best-known poems of Percy Bysshe Shelley is "Ozymandias of Egypt." Ozymandias is the Greek name for Ramses II, known as Ramses the Great, the pharaoh who ruled Egypt in the thirteenth century B.C.

Shelley's poem begins with a description of the ruins that are all that remain of the colossal statue of himself that Ozymandias had erected during his reign:

> . . . *Two vast and trunkless legs of stone*
> *Stand in the desert. Near them, on the sand,*
> *Half sunk, a shattered visage lies . . .*

On the face of the statue one can still see the "frown and wrinkled lip, and sneer of cold command," that are an indication of the kind of man Ozymandias was. If that is not enough to convince the viewer of his conceit and arrogance, he or she need only read the inscription that is still legible on the ruined statue's pedestal:

My name is Ozymandias, king of kings:
Look on my works, ye Mighty, and despair!

As colossal and awe-inspiring as the works of Ramses/Ozymandias were, they could not survive the ravages of time any more than their maker could attain the immortality he sought.

Nothing beside remains. Round the decay
Of that colossal wreck, boundless and bare
The lone and level sands stretch far away.

"Ozymandias of Egypt" was published in 1818, just four years before Shelley's death at the age of thirty. Its simple yet powerful message has made it one of the most frequently quoted works of nineteenth-century poetry. Its wide readership caused the name of the pharaoh who built on such a colossal scale—the magnificent temple of Abu Simbel was one of the works commissioned by Ramses II—to be converted into an adjective, *Ozymandian,* which means huge or colossal, like the massive monuments on which the pharaoh mistakenly counted to give him immortality.

pamphlet: a short, paper-bound or unbound booklet

A farmer might write to the Government Printing Office for a pamphlet on crop rotation. While sitting in the doctor's waiting room, a patient may peruse a pamphlet that tells how to prevent osteoporosis. A candidate's supporters frequently stand on street corners and pass out pamphlets just before an election. Romance is probably the last thing on any of these people's minds as they do so. But, ironically, pamphlets, which are now used mostly to disseminate information or political propaganda, take their name from the title of a twelfth-century Latin love poem.

"Pamphilus, seu de Amore" ("Pamphilus, or about Love") was a popular, widely disseminated poem that has been lost to us over the centuries. The first word of its Latin title, which means "loved by all," was translated into French as *pamphilet* and became *pamphlet* in English. We know little else about the poem, except that it was brief and either loosely bound or not bound at all. It may have been the medieval version of a paperback—with a thin parchment covering instead of the heavier boards used around full-length manuscripts.

The first documented use of the word *pamphlet* to refer to any short, loosely bound work is found in a fourteenth-century text, where it is used in contradistinction to the word *book*. After the invention of printing in the fifteenth century, *pamphlet* became the commonly used term for all such small booklets.

The form lent itself well to the mass production of polemical and propagandist treatises on current affairs, politics, religion, philosophy, etc. The first great age of pamphleteering came with the Reformation, in the early sixteenth century. Martin Luther and other Protestant leaders inveighed against the Pope and the Roman Catholic Church in their pamphlets. In France, so many pamphlets were printed and distributed by the Reformers that they were prohibited by several edicts.

From the seventeenth to the nineteenth century, pamphlets continued to be the preferred way to voice differences of opinion in most European countries and in America as well. In fact, they served the same function as modern-day newspapers, which eventually replaced them. While some religious groups and politicians still rely on pamphlets to get their message out, the word *pamphlet* now refers mostly to informational publications, brochures, instruction booklets, and the like.

pandemonium: great noise and/or chaos

The English word *demon* comes from the Greek *daimon,* which was used in ancient times to refer to a variety of supernatural beings—some friendly, some malevolent. To the early Christians, however, there was no such thing as a good demon: All these pagan spirits were sent by Satan to corrupt men and turn them away from the true God.

The Christian association of the Devil with demons led John Milton, in *Paradise Lost*, to coin the word *Pandemonium* to refer to the principal city in Hell. This gathering place of Satan and his entourage—"all the demons"—would naturally be lawless and chaotic. *Paradise Lost* was published in 1667, and by the mid-nineteenth century Milton's linguistic creation had become a synonym for a scene of great noise and confusion, so tumultuous that one might think all Hell had broken loose.

pander: to cater to low tastes; act as a procurer

The creation of the English word *pander* is an outstanding example of the power of the pen. The written word sometimes becomes more real than reality, and we find ourselves believing not what we know, but what we read.

The verb *to pander,* meaning to cater to low tastes or act as a sexual procurer, and the nouns *pander* and *panderer,* which are terms for a pimp or procurer, come from the name of Pandarus, a figure in Greek mythology. Pandarus appeared in Homer's *Iliad,* where he fought nobly on the side of Troy in the war between the Trojans and the Greeks. How, then, did his name come to be associated with such base activities?

The answer lies in the literary portraits of Pandarus that were painted by later authors, beginning with Boccaccio. In 1344, he wrote a romance, *Filostrato,* in which Pandarus became Pandaro, a comrade of Prince Troilus who procured the Greek maiden Criseida for his royal friend. Both Chaucer's *Troilus and Criseyda* and Shakespeare's *Troilus and Cressida* depicted Pandarus in the same light. Shakespeare made him Cressida's uncle, an uncouth fellow who urges her to accept Troilus's indecent proposal.

Due to the popularity of these later works, Homer's portrait was forgotten, and the Trojan hero was immortalized in our language, not for his gallant deeds on the battlefield, but for his ignoble activities outside the bedroom door.

Panglossian/panglossian: characterized by incurable optimism

Baron Gottfried Wilhelm von Leibnitz lived from 1646 to 1716 and formulated the philosophical doctrine of optimism. Optimism held that our world was the only world and must, therefore, be the best of all possible worlds. God in his infinite knowledge and goodness knew exactly what was best and would not create anything less. Leibnitz explained the existence of evil in the world by saying that it too was created by God and served a purpose: to accentuate goodness.

In 1759, François Marie Arouet, who wrote under the pen name Voltaire, expressed his opinion of optimism in his renowned satire, *Candide, ou L'Optimisme (Candide, or Optimism)*. The title character is a young man who has been adopted and raised by the Baron Thunder-ten-tronckh. When he is caught making love to the baron's daughter, Cunégonde, he is expelled from the castle and must make his way in the world.

The only schooling Candide has had came from his tutor, Dr. Pangloss, who was a brilliant exponent of optimism:

He could prove wonderfully that there is no effect without cause and that, in this best of all possible worlds, His Lordship the Baron's castle was the most beautiful of castles and Madam the best of all possible baronesses. . . . Those who have argued that all

*is well have been talking nonsense. They should have
said that all is for the best.*

Until his expulsion, Candide never had any reason
to doubt that all is for the best in this best of all
possible worlds. But now, alone in the world, he soon
finds himself questioning the veracity of Pangloss's
beliefs.

Candide is forced to join the Bulgarian army,
where he is treated brutally. He decides to desert and,
as he runs away, he passes through a village that has
been burned by the Bulgars in accordance with international law. What he sees is horrifying:

> *. . . old men riddled with shot looked on as their
> wives lay dying, their throats slit, and clutching their
> children to blood-spattered breasts . . . young girls
> lay disembowelled, having satisfied the natural urges
> of a hero or two, breathing their last; others, half
> burnt to death, cried out for someone to finish them
> off. Brains lay scattered on the ground beside severed
> arms and legs.*

Candide succeeds in escaping to Holland, where he
is reunited with Pangloss, who tells him that the baron
and his entire family, including Cunégonde, have
been killed by the Bulgars. Pangloss is now suffering
from syphilis. When Candide suggests that the disease
must have been created by the Devil, Pangloss reit-
erates the party line of optimism: ''It [syphilis] was

an indispensable part of the best of all worlds, a necessary ingredient.''

As Candide and Pangloss travel through the world, they are shipwrecked, get caught in Lisbon's great earthquake, and are arrested for heresy. Candide is flogged, then released, but Pangloss is hanged. In the midst of his grief over his tutor's death, Candide is reunited with Cunégonde, who did not die after all. But they are soon separated again, and both must endure many more misfortunes before they are reunited in Constantinople. By that time, Cunégonde has been reduced to washing dishes for the Prince of Transylvania and has become ugly and shrewish. Pangloss is found alive—the hangman was inexperienced—chained on a galley for having made advances toward a Turkish woman. Candide buys Pangloss's freedom, marries Cunégonde, and they and their friends retire to a farm, preferring to cultivate their garden rather than venture forth again into the best of all possible worlds.

Before the book ends, Voltaire directs one more barb toward Leibnitz, in the following interchange between Candide and Pangloss:

> *"Now then, my dear Pangloss!" Candide said to him. "When you were being hanged, and dissected, and beaten, and made to row in a galley, did you continue to think that things were turning out for the best?"*
>
> *"I still feel now as I did at the outset," replied Pangloss. "I am a philosopher after all. It wouldn't*

do for me to go back on what I said before, what
with Leibniz not being able to be wrong. . . ."

The name *Pangloss* is now used as a synonym for
an incurable optimist, and such a person is said to
have the Pangloss syndrome or to be *Panglossian.*

The name of Voltaire's young hero, Candide, has
also become a part of our language. A Candide is a
naive, ingenuous person who has no knowledge of
the world, like the boy who was thrown out of the
baron's castle and became easy prey for anyone who
wanted to take advantage of him.

paparazzi: photographers or reporters who
relentlessly follow celebrities

In the 1960 film, *La Dolce Vita*, there was a photographer named Signor Paparazzo. The character, and
his name, were creations of the famous Italian film-
wright and director Federico Fellini.

In a letter to one of the best-known American paparazzi, Ron Galella, Fellini explained the origin of the
name. He told Galella that when he was growing up in
Rimini, one of his classmates was a boy "who was always squirming, who was always talking so fast that
his words came out stuck together in an endless buzzing." A teacher gave the boy the nickname Paparazzo,
which is an Italian dialect word for a mosquito-like in-
sect that is always buzzing around in the air.

When Fellini was writing the script for *La Dolce Vita*, he remembered his classmate's nickname and gave it to his fictitious photographer. It was a fitting appellation for a character who constantly flitted around the rich and famous. Before long the real-life photographers and reporters who follow celebrities everywhere they go began to be known as *paparazzi*, the plural of paparazzo.

Like a swarm of buzzing insects, paparazzi cannot be brushed off; they follow their subject relentlessly, overwhelming him or her by their numbers and their constant, noisy movement. They descend all at once, hoping that their confused and disoriented victim will say or do something they can record in a candid photograph or sell as a journalistic scoop.

Patagonia: *See:* California

Peck's Bad Boy: anyone whose mischievous or tasteless behavior is a source of embarrassment or annoyance

When someone, whether a child or an adult, does things to annoy or embarrass others, we chidingly call that person *Peck's Bad Boy*. The allusion is to a fictional youngster who appeared in the 1883 novel, *Peck's Bad Boy and His Pa*, and in a series of humorous sketches by George Wilbur Peck.

The bad boy in these works was named Hennery, and he devoted a large part of his time to thinking up new tricks to play on his father. Mr. Peck's faculties were often impaired due to his having overimbibed, making him an easy target for many of Hennery's pranks. Hennery would do such things as line the band of his father's hat with limburger cheese just before Pa went out.

Today, a great many adult Peck's Bad Boys (and girls) are found among actors and rock stars, many of whom engage in outré behavior as a way of attracting publicity. Just like Hennery, who didn't care if he was punished as long as he was noticed, these show-offs don't mind if the publicity is unfavorable, as long as it focuses on them.

Pecksniff: a moralizing hypocrite

The works of Charles Dickens are filled with tableaux of life in nineteenth-century England: The lives of both the rich and the poor are described in minute, accurate detail, as are the streets in which they walked and rode and the buildings in which they lived, worked, and died.

But Dickens's works are far more than a realistic portrait of society at a certain time and in a certain place. The dreamer, the miser, the swindler, the hypocrite—all the character types that can be found in any cross-section of humanity, anywhere, anytime—come to life on the pages of his novels. His genius lay in his ability to create characters that are at once universal archetypes and unique, memorable individuals.

One of his most original creations is the character of Seth Pecksniff, who plays a central role in *The Life and Adventures of Martin Chuzzlewit* (1843). Pecksniff maintains a careful facade of piety and morality:

> *Perhaps there never was a more moral man than Mr. Pecksniff: especially in his conversation and correspondence. . . . He was a most exemplary man: fuller of virtuous precept than a copy-book. Some people likened him to a direction-post, which is always telling the way to a place, and never goes there. . . .*

He is, in fact the archetypal hypocrite, practicing just the opposite of what he preaches. Jealous of young Martin Chuzzlewit's influence with his grandfather, old Martin, and of Mary Graham's feelings for the young man, he summarily dismisses Martin from his architectural apprenticeship. Later, he attempts to blackmail Mary into marrying him by threatening to bring further ruin to Martin if she refuses. When Pecksniff's long-time employee, Tom Pinch, learns the truth about his boss, Pecksniff fires him, accusing him of making improper advances toward Mary. He justifies this treatment of Tom by telling old Martin Chuzzlewit, Mary's adopted father, that he has ''a duty to discharge, which I owe to society.'' Fortunately, Pecksniff receives his comeuppance when his schemes are revealed and Mary marries young Martin, who has been restored to his grandfather's favor.

Pecksniff was such a successful personification that his name has become a trope for a moralizing hypocrite. An adjective was also coined from the character's name: *pecksniffian* is the term applied to someone who is selfish and corrupt while hiding behind a facade of goodness. Less common, but still to be found in the dictionary, are the nouns *pecksniffery* and *pecksniffianism*, meaning the quality of being pecksniffian. (In all of these words, except the proper noun *Pecksniff*, the initial letter may be written in either upper or lowercase: i.e., pecksniffian/Pecksniffian, etc.)

Peter Pan/Peter Pan complex: a person who acts like a child; the pathological condition of never wanting to grow up

Sir James Matthew Barrie introduced the character of Peter Pan in his 1902 novel *The Little White Bird*, several chapters of which were republished in 1906 as the illustrated children's book *Peter Pan in Kensington Gardens*. In 1904 Barrie made Peter the central figure in a stage play entitled *Peter Pan, or The Boy Who Would Not Grow Up*. With the addition of a substantial amount of new material, Barrie turned his play into a novel, *Peter Pan and Wendy*, in 1911. He also wrote a film scenario in the 1920s and published a new version of the play in 1928.

The most popular of all these Peter Pan stories was far and away the 1904 play. It was in this stage version that Barrie introduced the Darling children—Wendy, John, and Michael—and their canine nursemaid, Nana. The children flew with Peter to his magical island of Never Land and met Tinkerbell and other fairies, mermaids, the lost boys, and a band of pirates led by the evil Captain Hook. After the children's return from the Never Land, Mrs. Darling wanted to adopt Peter, but he rejected her offer, saying "I don't want to go to school and learn solemn things. No one is going to catch me, lady, and make me a man. I want always to be a little boy and to have fun."

It was with these words in mind that psychologists coined the term *Peter Pan complex* to describe an individual's refusal to act in a responsible, adult fashion. Such people, who are overwhelmingly male, are referred to as *Peter Pan*s and, like their namesake, want only to stay young and have fun forever.

Barrie, it seems, was himself a victim of the Peter Pan complex. His childhood was perfect until the age of six, when his brother died. His mother was permanently changed by the tragedy, never fully regaining her former lightheartedness and joyful outlook on life. As a result, Barrie spent a lifetime trying to recapture the happy years before age six. His writings contain many references to his disenchantment with adulthood and his longing for the halcyon days of childhood. The theme recurs in his private journals, in the autobiographical novel *Sentimental Tommy*, and in the plays *Peter Pan, The Admirable Crichton, The Twelve-Pound Look, The Will*, and *Dear Brutus*.

It would be impossible to list the numerous stage, film, and television adaptations of *Peter Pan* that have been produced since its 1904 debut. Between 1904 and 1987 the play was performed in England at Christmas every year but 1940. The most popular American versions were the 1953 animated film by Walt Disney and the 1955 television production that starred Mary Martin as Peter.

(the) Peter Principle: the idea that people rise to the level of their incompetence and remain there

In his introduction to *The Peter Principle: Why Things Always Go Wrong*, Raymond Hull says that until he met Dr. Laurence Peter he was terribly distressed by the incompetence of those around him. Dr. Peter, it seems, had spent years amassing a vast collection of "incompetenciana," which he had studied at great length and which had led him to some startling conclusions. The incompetence that had so troubled Hull was finally explained to him by The Peter Principle, and he proceeded to collaborate with Dr. Peter to turn the latter's voluminous notes into a book.

Hull calls the Peter Principle "the most penetrating social and psychological discovery of the century" and warns the reader that he or she should not make the decision to read the book lightly:

> *If you read, you can never regain your present state of blissful ignorance; you will never again unthinkingly venerate your superiors or dominate your subordinates. Never! The Peter Principle, once heard, cannot be forgotten.*

When one reads on, one discovers that Laurence Peter learned about the existence of widespread incompetence after he graduated from college and became a teacher. After encountering incompetence on every level of the school system, he naively thought he could transfer to another system and find competent people. When all he found were more incompetents, he "began to suspect that the local school system did not have a monopoly on incompetence."

Eventually he came to the conclusion that "occupational incompetence is everywhere." He cites a number of cases, from government, private enterprise, and the military, which he says gave him a clue about the reason for incompetence: In each case, the employee had been promoted from a position of competence to one of incompetence. This led to the formulation of the Peter Principle: "In a Hierarchy Every Employee Tends to Rise to His Level of Incompetence."

Peter and Hull go on to elaborate on this notion:

*Everyone in business, industry, trade-unionism, pol-
itics, government, the armed forces, religion and education is so involved. All of them are controlled by
the Peter Principle. Many of them, to be sure, may
win a promotion or two, moving from one level of
competence to a higher level of competence. But
competence in that new position qualifies them for
still another promotion. For each individual, for you,
for me, the final promotion is from a level of competence to a level of incompetence.*

Given enough time, therefore, each employee will
rise to and remain at his or her level of incompetence.
This realization led to the formulation of Peter's Cor-
ollary, which states that "in time, every post tends to
be occupied by an employee who is incompetent to
carry out his duties." Fortunately, say the authors,
you rarely find a system in which everyone has already reached their level of incompetence. So something does get done: "Work is accomplished by those
employees who have not yet reached their level of
incompetence."

The Peter Principle, which was published in 1969,
immediately became a bestseller. Its mock-serious
tone and its hilarious, yet frightening examples of incompetence make it delightful reading. At the same
time, it exposes a societal problem that cannot be denied nor, it seems, remedied. More than twenty-eight
years after its publication, Peter's and Hull's
observations and conclusions are still valid. This is
proven by the fact that we still find myriad examples
of incompetence that cause us to say, with dismay,

that "the Peter Principle is at work" or "it's a perfect case of the Peter Principle."

Peyton Place: any place that is a hotbed of covert sexual activity

If Grace Metalious had had her way, her 1956 best-seller would have been called *The Tree and the Blossom*, and the English language would have contained one less literary allusion. As it turned out, Metalious was overruled, and the title *Peyton Place* became a household word.

Metalious wanted the title to symbolize the parents and children in the book, with the blossom falling not far from the tree. She used the same image in a scene between her young heroine, Allison MacKenzie, and Dr. Matthew Swain, who quotes the following line of poetry: "I saw the starry tree Eternity, put forth the blossom Time." Kitty Messner, owner of Julian Messner, Inc., the publisher that had purchased Metalious's novel, thought the symbolism was quite appropriate. When Aaron Sussman, head of the advertising agency handling the novel, told her the title was too poetic and the book would never sell, she challenged him to come up with something better.

In 1940 Henry Bellamann had written a novel about the scandalous goings-on in a small town. *King's Row* had been a huge success and Sussman

saw many parallels between it and Metalious's novel.
(In fact, Grace Metalious had read *King's Row*, and
its influence on her work is apparent. Corruption and
illicit sexual activity are pervasive in both locales; the
townspeople know each other's deep, dark secrets,
but never reveal them to outsiders.) One of Bellamann's characters was a corrupt businessman named
Peyton; Sussman suggested that a book entitled *Peyton Place* might capitalize on, and repeat, the success
of *King's Row*.

Sussman's strategy worked, and one week before
it was published *Peyton Place* was already number
four on the best-seller list. In addition, 20th Century
Fox had already made a bid for the film option. The
novel finally appeared on September 24, 1956, and
within one month 104,000 copies had been sold. The
fact that it had been banned in many U.S. cities and
in Canada only served to fuel sales in areas where it
was available. It remained on the best-seller list for
twenty-six weeks.

The book's initial success was repeated in 1957,
when it became a film starring Lana Turner and Diane
Varsi as Constance and Allison MacKenzie. The
novel *Return to Peyton Place* appeared in November
1959, but, although it bore Metalious's name, most of
it had been written by Warren Miller from a short
screen treatment Metalious had produced for Hollywood. (The movie version of *Return to Peyton Place*
finally appeared in 1961, starring Eleanor Parker and
Carol Lynley.)

Peyton Place achieved its greatest success on tele-

vision. Dorothy Malone and Mia Farrow played the
MacKenzies on an incredibly popular series that ran
for half an hour—first twice weekly, then three nights
a week—from September 1964 to June 1969. That
series was followed by a daytime serial, *Return to
Peyton Place* (1972–1974), and two television movies, *Murder in Peyton Place* (1977) and *Peyton Place:
The New Generation* (1985). Nine paperback books,
based on the television shows, also appeared, but
Grace Metalious had no hand in writing any of these.

Metalious only published two other novels: *The
Tight White Collar* in 1960 and *No Adam in Eden* in
1963. Although they received decent reviews, neither
made any great impact on the publishing world and
both are all but forgotten today. Not so *Peyton Place*:
The name of Metalious's fictitious New England town
remains a common synonym for a hotbed of covert
sexual activity, whether it be a community, a country
club, a school, or an office.

Pickwickian/pickwickian: resembling Samuel Pickwick in manner and/or appearance; intended or taken in a sense other than the literal
one

Charles Dickens's first full-length novel was *The
Posthumous Papers of the Pickwick Club*, better
known to the public as *The Pickwick Papers*. The
papers in question are the chronicles of the adventures

of Samuel Pickwick and three of his fellow members of The Pickwick Club: Tracy Tupman, Augustus Snodgrass, and Nathaniel Winkle. As the "Corresponding Society of the Pickwick Club," the three friends are entrusted with the task of traveling throughout England, forwarding ". . . authenticated accounts of their journeys and investigations, of their observations of character and manners, and of the whole of their adventures . . . to the Pickwick Club, stationed in London."

Samuel Pickwick, founder of the club, is a genial, rotund fellow who has devoted his life to the advancement of learning: ". . . the man who had traced to their source the mighty ponds of Hampstead, and agitated the scientific world with his Theory of Tittlebats . . ." Middle-aged, bald, wearing circular spectacles, a waistcoat, and gaiters, Pickwick is the quintessential English gentleman, much respected and admired by his fellow club members.

The hilarious adventures that Dickens set down in 1836 made the name of Pickwick a household word in England. To this day, we use the adjective *Pickwickian* to describe a person who, like Samuel Pickwick, is honest, generous, gentlemanly—and somewhat naive. We also refer to someone who has the same physique as Mr. Pickwick—round, with a substantial "corporation" up front—as Pickwickian.

Obesity, especially in men, often leads to obstructive sleep apnea, a condition in which the upper airway narrows so much that air cannot pass through it, and the sleeper is unable to breathe. He or she usually wakes up gasping, but a severe obstruction can lead to unconsciousness and death. Recognizing that someone of Mr. Pickwick's proportions is most likely to suffer from obstructive sleep apnea, physicians now give the condition an alternate name: the pickwickian syndrome.

The Pickwick Papers also gave us the expression *in a Pickwickian sense,* meaning in a sense other than the literal or commonly accepted one. The passage in which the expression originated is found at the very beginning of the novel, when a certain Mr. Blotton of Aldgate calls Mr. Pickwick a humbug. (In its ordinary sense, a humbug is someone who is pretending to be something he is not: in other words, a deceiver.) This accusation naturally causes an uproar among the club's members, until Pickwick asks Blotton if he used the expression in a common sense. Blotton responds that he used the word "in its Pickwickian sense . . . personally, he entertained the highest regard and esteem for the honourable gentleman; he had merely considered him a humbug in a Pickwickian point of view."

Pickwick is "much gratified by the fair, candid, and full explanation of his honourable friend." As a Pickwickian, he understands completely that an insult isn't always an insult. In fact, coming from a friend or family member, an insult may be used as a term of endearment. Often, when a mother calls her child a little monster, or one friend calls another a creep, the words are being used in a purely Pickwickian sense.

pilgrim's progress: a moral journey, an attempt to attain salvation

John Bunyan wrote *The Pilgrim's Progress from This World to That Which Is to Come* in 1675, while he was in prison for his religious beliefs. Bunyan became interested in religion after reading some devotional works in the late 1640s. He went through an intense spiritual struggle, finally joining the Baptist church. As a lay preacher, he violated the laws against nonconformist preaching and was imprisoned from 1660 to 1672. During that time he studied the Bible and wrote several of his works, including his autobiography.

The Pilgrim's Progress is an allegorical tale of man's search for salvation. Christian, the hero of the tale, sets off to find the Celestial City (i.e., heaven). On his journey he passes through several imaginary realms, which are symbolic of the obstacles that stand in the way of man's salvation, and he meets many allegorical characters who personify both the good and bad traits of human beings.

After many terrifying experiences, Christian reaches the country of Beulah, in which the Celestial City is located. Bunyan describes Beulah, "whose air was very sweet and pleasant . . . here they heard continually the singing of birds, and saw every day the flowers appear in the earth, and heard the voice of the turtle in the land. In this country the sun shineth night and day. . . ."

As Christian and the other pilgrims approach the

Celestial City, they see that, "It was builded of pearls
and precious stones, also the streeet thereof was paved
with gold. . . ." They then cross the river that is the
city's boundary, led by two ministering spirits. A
heavenly host comes to meet them and they are told:

> *You are going now . . . to the paradise of God,*
> *wherein you shall see the tree of life, and eat of the*
> *never-fading fruits thereof: and when you come there*
> *you shall have white robes given you, and your walk*
> *and talk shall be every day with the King, even all*
> *the days of eternity. There you shall not see again*
> *such things as you saw when you were in the lower*
> *regions upon the earth: to wit, sorrow, sickness, af-*
> *fliction, and death. . . .*

It is only the righteous who are able to complete
the journey to the Celestial City, according to Bunyan. The term *pilgrim's progress,* therefore, has become another way of referring to a person's attempt
to find salvation. Even if one's goal is not to attain
heaven in the traditional sense, one can embark on a
pilgrim's progress in an effort to attain a higher level
of morality or spirituality.

See also: **slough of despond, Vanity Fair.**

podsnappery/Podsnappery: a pompous, self-
satisfied attitude

Chapter eleven of Charles Dickens's *Our Mutual
Friend* is entitled "Podsnappery." There was no such

word before Dickens coined it from the name of one
of the characters in the novel, but *podsnappery* is still
in use today by those familiar with Dickens's works.

Dickens's introduction of Mr. Podsnap sums up
this upper-middle-class man's attitude toward the
world around him:

> *Mr. Podsnap was well to do, and stood very high in*
> *Mr. Podsnap's opinion. Beginning with a good in-*
> *heritance, he had married a good inheritance . . . and*
> *was quite satisfied. He never could make out why*
> *everybody was not quite satisfied, and he felt con-*
> *scious that he set a brilliant social example in being*
> *particularly well satisfied with most things, and,*
> *above all other things, with himself.*

The rest of the chapter is a brilliant satirical portrait
of Mr. and Mrs. Podsnap and their daughter, their
lifestyle, and their values. Podsnap lives in a well-
defined, well-ordered universe and admits nothing
into his life that might be disturbing. Any unpleas-
antness is swept away with a flourish of his arm and
the words, "I don't want to know about it," or "I
don't admit it." When a guest at his daughter's birthday party mentions that half a dozen people have died
of starvation in the streets of London recently, Podsnap is appalled. In Podsnap's world such talk is im-
polite and not in good taste, particularly after dinner.
He maintains that if it is true—and he doesn't admit
that it is—it must have been their own fault. He further maintains that "Providence has declared that you

shall have the poor always with you.'' (As Dickens points out, ''. . . he always knew exactly what Providence meant. . . . And it was very remarkable that what Providence meant, was invariably what Mr. Podsnap meant.'')

Our Mutual Friend was published in 1864, just six years before Dickens's death. It is not a cheerful book, being filled with materialism, deceit, and death. It is, however, a masterpiece of social satire and, to many critics, reflects the aging Dickens's growing pessimism vis à vis the possibility of achieving equality for all classes of society.

Pollyanna: a foolish optimist

Have you ever met a person who, no matter how bad things got, always managed to remain optimistic? If so, you probably referred to this ever-cheerful individual as a *Pollyanna*: someone who refuses to see things the way they really are and holds on to his or her foolish optimism even in the worst of times.

The original ''glad girl'' is eleven-year-old Pollyanna Whittier, an orphan who is sent to live with her aunt, a stern, embittered old maid. As soon as Pollyanna arrives, she begins finding things to be glad about in situations that would plunge anyone else into deep despair. When she's housed in a Spartan room in the attic of her aunt's mansion, she's glad there are no pictures on the walls or curtains on the windows or rugs on the floor. Looking out the window, she declares:

> *Look—'way off there, with those trees and the houses*
> *and that lovely church spire, and the river shining*
> *just like silver. Why, Nancy, there doesn't anybody*
> *need any pictures with that to look at. Oh, I'm so*
> *glad now she let me have this room!*

Pollyanna explains to her aunt's maid, Nancy, that she has been playing "the glad game" since she was a little girl. Her father was a missionary, and nearly all the family's belongings came from donations sent to them in missionary barrels. Once, Pollyanna had been hoping for a doll, and her father had written asking if one could be donated. But when the barrel arrived, there was no doll: only a pair of child-sized crutches. Pollyanna was disappointed, but her father told her she should look on the bright side and "just find something to be glad about." In this case, he suggested she just be glad that she didn't need the crutches.

Pollyanna hasn't been living with her aunt very long before she has everyone in town playing the glad game. Her optimism is infectious, touching even her aunt and allowing her to open her heart to Pollyanna and to the man she loved but quarreled with long before.

Pollyanna was the creation of Eleanor H. Porter. Ms. Porter's novel, *Pollyanna*, appeared in 1913 and was followed, in 1915, by *Pollyanna Grows Up*. The first film version of *Pollyanna* was made in 1920 and starred Mary Pickford. Disney Studios remade the film in 1960, with Hayley Mills playing the part of the glad girl.

Pooh-Bah: a very important person, a big cheese

The comic operas of William Schwenck Gilbert (text) and Arthur Seymour Sullivan (music) began to be produced at London's Savoy Theatre in 1881 by Richard D'Oyly Carte. *The Mikado or the Town of Titipu*, which was written in 1885, was one of their most popular collaborations. The opera is set in Japan, and Mikado is the title foreigners once used to address the Emperor of Japan.

One of the characters in *The Mikado* is a man named Pooh-Bah. Among the titles he holds are: First Lord of the Treasury, Lord Chief Justice, Commander-in-Chief, Lord High Admiral, Master of the Buckhounds, Groom of the Back Stairs, Archbishop of Titipu, and Lord Mayor. To simplify matters, he is generally referred to as ''The Lord High Everything Else.''

The many theatergoers who attended performances of *The Mikado* soon began to apply the name *Pooh-Bah* to people of great importance, those we would today call big cheeses or VIPs.

portmanteau word: a word made by combining parts of other words

In *Through the Looking-Glass*, Lewis Carroll's young heroine finds a whole new world on the other side of a mirror. In that world, everything is backward. When she picks up a book, she cannot read it until she holds it up to the mirror. Then, although she can make out the words, she has no idea what they mean.

Later in the story, when she meets Humpty Dumpty, she asks him to explain the poem "Jabberwocky," which was in the book. Alice has never heard of many of the words, and Humpty must translate them as though they were in another language. When he explains the word *slithy,* he says it means lithe and slimy. "You see," he continues, "it's like a portmanteau—there are two meanings packed up into one word." Another portmanteau word that appears in the poem is *mimsy:* a combination of flimsy and miserable.

In French, *porter* means to carry, and *manteau* is the word for a coat or a cloak. The British call a large suitcase that opens into two hinged compartments a *portmanteau.* The fact that both sides can be packed separately and then joined together to make one suitcase formed the basis of Carroll's colorful metaphor.

While neither *slithy* nor *mimsy* have become a part of the English language, the word *chortle,* which Carroll also created, did. Many other combination words are now used in English—brunch, smog, motel, transceiver, workaholic, to name a few—and Lewis Carroll's linguistic invention is now the accepted term for them.

See also: **chortle, jabberwocky.**

(a) pound of flesh: an excessively high price exacted for a favor

At the beginning of *The Merchant of Venice*, Bassanio tells his friend, Antonio, that he is in love with Portia, a rich heiress whom he is trying to impress. When he asks Antonio to lend him some money so that he can compete with her other suitors, Antonio agrees, although his own funds are invested in a shipping venture, and he himself will have to borrow the money.

Antonio and Bassanio go together to see Shylock, a Jewish moneylender. Although Antonio has no use for Jews and has often insulted Shylock in the past, and Shylock despises Christians, the two men come to an agreement. Shylock will lend the money, interest free, but will claim one pound of Antonio's flesh if the latter defaults. Confident that his ships will bring back a profit, Antonio accepts Shylock's gruesome terms.

When one of Antonio's ships is lost, and he cannot pay back the loan, Shylock is delighted at the prospect of collecting his fee. Motivated by his hatred of Christians, which has intensified since his daughter eloped with one, he rejects all pleas for mercy.

The case will be heard by the Duke of Venice, who has called on a Paduan scholar for his opinion. Disguised as a lawyer sent by the scholar, Bassanio's beloved, Portia, interrogates Antonio and Shylock. Shylock keeps insisting that the wording of the contract is quite specific: He is entitled to one pound of Antonio's flesh. The clever Portia then turns his own words against him, when she rules that he be allowed to take one pound of flesh, but he must do it without spilling a drop of Antonio's blood—for the contract does not entitle him to anything but flesh.

The image of someone carving a pound of flesh from another's body in payment for a loan is so grotesque, so disturbing, that it left an indelible impression on Elizabethan theatergoers. Before long the phrase *a pound of flesh* became a popular way of referring to an exorbitant price demanded by someone in return for a favor, and it remains one of the most vivid literary allusions in the English language.

See also: **shylock.**

primrose path: a path of ease or pleasure; the way to disaster

In Act I, Scene 3 of *Hamlet*, Laertes cautions his sister, Ophelia, against being romantically involved with Prince Hamlet. Knowing that Laertes is about to leave for Paris, a city well known for its pleasures, she re-

sponds by suggesting that he practice what he
preaches:

> *Do not, as some ungracious pastors do,*
> *Show me the steep and thorny way to heaven,*
> *Whiles, like a puff'd and reckless libertine,*
> *Himself the primrose path of dalliance treads. . . .*

Long before William Shakespeare wrote his Elizabethan dramas, the primrose had been associated
with youth and sensual pleasure. Shakespeare's audience was bound to understand the reference and realize that Ophelia is suggesting that her brother is far
more likely to be corrupted by the lifestyle he is about
to adopt than she is by Hamlet.

Shakespeare used a variation of the phrase in *Macbeth*, Act II, Scene 3—when the porter speaks jest-
ingly of all the people who ''go the primrose way to
the everlasting bonfire.'' In this case, the primrose
way leads not just to an idle, corrupt life but to eternal
damnation.

Today, when we say someone is going down the
primrose path, we are predicting disaster for him or
her. They might be enjoying themselves for the moment, but one day they'll have to pay the price for
the life of indulgence they have led.

quixotic: idealistic and impractical

In the popular Broadway musical *Man of La Mancha*, the title character sang a song called "The Impossible Dream." Its lyrics summed up the personal credo of Don Quixote, an elderly Spanish gentleman who took it upon himself to "right the unrightable wrong" and "fight the unbeatable foe."

Don Quixote of La Mancha, Ingenious Gentleman was written by Miguel de Cervantes Saavedra at the beginning of the seventeenth century. It is generally agreed that Cervantes intended his novel to be a satire on the romances of chivalry that were immensely popular throughout Europe at the time. He tells us that as a result of reading too many of these romances, Don Quixote's "brain dried up and he lost his wits." The old man's delusions of grandeur are certainly proof of that: He believes his old nag, Rocinante, is a fine steed; he mistakes windmills for giants and sheep for soldiers; he is convinced of the nobility of his "lady," whom he calls Dulcinea, but who is really a local farmer's daughter named Aldonza.

But Cervantes's genius made *Don Quixote* much more than a satire. As mad as its hero is, we cannot help but admire him. He is pure of heart, an innocent surrounded by worldliness and corruption. Forging onward, Don Quixote maintains his ideals in the face of defeat after defeat. He continues to "dream the impossible dream" long after anyone in his right mind would have given up and gone home.

In the end, Don Quixote does go home, declaring that he is cured of his folly. He will no longer act the part of the knight errant, facing his enemies on the jousting field and rescuing damsels in distress. But once he abandons his dreams, Don Quixote sinks into a state of melancholy. Formerly the voice of reason, Sancho Panza now urges his master to take up arms again and seek new adventures: ". . . in your books of chivalries . . . it's a common thing for one knight to overthrow another, and the one that's conquered to-day may be the conqueror to-morrow."

With nothing to live for, Don Quixote lets himself die, and we can't help but regret, as he once did, that he wasn't born in a different age: one in which his noble ideals would have been admired instead of scoffed at.

Today, we refer to a person who is overly idealistic as *quixotic*. Like the gentleman of La Mancha, such an individual takes on all kinds of impossible causes or projects, refusing to take into account the practical aspects that are bound to get in the way of their accomplishment.

The name of Cervantes's hero has also been immortalized in an English verb, *to quixotize*, which means to make or to be quixotic. *Quixotism* is quixotic action or thought. And, finally, a *quixote* or *Quixote* is a person given to lofty, utterly impractical schemes.

See also: **(to) tilt at windmills.**

Rabelaisian: lusty, ribald

In the author's prologue to his monumental work, *Gargantua and Pantagruel*, François Rabelais wrote the following:

> *Most illustrious Drinkers and you, most precious Syphilitics, for it is to you, not to others, that my writings are dedicated.*

He went on to say that his intention was to bring laughter to his readers, but he also hinted at a deeper meaning to his work, suggesting that the reader "break the bone and suck the substantific marrow." And, in fact, a large part of *Gargantua and Pantagruel* is a satire on the religious, political, legal, and social life of France in the early sixteenth century. Rabelais, who lived at the close of the Middle Ages, was one of the first Renaissance men, forward-

looking and concerned more with the secular life of
man than with his religious salvation.

The bone within which Rabelais couched his satirical marrow was the broad, coarse, ribald humor of
his time. By modern standards, most of *Gargantua
and Pantagruel* would be considered obscene. But, as
scholars have pointed out, it was not uncommon for
writers, orators, and even preachers of Rabelais's time
to employ vulgarities. It was also a characteristic of
popular entertainment: The stories, jokes, and songs
exchanged by the lower classes were full of double
entendres and scatological references.

Rabelais refers to the attraction between men and
women and the sex act in popular terms, saying that
Gargantua's mother, Gargamelle, was "a pretty
wench with a good mug on her." She and her husband "often played the beast-with-two-backs, rubbing
their bacons together hilariously, and doing it so often
that she became pregnant with a fine son. . . ." He
then proceeds to recommend that a man commit adultery with a woman who is already pregnant, so there
is no chance of her becoming pregnant with his child
and causing a scandal.

Rabelais's comments on drinking are equally
shocking to those of us who have been brought up
with the influence of the Puritans. He devotes an entire chapter in the first book of *Gargantua and Pantagruel* to the great benefits of drink. In "The
Remarks of the Drunkards" Gargantua's father and
his cronies share their thoughts on imbibing. One
states, "Sinner that I am, I never drink without thirst,

if not present, at least future—to head it off, you understand. I drink for the thirst to come. I drink everlastingly. With me, it's an eternity of drinking and a drinking of eternity.'' And the others continue in the same vein, praising the benefits of drunkenness.

Rabelais's humor often consists of what we call today ''bathroom jokes''. In the chapter entitled ''How Grandgousier Learned of Gargantua's Marvelous Mind through the Latter's Invention of a Rump-Wiper,'' Gargantua goes through a long, detailed list of the many objects he has used to wipe his bottom in an effort to find the best one for the job. He concludes, ''that there is no rump-wiper like a good downy goose . . . you will feel in your bunghole a miraculous pleasure, from the softness of the down as well as from the moderate heat of the goose, which is readily communicated to the rump-gut and other intestines, until it reaches the region of the heart and brain.''

With such passages in mind and from the great gusto with which Gargantua, Pantagruel, and the rest of Rabelais's characters live their lives, the adjective *Rabelaisian* was created. It is used to describe a bold, lusty attitude toward life's pleasures and a way of communicating that, like Rabelais's writing, is unrestrained, uncensored, and ''tells it like it is.''

See also: **gargantuan.**

(run a) Red Queen's race: get nowhere in
spite of one's efforts

Alice, the young heroine of Lewis Carroll's *Alice's
Adventures in Wonderland*, finds herself in another
strange world when she goes *Through the Looking-
Glass*. In this sequel, published in 1872, Alice meets
a whole new cast of characters, including a group of
red and white chess pieces.

In Looking-glass country everything is reversed, so
it stands to reason that the only way Alice can meet
the Red Queen is by walking *away* from her. The Red
Queen's country is divided up into squares, just like
a chessboard, and no sooner does Alice express the
wish to be part of the game of chess than the Red
Queen tells her she can start out as a pawn and, when
she reaches the eighth square, she'll become a queen.
Taking Alice by the hand, she begins to run. She runs
so fast that Alice can barely keep up with her, and
she keeps yelling "Faster! Faster!" Alice finally gets
the breath to ask, "Are we nearly there?" and the
Red Queen's response is "Nearly there! Why, we
passed it ten minutes ago! Faster!"

When they finally stop and Alice looks around, she
tells the Red Queen that she believes it's the same
place they started from and everything is just as it
was. "Of course," replies the Queen. "What would
you have it?"

"Well, in our country," says Alice, "you'd generally get to somewhere else—if you ran very fast for
a long time as we've been doing."

"A slow sort of country!" replies the Queen. "Now, here, you see, it takes all the running you can do, to keep in the same place. If you want to get somewhere else, you must run at least twice as fast as that!"

When we say someone is *running a Red Queen's race*, therefore, we mean they are getting nowhere fast. In spite of all their efforts, they can't seem to make any progress. Like Alice and her animated chess piece, they are bound to end up exactly where they started.

Rip Van Winkle: someone who is out of step with the times; someone who sleeps a lot

Imagine what it would be like to wake up in 1996 after having gone to sleep in 1976. What would you think when you heard people talking about faxing, surfing the Internet, the Russian democracy, AIDS, or the trial of the century? You would be just as confused as Rip Van Winkle was when he woke up after sleeping for twenty years.

The story of Rip Van Winkle appeared in Washington Irving's *The Sketch Book of Geoffrey Crayon, Gent.*, which was published in 1819. Other famous stories in the book include "The Legend of Sleepy Hollow" and "The Spectre Bridegroom." In *The Sketch Book* Irving claimed to have found the tale among the papers of Diedrich Knickerbocker, a fictitious Dutch settler of New York City. In reality, the story may be based on a folktale from the Orkney Islands.

Irving's tale takes place in New York's "Kaat-skill" Mountains some time before the Revolutionary War. Rip Van Winkle is a jolly, lazy fellow, who likes nothing better than to gather with his cronies at the local inn. He and his shrewish wife have a son and a daughter. When he can no longer stand being hen-pecked, Rip generally escapes into the mountains with his dog, Wolf. On one of these occasions, he meets a man dressed in antique Dutch fashion, who asks him to help carry a keg up the mountainside. At the top, they come upon a group of men who are playing nine-pins. The keeper of the keg directs Rip to serve the players, which he does. No one offers Rip anything to drink, however, and when the others are not look-ing Rip steals several drinks. He is suddenly over-come and falls into a deep sleep.

When Rip wakes up, the people are gone and so is his dog. His gun is covered with rust. He hurries home, only to find his house abandoned. He goes to the inn, which is under new ownership, and scarcely recognizes anyone. When he asks if anyone knows Rip Van Winkle, the crowd points at a young man: his own grown-up son. He then meets his daughter, who is now married and has a child of her own. Rip has apparently slept for twenty years. When he set out for his walk in the woods, New York was a col-ony ruled by King George III of England. Rip is told that he is now a free citizen of the United States of

America. Some of the townspeople doubt Rip's story at first.

It was determined, however, to take the opinion of old Peter Vanderdonk . . . the most ancient inhabitant of the village. . . . He recollected Rip at once, and corroborated his story in the most satisfactory manner. He assured the company that it was a fact . . . that the Kaatskill mountains had always been haunted by strange beings. That it was affirmed that the great Hendrick Hudson, the first discoverer of the river and country, kept a kind of vigil there every twenty years, with his crew of the Half-moon . . . his father had seen them in their old Dutch dresses playing at nine-pins in a hollow of the mountain; and that he himself had heard, one summer afternoon, the sound of their balls, like distant peals of thunder.

Irving's *Sketch Book* established him as one of America's most popular writers, and his tales have become part of our folklore. They have been read by generations of young Americans, and are so well-known that it is common to refer to someone who is behind the times as another *Rip Van Winkle*. The name of Irving's hero is also applied, for obvious reasons, to a person who sleeps more than most.

(the) road less traveled: the unconventional way

Robert Frost (1874–1963) is considered by many to be primarily a New England poet. He spent most of his life in Massachusetts and New Hampshire, and most of his poems describe the inhabitants and the landscape of those states. But Frost's work transcends time and place. His poems are filled with symbolism, and his images have both literal and figurative meanings. A good example of this is found in "The Road Not Taken."

In this well-known poem, the narrator recounts how "Two roads diverged in a yellow wood." He stood looking at the paths, wishing he could take both, but he knew he had to make up his mind and choose one. Finally, he says, "I took the one less travelled by, And that has made all the difference."

Of course the wood symbolizes life, in which we must make choices regarding home, family, career, etc. Becoming a poet is not the conventional thing to do, and most people choose a more secure way of earning a living. So, in his own life, Frost did take the road less traveled. And it did make all the difference: He received four Pulitzer Prizes for poetry and forty-one honorary degrees in the United States; was elected to the National Institute of Arts and Letters and the American Academy of Arts and Letters; traveled to South America, Israel, Greece, and Russia as an ambassador of goodwill; was awarded the Congressional Gold Medal; and represented the arts at the inauguration of John F. Kennedy.

He also left his mark on the English language: When we use his phrase *the road less traveled*, we mean the unconventional way. It may not be the path most people choose, but it is one that can lead to great and glorious things if we have the courage to set forth on it.

See also: **miles to go before I sleep.**

robot: a mechanical being; a person who goes through life automatically, without thinking or varying his or her routine

There certainly aren't many words in the English language that come from Czech. One of the few, if not the only one, that does has become extremely common in twentieth-century parlance: the word *robot.*

In the Czech language, *robota* means drudgery or forced labor. In 1920 Czech writer Karel Capek introduced his play, *R.U.R.*, in which mechanical creatures did man's work. In 1923 the play was translated into English as *Rossum's Universal Robots* and performed on the London stage. Its success soon put the word *robot* and several of its derivatives (*robotism*—machinelike behavior in a human being; *robotization*—the act of turning a human being into a robot; *robotize*—to turn a human being into a robot; *robotic*—resembling a robot) into English dictionaries.

Karel Čapek was born in 1890 and studied philosophy before becoming a writer and journalist. His literary contribution ranged from science fiction to psychological studies, mysteries, and travel books. He was the most popular writer of the first Czech Republic (1918–1938) and a staunch supporter of its founder, President T. G. Masaryk.

At the beginning of his literary career he collaborated with his brother, Josef Čapek, on several works. One of these, *The Life of Insects* (1922), reprised the theme of *R.U.R.*: the problems man faces in a centralized, machine-dominated society. Čapek was a strong believer in democracy and humanism; the themes of antitotalitarianism and personal freedom run through much of his science fiction.

Čapek died in Prague on December 25, 1938, just two and a half months after Czechoslovakia had been forced to cede a large part of its territory, including the Sudeten, to Germany. His untimely death spared him from having to watch when, on March 15, 1939, Hitler appeared in Prague and announced that Čapek's beloved Czechoslovakia was now a "protectorate" of the Third Reich.

Romeo: a great lover

Romeo and Juliet has always been one of Shakespeare's most popular plays. It was probably written between 1594 and 1595. By the time the first edition

was published in 1597, the printer was able to boast
that the play had "been often (with great applause)
plaid publiquely."

The play has been performed regularly ever since.
Subsequent productions often differed greatly from
the original version, as in a London production of the
1670s, in which at the end of every other performance
the lovers survived. In 1750 two adaptations ran simultaneously on the London stage, vying for the attendance of theatergoers in what was dubbed the
"Romeo and Juliet War."

Stage performances continued throughout the nineteenth and early twentieth centuries, and, since the
advent of film, at least seventeen movie versions, in
six languages, have appeared. Numerous operas, symphonies, and ballets, as well as the modernized drama,
West Side Story, have all been inspired by Shakespeare's play.

It is no wonder, then, that the names Romeo and
Juliet have become a synonym for a pair of young
lovers, particularly those whose love is thwarted. In
addition, the name *Romeo* has entered our language
as a common epithet for a great lover or a ladies'
man. In the latter sense, modern usage has strayed
considerably from the literary source: Once Shakespeare's Romeo caught sight of Juliet, he never
looked at another woman; today's Romeos are less
interested in the quality of their relationships than in
the quantity.

Incidentally, Shakespeare did not invent the story
or the names of Romeo and Juliet. He adapted several

earlier tales, including the 1530 Italian version by
Luigi Da Porto, who was the first writer to name the
young lovers Romeo and Giulietta.

See also: **Montagues and Capulets.**

Romeo and Juliet: *See* Romeo.

(to) rube goldberg: to accomplish by extremely complex, roundabout means what seemingly could be done simply

Reuben Lucius Goldberg was born in San Francisco
in 1883. At the insistence of his father, he studied
engineering at the University of California but immediately after graduation went to work as a sports
cartoonist at the *San Francisco Chronicle.* In 1907 he
moved to New York to draw sports cartoons for the
Evening Mail.

In 1914 he drew a complicated machine that was
supposed to help people lose weight. It was so absurd—and so realistic, thanks to Goldberg's engineering background—that it was a sensation among
newspaper readers. From then on Goldberg included
similar contraptions in his cartoons on a regular basis.

Goldberg reached national fame with his comic
strip *Boob McNutt.* Boob appeared in newspapers,
magazines, on radio, on stage, and even on billboards.
His goofiness and ineptitude made the name Boob

McNutt a synonym for a person who is not too bright: in other words, a dim bulb.

At the height of the strip's success, Goldberg astonished fellow journalists and the public by giving it up and becoming a magazine writer. In 1939 he began drawing serious cartoons for the editorial page of the *New York Sun*. One of these, on the subject of atomic power, won a Pulitzer Prize in 1948.

Goldberg is best remembered, however, for the ridiculous inventions he continued to draw throughout the years. Much of his inspiration came from his engineering studies, and he used his artistic skill to satirize the machine age and the many needless gadgets that were being marketed to and purchased by the American public.

Goldberg's lunatic contraptions promised to take the drudgery out of many daily tasks: "Self-Working Corkscrew," "Awning That Lowers Itself," "Self-Watering Palm Tree," "Simple Way to Make Your Own Toast," "No More Summer Bugs," "No More Parking Problems," etc. "A Simple Bookmark" is a good example of how Goldberg could complicate anything:

. . . the operator by lifting his reading glasses releases a flock of moths who eat a woolen sock which drops a tear-gas bomb which causes a small dog to weep into a sponge whose added weight puts into operation a magic lantern which casts on the book's cover the likeness of a man who has stolen the wife of an angry dwarf who plunges a dagger through the

*picture and into the book, stopping when he strikes
a pet flea who jumped between the pages to sleep
when the book was laid down. The flea says "Ouch!"
and kicks open the book at the right page.*

As a result of Goldberg's many similar "technological breakthroughs," complicating things unnecessarily has come to be called *rube goldberging*. The
adjective *rube goldbergian* was also coined and is
applied to anything that is unnecessarily complex and
convoluted. Finally, a complicated contraption that
makes life harder when it is supposed to simplify
things is called a Rube Goldberg device.

Runyonesque: dealing with colorful, somewhat shady or underworld characters

When Damon Runyon died in 1946, his long-time
friend, journalist Walter Winchell, founded the Damon Runyon Cancer Fund in his memory. Its first
contributors were members of the mob, including underworld don Frank Costello, who donated $25,000.
During his life, Runyon was friends with a number
of other gangsters: Al Capone, his neighbor in Florida, gave Runyon his favorite dogs as a keepsake
when he was sent to prison in 1932. Runyon just
seemed to gravitate naturally to those who lived on
the fringe of—or beyond—respectable society.

He seems to have inherited the predilection from

his father, a rough-and-ready man who was born in
Kansas, where he later started a local newspaper. Alfred Damon Runyon, Sr. was an Indian fighter, a gam-
bler, and a drunkard. He had great respect for
"independent" men—gamblers, sportsmen, and out-
laws—and a great deal of curiosity about their way
of life and their exploits.

After Runyon, Sr.'s marriage and the birth of his
three children, he moved his family to Colorado.
There his wife died of tuberculosis, and he sent his
two daughters back to Kansas to live. His son, Al, Jr.,
remained in Colorado with him, where he became "a
newspaper and saloon orphan." The boy left school
in the fourth grade. He began smoking at nine, drinking whiskey at fifteen, and packing a six-shooter.

At fourteen, Al Runyon, Jr., got his first newspaper
assignment from the Pueblo, Colorado, *Evening
News*: to cover a lynching. At fifteen, he was a full-
time reporter. Before he was out of his teens, Runyon
had seen action in the Spanish-American War and had
spent considerable time as a railroad hobo, riding
around Colorado between newspaper jobs.

The school of hard knocks had prepared Damon
Runyon, as he was now known, well for the job of a
sports reporter in New York City. He arrived there in
1910, at the age of thirty. By the early 1920s, Runyon
had become a star reporter for the Hearst newspaper
chain. Although by then he was married and the father
of two children, he was rarely at home, preferring to
crash in a variety of places closer to the action of
Broadway.

There he hung out at Lindy's restaurant, in the company of racketeers, show people, bookies, gamblers, and small-time hustlers. After covering a baseball game, a prizefight, or the action at the racetrack, Runyon spent the night making the rounds of the card and dice games, then moving on to New York's nightclubs. Having given up alcohol in 1910, Runyon drank only coffee, listening to and watching the crowd carefully. What he picked up went straight into his short stories, particularly the *Guys and Dolls* series that was published in 1932 and became a smash hit on Broadway in 1952.

Runyon had a remarkable memory and a real ear for language. He was able to sit at the racetrack or in a speakeasy and memorize the conversations he heard, reproducing them perfectly back at his typewriter. This authentic street language, coming from the mouths of characters like Angie the Ox, Apple Annie, Joe the Joker, and Regret the Horseplayer, is what sets Runyon's stories apart from those of other writers. Runyon's style is so unique that a word was coined from his name to describe it: *Runyonesque*.

The following passage is a typical example of Runyonesque writing, from the short story "Dream Street Rose":

"Listen," Charley says, "understand that I do not say the guy does not deserve what he gets, and I am by no means hollering copper, but," Charley says, "if he knocks himself off, how does it come the rod

*is still in his lap where Dream Street Rose says her
friend tosses it?''*

To this day, colorful street language and the characters who use it—underworld figures, police and
their informants, bookies, and the like—are termed
Runyonesque in honor of Damon Runyon and the
company he kept.

S

sad sack: a blundering misfit

A person who never seems to be with it, who doesn't quite fit in, and who is always making mistakes is commonly dubbed a *sad sack*.

The term comes from U.S. Army slang for someone who is depressed or inept: a pathetic case. Although the term was in use before World War II, it was during the war that it was popularized among soldiers through a cartoon produced by George Baker. In 1942 Baker introduced a character that he called Sad Sack in a comic strip produced for *Yank*, a U.S. Army magazine.

Sad Sack was a fellow who, no matter how hard he tried, could never do anything right. His physical demeanor was an indication of his personality: skinny, slouched over, dressed in a baggy, ill-fitting uniform, the comic-strip G.I. always looked as though he bore the weight of the world on his shoulders.

Somehow Sad Sack managed to screw up every assignment he was given, and his commanding officer, Sarge, responded by heaping verbal abuse on the inept soldier and giving him the worst duty he could think of. The hapless Sad Sack took it all, shrugging his shoulders and resigning himself to his fate.

By the time the war ended, the adventures of Sad Sack had become popular enough for civilian newspapers to pick up the strip, and the expression sad sack soon spread from the military to the general populace.

Beginning in 1949 and continuing into the 1950s, the adventures of Sad Sack were published in comic-book form by Harvey Comics. *Sad Sack and the Sarge* and *Sad Sack's Army Life* were two of the titles in the popular series.

Sadie Hawkins Day: an unofficial holiday when females can take the initiative in asking males for dates or proposing marriage

Since 1937 the first Saturday in November has been observed as *Sadie Hawkins Day* in the United States. On this day women and girls are encouraged to stop waiting for their favorite man or boy to ask them out or propose to them and to take the initiative themselves.

The tradition began in the fictional town of Dogpatch, U.S.A. Sadie Hawkins, who made her first appearance in the comic strip *Li'l Abner* in November 1937, was the daughter of the wealthiest and most powerful resident of Dogpatch. None of the local young men were willing to marry her or even go out with her, however, because she was also the ugliest female anyone had ever laid eyes on. Finally, Sadie's father, the redoubtable Hekzebiah Hawkins, intervened to keep Sadie from becoming an old maid.

Hekzebiah made all the unmarried men in the town line up and, as he fired his pistol, head for the hills. His second shot was a signal to all the single women to begin the pursuit. Any man caught by a woman, including the one Sadie brought back kicking and screaming, was obliged to marry his captor, no matter how ugly she was. Most of Dogpatch's spinsters were just as ugly as Sadie Hawkins, so they were all too willing to make the chase an annual event. (After years of trying, Daisy Mae finally captured Li'l Abner on Sadie Hawkins Day in 1952.)

Followers of *Li'l Abner*—particularly college students—liked the idea that turnaround is fair play so much that 10 colleges celebrated Sadie Hawkins Day that first year. By 1940 more than 350 colleges and towns held Sadie Hawkins Day dances and celebrations. The popularity of the "holiday" reached its peak in the 1940s and 1950s.

Li'l Abner was created by Al Capp (Alfred C. Caplin) in August 1934. The title character, who was anything but little, was a member of the Yokum clan, whose name is a combination of the words *yokel* and *hokum*. The strip introduced the American public to the ways of Southern hill folk, or hillbillies, as they came to be popularly called. The strip first ran in 8 newspapers; by the time Capp stopped producing it in 1977, it was being carried by more than 500 papers and was one of the most popular strips in the history of American cartoons.

Al Capp's fame was hard won. After graduation from high school he attended a total of nine art schools, each for a very short time, before he got his first job. At the age of nineteen he was hired by the Associate Press Feature Service in New York to draw a comic strip called *Mr. Gilfeather*, which appeared in eighty newspapers. Capp became the youngest nationally syndicated cartoonist but, by his own admission, his work was not very good, and he quit after only six months. He went back to art school and stuck with it this time.

One day in 1933 Capp was walking down the street with a roll of drawings under his arm, when he caught the attention of Ham Fisher, the creator of the popular comic strip *Joe Palooka*. Fisher hired him as his assistant, and Capp remained with Fisher until the following year, when he was offered a contract by United Feature Syndicate. The success of the comic strip *Li'l Abner* led to a movie of the same title, written by Capp and released in 1940. During the 1940s several short cinema cartoons were made featuring the residents of Dogpatch. A musical version of *Li'l Abner* was produced for the New York stage during the 1950s, and the play was made into a film in 1959.

sadist: one who enjoys inflicting pain on others

Donatien-Alphonse-François, Comte de Sade, lived for seventy-four years. He spent twenty-seven of those years in French prisons for engaging in illicit sexual activity and for publishing books that were judged to be obscene.

The Comte, or Marquis, de Sade, as he is better known, was born in Paris in 1740 to one of the most respected families in the south of France. He served in the French military during the Seven Years' War and became governor-general and lord of several provincial areas. Although de Sade married well and had two sons by his wife, he led the life of a libertine.

Soon after his marriage in 1763, he was convicted of debauchery and acts of violence, and he was arrested repeatedly during the next decade. In 1772, after an incident involving four girls, de Sade was sentenced to death in absentia for "crimes of poisoning and sodomy." He was eventually captured, and, although the death sentence was commuted, he was imprisoned. He escaped and during the next seventeen years was involved in one sexual scandal after another. He was constantly being arrested and imprisoned, then escaping and being recaptured.

After his release from prison in 1790, de Sade seemingly went straight for a while. He held a position in the revolutionary government and made several patriotic addresses. He was mistakenly imprisoned during the Reign of Terror, but was released unharmed and went to live with a Parisian actress. The publication of

Justine, or the Misfortunes of Virtue, in 1801, got de
Sade into trouble with the authorities once more due
to its graphic descriptions of incest, homosexuality,
group sex, and sexual abuse. He spent two years in
prison before he was moved to a lunatic asylum outside Paris. Even there he was involved in scandals
until his death in 1814.

Most of de Sade's works were written in prison and
published in unofficial editions. They include: *Justine*,
which was written in 1791; *Juliette* (1792); *The 120
Days of Sodom* (written in 1785 but not discovered
and published until the early twentieth century); *Aline
and Valcour* (1795); *Philosophy in the Bedroom*
(1795); and *Crimes of Love* (1800). All include scenes
of sexual activity accompanied by violence. Time and
again de Sade writes about individuals who are sexually aroused by inflicting pain on their partner or
partners. Orgies, bondage, incest, sex with children—
all this and more is described in vivid detail by the
author. Because of this, de Sade's works are still considered obscene and banned in many countries.

A good number of respected writers and critics
have found redeeming social value in de Sade's works
and view him as "the type of the eternal rebel, the
example of man seeking, in unbounded fury, to sur-
pass the limits of the human condition." But de
Sade's name has not gone down in history—or in
language—as the prototype of the rebel. Rather, he is
remembered as the practitioner and proponent of deviant sexual acts. His name gave us the clinical terms
sadist and *sadism* to refer to those individuals in

whose twisted minds pain and pleasure are interdependent and to the unorthodox activities they engage in.

See also: **masochist.**

salad days: one's youth

In Act I, Scene 5 of William Shakespeare's *Antony and Cleopatra*, Cleopatra's attendant, Charmian, teases her mistress for singing the praises of Mark Antony the same way she once extolled Julius Caesar. Cleopatra explains away her romance with Caesar by telling Charmian that at the time she was too young to know any better. Those were, she says, ''My salad days, when I was green in judgment, cold in blood. . . .''

Cleopatra is saying that, at the age of twenty-one, when she became Caesar's mistress, she was as green and cold as a leaf of lettuce. By this she means that she was inexperienced and her passions had not yet been awakened. Now that she is almost forty, she has some basis for comparison and knows that her feelings for Mark Antony are authentic.

Shakespeare's vivid, evocative metaphor impressed theatergoers so much that it became a popular figure of speech. Today we frequently use the term *salad days* when referring to our youth, to the days when, like the young queen of Egypt, we still had a lifetime of loving and learning before us.

sapphism/Sapphism: *See* **lesbian/Lesbian.**

Scrooge: a miser; a mean-spirited person

Many artistic works become Christmas traditions, to be read, performed live, or replayed year after year: Handel's *Messiah*; the films *Miracle on 34th Street* and *Holiday Inn*; Clement Moore's *'Twas the Night Before Christmas*; Frank Church's *Yes, Virginia, There Is a Santa Claus*; and Charles Dickens's *A Christmas Carol*.

When it first appeared, in 1843, *A Christmas Carol, in Prose. Being a Ghost Story of Christmas* was a huge success. Readers loved the sentimental story of the heartless miser who repents on Christmas Day. In the century and a half since the book's first publication, it has been adapted over and over again. There have been numerous stage productions, including an opera by Thea Musgrave. At least seven silent films were made of the story. To date, there have been four sound films (1935, 1938, 1951, 1970). The 1951 version, entitled *A Christmas Carol* and starring Alastair Sim, is the classic that is rerun on television each year; the *Scrooge* of 1970 starred Albert Finney and was a musical. Alastair Sim also provided the voice of Scrooge in a 1971 animated film version. A 1979 TV movie starred Henry Winkler as a modern-day Scrooge. And, in *Mickey's Christmas Carol*, Walt Disney introduced the character of Scrooge McDuck, while Bob Cratchit was played by Mickey Mouse.

Scrooge is first warned by the ghost of his business partner, Jacob Marley, that unless he mends his ways, he will be doomed to walk the earth, in torment, for eternity. He is then visited by the Ghosts of Christmas Past, Present, and Yet to Come, who show him what he once was, what he has become, and what lies in store for him if he does not repent. As a result of these visions, Scrooge becomes a different man. His love of money vanishes and is replaced by his love of mankind.

As heartwarming as readers found Scrooge's metamorphosis, it was Dickens's original portrait of him— as a solitary, cold, immovable being—that made a lasting impression on them. Likewise, today, when we call someone a *Scrooge*, we are alluding not to the kindhearted fellow who sent a Christmas turkey to the Cratchit family and became a second father to Tiny Tim, but to the mean-spirited miser so brilliantly described by Dickens at the beginning of his story:

Oh! But he was a tight-fisted hand at the grindstone, Scrooge! a squeezing, wrenching, grasping, scraping, clutching, covetous old sinner! Hard and sharp as flint, from which no steel had ever struck out generous fire; secret, and self-contained, and solitary as an oyster. . . . He carried his own low temperature always about with him. . . . External heat and cold had little influence on Scrooge. No warmth could warm, no wintry weather chill him. No wind that blew was bitterer than he, no falling snow was more intent upon its purpose, no pelting rain less open to entreaty.

sea change: a dramatic alteration or meta-morphosis

At the beginning of William Shakespeare's romance play, *The Tempest*, the magician Prospero conjures up a violent storm in the waters around his island. The ship in which King Alonso of Naples and his son, Ferdinand, are traveling is wrecked, and Prospero arranges for the father and son to be separated.

In Act I, Scene 2, Ferdinand, who believes his father has drowned in the storm, hears a disembodied voice singing about the king:

> *Full fathom five thy father lies;*
> *Of his bones are coral made;*
> *Those are pearls that were his eyes:*
> *Nothing of him that doth fade,*
> *But doth suffer a sea-change*
> *Into something rich and strange.*

Ariel, the spirit who is singing, is referring to the metamorphosis that all things undergo when they are submerged in the ocean for a long period of time. The continual action of saltwater washing over an object—or a body—in time transforms it into something entirely different.

Of course, the sea doesn't really change flesh and bones into coral and pearls, but the power of Shakespeare's image made it a lasting metaphor for a transformation: a dramatic alteration, especially into something richer or finer.

serendipity: wealth or good fortune that one
stumbles upon when one is not looking for it

Horace Walpole is best known for two literary accomplishments: *The Castle of Otranto*—the earliest English Gothic novel—and his voluminous *Letters*—posthumous publications of his correspondence with the major political, social, and literary figures of his time.

Walpole lived from 1717 to 1797. In 1739 he met Horace Mann, who was soon to become British minister to the court of Tuscany. The two men began a correspondence that was to last until Mann's death, forty-five years later, and that added a word to the English language.

It was in a letter written to Mann on January 28, 1754, that Walpole coined the word *Serendipity*, writing: ". . . this discovery, indeed, is almost of that kind which I call Serendipity, a very expressive word."

Walpole began the word with a capital S because, as he explained to Mann, it was formed from *Serendip* (*Sarandīb* in Arabic), an old name for Ceylon or Sri Lanka, as it is called today. He explained further that the name was part of

> *a silly fairy tale, called* The Three Princes of Serendip: *as their highnesses travelled, they were always making discoveries, by accidents and sagacity, of things which they were not in quest of. . . .*

Walpole goes on to say that "no discovery of a thing you *are* looking for, comes under this description."

Although we no longer capitalize the word *seren-dipity,* it still carries the original connotation given by Walpole: accidental, unsought good fortune, which comes our way when we least expect it.

Shangri-La: a safe haven, a place of refuge from the cares of the world

Since the administration of Franklin D. Roosevelt, U.S. presidents have found temporary escape from the hectic life of Washington, D.C., at a retreat in the Maryland hills. Now known as Camp David, in honor of the grandson of Dwight D. Eisenhower, the origi-nal name of this secluded spot was Shangri-La.

The term *Shangri-La* has come to mean any safe haven or place of peace in which we can escape from the worries and cares of the world. The original Shan-gri-La was a fictional mountain kingdom in Tibet where there was no sickness, people lived to a great age, and war was unheard of. This mythical land was created by James Hilton, in his 1933 novel, *Lost Ho-rizon.*

The novel tells the story of a young Englishman named Hugh Conway, who is presumed dead after his plane is hijacked. In reality, he and his fellow pas-sengers have been flown to Shangri-La, where they are introduced to a world in which time has stood still. The Tibetan word *la* means mountain pass, and the only entrance to this earthly paradise is through a

narrow pass that leads to the valley of Karakal or Blue
Moon. There, on a rocky shelf partway up the mountain called Blue Moon, stands a magnificent monas-
tery where the reluctant travelers are housed.

Taking Conway into his confidence, the high lama
of Shangri-La reveals that he is in fact a French priest
who arrived there in 1719, at the age of thirty-eight.
He predicts that the world will soon be torn apart by
a terrible war, and that the only safe haven will be
Shangri-La. He knows that his death is approaching,
and he wants Conway to be his successor. He paints
a beautiful picture of the life that can be his in Shangri-La:

> *The years will come and go, and you will pass from
> fleshly enjoyments into austerer but no less satisfying
> realms; you may lose the keenness of muscle and
> appetite, but there will be gain to match your loss;
> you will achieve calmness and profundity, ripeness
> and wisdom, and the clear enchantment of memory.
> And, most precious of all, you will have time—that
> rare and lovely gift that your Western countries have
> lost the more they have pursued it.*

Conway is torn between two worlds: He longs to
stay in Shangri-La, but he finally consents to help his
friend and the beautiful young Chinese woman he has
fallen in love with to find their way back to "civilization."

Conway is later found in a mission hospital, where
he is suffering from amnesia. He had been brought to

the mission by a Chinese woman: "Most old of any one I have ever seen," is how the doctor describes her. As Conway's memory returns, he tells his incredible story to a fellow Englishman, who arranges his passage back to England. But Conway disappears, and it is apparent that he has headed back to Tibet, in search of the hidden valley of Blue Moon.

Lost Horizon was turned into a film, directed by Frank Capra and starring Ronald Colman, in 1937. Due to the enormous success of both the book and the movie, it wasn't long before the word *Shangri-La* gained prominence in the English language.

"Shangri-La" was also the title of a popular song of the 1950s, and Peter Finch starred in a musical version of *Lost Horizon* in 1972.

(a) Sherlock/sherlock: a detective; a person who has excellent powers of deduction

Christopher Morley concludes his preface to *The Complete Sherlock Holmes* with "A blessing, then, on those ophthalmic citizens who did not go to that office at 2 Devonshire Place, near Harley Street, where in 1891 Dr. A. Conan Doyle set up consulting rooms as an eye specialist."

Arthur Conan Doyle was indeed an unsuccessful eye doctor. As a means of supplementing his income, he decided to try his hand at writing and ended up creating the most popular detective in literary history.

The first Sherlock Holmes adventure was *A Study in Scarlet*, which appeared in 1887 and for which the author received the sum of twenty-five pounds. The book was not much of a success, but an American publisher encouraged Conan Doyle to write a sequel, which he did in 1890 *(The Sign of the Four)*.

Conan Doyle's eccentric detective didn't catch on with the public, however, until he appeared in a series of short stories in the *Strand Magazine*. These were collected in 1892 as *The Adventures of Sherlock Holmes* and in 1894 as *The Memoirs of Sherlock Holmes*. In the last of these stories, "The Final Problem," Sherlock Holmes and his archenemy, Dr. Moriarty, both perish. Fans of Holmes protested so vigorously that Conan Doyle was forced to bring Holmes back to life in *The Hound of the Baskervilles* (1902). More Holmes stories and novels followed until 1927: *The Return of Sherlock Holmes, The Valley of Fear, His Last Bow*, and *The Case Book of Sherlock Holmes*.

There have probably been more sequels, spinoffs, plays, films, television and radio shows, and critical commentary on the Sherlock Holmes stories than on any other works of fiction. In *Imaginary People*, David Pringle provides a four-page list of these, which should interest serious students of "Sherlockiana."

Some of the more interesting facts given by Pringle include the origin of Holmes's deerstalker hat and Inverness cape: The hat was the creation of artist Sidney Paget, who illustrated the stories in the *Strand Magazine*; the cape is thought to have been worn for the first time by American actor-playwright William Gillette. Gillette wrote and starred in *Sherlock Holmes* on the New York stage in 1899. He continued to perform in the play for the next thirty years and also starred in the 1916 film version.

Conan Doyle said that the character of Sherlock Holmes was suggested in part by Dr. Joseph Bell of the Edinburgh Infirmary, under whom he had studied. Bell's diagnostic skills were so amazing that his pupils and patients were constantly astounded by them. Holmes, as readers are aware, was possessed of equally amazing powers of deduction. He claimed that "From a drop of water, a logician could infer the possibility of an Atlantic or a Niagara without having seen or heard of one or the other. So all life is a great chain, the nature of which is known whenever we are shown a single link of it." Holmes excelled at deducing great quantities of information from the smallest bit of evidence: a footprint, a bit of cigarette ash, a person's fingernails, etc.

Arthur Conan Doyle died in 1930, having left an indelible mark on English literature and on our language. The name *Sherlock* or *Sherlock Holmes* is now synonymous with the word *detective,* and anyone who has excellent powers of deduction may be called by the name of Conan Doyle's sleuth. A verb, *to sherlock,* has also been coined from his name, and it means to investigate or play detective. Finally, the adjective *sherlockian* is used to describe deductive powers such as those possessed by Sherlock Holmes.

The actor who is best remembered by most of us

as Sherlock Holmes is Basil Rathbone, who starred in a series of fourteen British films made between 1939 and 1946. Rathbone's equally memorable costar was Nigel Bruce, who played the somewhat slow-witted, bumbling Dr. John Watson. In *A Study in Scarlet*, Watson meets Holmes when he is looking for someone to share the cost of lodgings. At first Watson does not know what to make of Holmes's eccentricities or of his claims to be able to solve any crime presented to him, often without even leaving his rooms. But after seeing Holmes in action Watson becomes his biggest fan. He accompanies Holmes on many of his investigations, and his failure to observe details—coupled with a tendency to jump to conclusions—makes him the perfect foil for Holmes. "Elementary, my dear Watson," is Holmes's way of beginning the inevitable explanation Watson requires.

The interaction between the brilliant detective and his dim roommate has led to the use of the name *Watson* to denote a somewhat slow-witted, but devoted, sidekick.

(a/the) shot heard round the world: an act of great importance, which has far-reaching consequences

A shot heard round the world is an act or event that is bound to have far-reaching consequences. The first such shot, which was commemorated by Ralph Waldo

Emerson, wasn't literally heard around the globe, but its repercussions were certainly felt far from Concord, Massachusetts, where it was fired on April 19, 1775.

On that day, British troops marched to Concord to seize a cache of weapons they believed were being hidden there by American patriots. The famous midnight ride of Paul Revere served to alert the citizens that the British were on their way, and Colonial militiamen met the redcoats on the green at Lexington. A second confrontation took place at Concord Bridge, and it was there:

> *By the rude bridge that arched the flood,*
> *Their flag to April's breeze unfurled,*
> *Here once the embattled farmers stood,*
> *And fired the shot heard round the world.*

The American Revolution had begun, and that first shot would be followed by many more, until the American colonists won their independence. Not only did that first shot have great significance for the Americans and the British, but it had a tremendous impact on the rest of the world as well. On July 14, 1789, echoes of the shot fired at Concord were heard in Paris, France, as the people stormed the Bastille and overthrew the monarchy of King Louis XVI.

The lines quoted above come from the "Concord Hymn," written by Ralph Waldo Emerson in 1836. Emerson's hymn was sung at the dedication of the Concord Monument, commemorating the battles of Lexington and Concord.

shuffle off this mortal coil: die

During his famous "To Be or Not To Be" soliloquy, Prince Hamlet of Denmark expounds on the pros and cons of committing suicide. One of the things that is stopping him is his fear of what will come after death:

> ... To die, to sleep;
> To sleep: perchance to dream: ay, there's the rub;
> For in that sleep of death what dreams may come
> When we have shuffled off this mortal coil,
> Must give us pause. ...

In *Brush Up Your Shakespeare!* Michael Macrone explains that in Elizabethan England the word *coil* generally meant a fuss or to-do. Within the context of the speech, he therefore interprets Shakespeare's use of the words "mortal coil" to mean this tumultuous world of mortals. Hamlet, therefore, is concerned about what will come after he has departed from this life into the next.

Hamlet, Prince of Denmark was first presented in 1600 or 1601. To this day it remains Shakespeare's most frequently produced play. And Hamlet's soliloquy in act 3, scene 1 remains one of the most frequently quoted passages in literature. Quotations such as "To be or not to be, that is the question," "Thus conscience does make cowards of us all," and "The undiscovered country, from whose bourn no traveller returns" are often sprinkled into philosophical or moral discussions by devotees of Shakespeare. In the same way, the figure of speech *shuffle off this mortal coil,* is often substituted for the less poetic, less erudite verb *to die.*

shylock: a loan shark; an exacting creditor

Throughout the Middle Ages, European Christians were forbidden from charging interest on loans they made to one another. However, canonical law did not apply to transactions between Christians and Jews, and the latter soon became the professional moneylenders of Europe. Although they were expelled from England in 1290, the Jews retained a reputation there, as elsewhere, for being avaricious and ruthless in their dealings with the Christians who came to them for loans.

When William Shakespeare decided to write *The Merchant of Venice* sometime between 1596 and 1598, he borrowed his plot from a collection of Italian stories called *Il Pecorone (The Simpleton).* But Giovanni Fiorentino's moneylender did not charge interest, and Shakespeare replaced him with a usurious Jew named Shylock, whom he based on the villainous title character of *The Jew of Malta,* a play written by Christopher Marlowe in 1592. Shylock is, therefore, a combination of the miser—a stock figure in comedy since the Middle Ages—and the stereotype of a Jew that was accepted by Shakespeare and his contemporaries.

While there are several subplots running through *The Merchant of Venice*, the main plot involves a businessman named Antonio who, in order to help a friend, asks for a loan from Shylock. Shylock agrees to lend him the money, with the stipulation that he will accept no interest but will be entitled to one pound of Antonio's flesh if the latter defaults. Meanwhile, Shylock's daughter, Jessica, elopes with a Christian, taking much of her father's fortune with her. Her betrayal and his financial loss intensify Shylock's hatred of all Christians, and when he learns that Antonio cannot repay the loan he delights in the macabre prospect of claiming his pound of flesh. The cruel Shylock refuses all pleas for mercy, and it is only because Antonio's friend, Portia, finds a loophole in the contract that his life is saved.

For nearly one hundred fifty years the part of Shylock was played as low comedy. He was portrayed as a typical miser who cared about his money above all else. Then, in 1741, Charles Macklin astonished London audiences by representing Shylock as a tragic, dignified figure. Since then, there have been many interpretations of *The Merchant of Venice* that have focused on Shylock as a victim of religious prejudice. Unfortunately, this modern view of Shakespeare's Jewish moneylender came too late to prevent his name from becoming a widely used synonym for someone who lends money at usurious rates and exacts a heavy penalty if it is not repaid: in other words, a loan shark. The name has even been made into a verb—*to shylock*—which means to charge an exorbitant rate of interest on a loan.

See also: **(a) pound of flesh.**

silent spring: ecological disaster

There was a strange stillness. The birds, for example—where had they gone? Many people spoke of them, puzzled and disturbed. The feeding stations in the backyards were deserted. The few birds seen anywhere were moribund; they trembled violently and could not fly. It was a spring without voices. On the mornings that had once throbbed with the dawn chorus of robins, catbirds, doves, jays, wrens, and scores of other bird voices there was now no sound; only silence lay over the fields and woods and marsh.

The above description is part of Rachel Carson's "Fable for Tomorrow," with which she began her 1962 bestseller, *Silent Spring*. The fable tells of an American town that was once beautiful and prosperous, surrounded by rich farmland, teeming with wildlife, where "all life seemed to live in harmony with its surroundings." Then, suddenly, the flora and fauna began to die; the people became ill and many of them died as well; the once-flourishing community was soon a wasteland. Why? Because, explains the author,

some weeks before, a white granular powder had
fallen onto the roofs and lawns, into the fields and
streams. Man, through his thoughtless, indiscriminate
use of chemicals, had caused this disaster.

Carson went on to say that the town in her fable
did not exist, but that one or more of the disasters
that befell it had occurred in real communities
throughout the United States. *Silent Spring* was her
attempt to stop man's destruction of his environment
before it was too late.

Rachel Carson received an undergraduate degree in
biology and did graduate work in genetics and development at Johns Hopkins University. From 1936
to 1952 she was a biologist and editor for the U.S.
Fish and Wildlife Service. In 1951 she wrote *The Sea
Around Us*, which was a bestseller for eighty-six
weeks and was eventually translated into thirty languages. It was followed, in 1955, by *The Edge of the
Sea*. In 1958 she began collecting data from scientists
all over the world on the effects of synthetic pesticides and other deadly chemicals on living things.

At a time when most people were blissfully unaware of the effect of "progress" on ourselves and
our planet, *Silent Spring* raised disturbing questions.
What effect was the widespread spraying of pesticides
having on our water supply? What was the connection
between such chemicals and cancer? How safe were
the fruits and vegetables we were putting on our ta-
bles? Did long-term exposure to man-made chemicals
cause genetic damage to living cells?

Since the publication of *Silent Spring* many dangerous pesticides, such as DDT, have been banned from use. Governments around the world have tightened controls on industry and other sources of pollution. Unleaded gasoline is no longer marketed in the United States, and emission controls are required on vehicles. Fluorocarbons are banned from use as aerosol propellants and refrigerants. We have a long way to go before we can say with certainty that our planet is out of danger, but we have begun to reverse the destructive trend that so alarmed Carson.

The expression *silent spring* is now used frequently as a synonym for ecological disaster. Hopefully, the impact of Carson's book and the actions it spurred will keep us from ever experiencing a silent spring like the one she described so eloquently.

Simon Legree: a hard, merciless taskmaster; a slavedriver

It is said that when Abraham Lincoln was introduced to Harriet Beecher Stowe his first words were, "So this is the little lady that made this big war." Whether or not the story is true, Stowe probably did more than any other single person of her time to galvanize public opinion in America against slavery.

Uncle Tom's Cabin was first published, in serial form, in the abolitionist journal *National Era*. During the time it ran—from June 5, 1851 to April 1, 1852—it was immensely popular among subscribers, many of whom wrote to praise its interest and pathos. On March 20, 1852, *Uncle Tom's Cabin* was released in book form. The first edition of five thousand copies was sold out in two days. One year later, over three hundred thousand copies had been printed and sold in the U.S. In addition, over one and a half million copies were soon sold in England, where Stowe's work was not copyrighted.

Stowe's original title for her work was *Uncle Tom's Cabin or, The Man That Was a Thing*. Although she changed the subtitle to *Life Among the Lowly* before the first installment appeared, the theme remained the same: Slavery denied men and women the most basic physical, emotional, and spiritual rights, reducing them to nothing more than things. And nowhere in *Uncle Tom's Cabin* are Blacks more dehumanized than on the plantation of Simon Legree.

Legree buys Tom and other Blacks at the slave market in New Orleans. His first speech to his new possessions is designed to strike fear into their hearts:

> *. . . this yer fist has got as hard as iron knocking down niggers. I never see the nigger, yet, I couldn't bring down with one crack. . . . I don't keep none o' yer cussed overseers; I does my own overseeing; and I tell you things is seen to. You's every one of ye got to toe the mark, I tell ye; quick,—straight,—the moment I speak. That's the way to keep in with me. Ye won't find no soft spot in me, nowhere. So, now mind yerselves; for I don't show no mercy!*

Legree is true to his word: His slaves are fed poorly, worked mercilessly, punished brutally, and humiliated constantly. Tom receives even worse treatment than the others for, "Legree . . . rated him as a first-class hand; and yet he felt a secret dislike to him,—the native antipathy of bad to good." Tom is singled out for even more abuse than his peers and, finally, when he refuses to reveal the whereabouts of two runaways, is flogged to death by Legree's henchmen.

Today, long after the North won the Civil War and slavery was abolished throughout the United States, *Uncle Tom's Cabin* remains one of the best-known works in American literature. Although critics have often denigrated the novel for its sentimentality and lack of literary artistry, these seem to be exactly the qualities that made it so popular with the masses. To the sophisticated reader of today, saintly Little Eva, righteous Uncle Tom, and blackhearted Simon Legree may seem to be simplistic, one-dimensional characters. But to Stowe's nineteenth-century readers, they were believable personifications of good and evil. Their powerful, moving portraits left an indelible impression on Stowe's readers and, in more than one case, on the English language. One of them soon became—and remains—a linguistic symbol of brutality and cruelty. Even those who have never read *Uncle Tom's Cabin* have no doubt heard the name *Simon Legree* and have perhaps used it themselves to characterize a harsh, cruel taskmaster who shows no mercy to his underlings.

See also: **(grow like) Topsy, Uncle Tom.**

Sleeping Beauty: a woman who is asleep; a woman whose full potential remains unrealized

Charles Perrault's collection of fairy tales, *Histoire ou Contes du temps passé*, was published in French in 1697 and translated into English by Robert Samber in 1729. The first tale in the collection was that of "La Belle au bois dormant" or "Sleeping Beauty."

As Perrault retold it, the story of *Sleeping Beauty* began with the birth of a princess, a child for whom the king and queen had hoped and prayed for many years. The royal couple was so delighted that they asked all the fairies they could find to be godmothers to the princess. Each of the fairies gave the princess a gift: They gave her beauty, wit, and grace; they endowed her with the ability to dance, sing, and play any musical instrument to perfection.

Unfortunately, the king and queen had forgotten about the existence of one old fairy. She appeared unexpectedly at the christening banquet and, when it was her turn to give a gift to the baby princess, she announced that the child would prick her hand on a spindle and die of the wound. Another fairy, who had not yet bestowed her gift on the princess, tried to undo some of the harm caused by the old fairy by amending her curse: She assured the king and queen that their child would not die, but would sleep for a hundred years, after which time she would be woken by the son of a king.

In spite of all the precautions taken by the king and queen, the princess came into contact with a spindle and pricked her hand on it. She immediately fell into a deep sleep and the king and queen ordered that no one was to enter the palace where she slept. The abandoned palace was instantly surrounded by a dense, impenetrable wood where the sleeping princess lay for the next one hundred years.

As the good fairy had predicted, a prince heard the story of Sleeping Beauty and set out to find her enchanted palace. As he approached her bed, she woke. The two fell in love, but the prince concealed his involvement with the princess from his parents. By the time they learned of it, the princess had given birth to two children.

In Perrault's version of the story, the prince kept his new family a secret because his mother was an ogress—one of a race of beings that have an appetite for human flesh, particularly that of children. When she found out about the princess and her offspring, she attempted to kill them but was foiled at the last minute and committed suicide. In the Italian version of "Sleeping Beauty" that appeared in Basile's *Pentamerone* of 1636, the princess was raped by the prince as she slept. She gave birth to two children, who were looked after by fairies while she remained unconscious. One of the children eventually sucked the splinter from its mother's hand and she woke up. The prince returned, was overjoyed to learn that he had two children, and he and Sleeping Beauty fell in love. However, in this version the prince already had a wife, and it was she who plotted the demise of her rival and her rival's offspring.

Nearly every child who has grown up in England or America has heard or read Perrault/Samber's tale of *Sleeping Beauty*. The name of the heroine is so well-known that it is used in English both literally and figuratively. In the literal sense, we often call a female Sleeping Beauty when she is out like a light. Figuratively, the term *Sleeping Beauty* is used to refer to a girl or woman who, for one reason or another, has failed to reach her full potential. Like the beautiful princess in the enchanted palace, she needs to wake up from her lethargy and get back into the world of the living.

slough of despond: deep despair or depression

John Bunyan's allegorical tale, *The Pilgrim's Progress*, deals with the spiritual journey of a man called Christian. Christian sets out for the Celestial City, but on the way he passes through a number of places where he is tempted to abandon his noble goal.

One of these places is called the Slough (pronounced *slew*) of Despond. Christian and his companion, Pliable, are not paying attention and fall suddenly into a bog or slough, the name of which is Despond. Christian, who is carrying a great weight of sin on his back, begins to sink in the mire. Pliable is angry because he did not expect the way to the Celestial City to be so difficult. Extricating himself from the mire, he returns home. Fortunately for Christian, a man called Help arrives on the scene and pulls him out.

Christian asks Help why someone doesn't repair the road so travelers won't fall into the Slough of Despond, and Help replies:

This miry slough is such a place as cannot be mended: it is the descent whither the scum and filth that attends conviction for sin doth continually run, and therefore it was called the Slough of Despond; for still as the sinner is awakened about his lost condition, there arise in his soul many fears and doubts, and discouraging apprehensions, which all of them get together, and settle in this place. And this is the reason of the badness of this ground.

In other words, the Slough of Despond is a symbol for the depression and hopelessness into which sinners fall when they realize the magnitude of their alienation from God. But, according to Bunyan, this sense of hopelessness need not keep them from their savior; with help they can overcome their feelings of depression and unworthiness and get back on the road to salvation.

The Pilgrim's Progress was published in 1678 and became one of the most widely read books in the English language. It gave rise to several literary allusions, including the use of the term *slough of de-*

spond to mean any state of depression or despair into which a person may fall.

See also: **pilgrim's progress, Vanity Fair.**

something's rotten in Denmark: there's something wrong under the surface of things

Most of us who use the expression *something's rotten in Denmark* to indicate that something is wrong or fishy know that it comes from William Shakespeare's *Hamlet, Prince of Denmark.* What few know, however, is that it was not Hamlet who made the observation and that the phrase as we commonly use it is a misquote.

As the play opens, we learn that the ghost of Hamlet's father has appeared to the sentries at Elsinore Castle. Bernardo and Marcellus have seen the ghost and have invited Horatio to keep watch with them. When the ghost appears, Horatio tries to speak to it, but it walks away from him and vanishes into the night.

Hamlet is informed of the apparition, and the following night he too keeps watch. The ghost leads him away from the others and addresses him. (In the following scene he will reveal to Hamlet that he did not die of natural causes but was murdered by his brother, with the complicity of his own wife.) As Hamlet walks away after the ghost, Marcellus wants to follow him, telling Horatio, "Something is rotten in the state of Denmark."

Over the centuries the phrase came to be used in shortened form and, for some unknown reason, attributed to Hamlet rather than Marcellus by those who had not read the play.

sour grapes: denigrating something that we cannot have

While walking along, a fox spies some grapes on a vine overhead. He makes several attempts to gather them, but they prove to be just out of his reach. Abandoning the effort, he walks away saying, "Oh, well, they were probably sour anyway."

This little fable contains an eternal truth: Like the fox, people, when they cannot get what they want, often pretend that they didn't really want it. By denigrating the object to others, they conceal their disappointment from the world and, perhaps, from themselves. The expression *sour grapes* refers to this ploy and comes from the fable summarized above, which is generally assumed to date from the sixth century B.C.

"The Fox and the Grapes" is one of the tales we refer to as *Aesop's Fables*, although some scholars doubt that Aesop ever existed at all. According to tradition, Aesop was a slave who lived on the island of Samos from about 620 to 564 B.C. The oldest in-

formation about Aesop comes from Eugeon, whose
writings date from the fifth century B.C. Eugeon and
later writers relate many stories about Aesop's life:
that he was Thracian or Phrygian, that he was put to
death by the Delphians, that he was freed from slavery, that he was a public defender who used his fables
in his judicial arguments, that he was deformed, etc.
None of these stories has ever been proved.

All that we do know for sure is that a collection of
fables attributed to Aesop existed in the ninth century
and was accepted by Greek scholars as his work. But
collections of fables existed long before then, and we
can be fairly certain that the ones that are today called
Aesop's Fables came from a variety of sources.
(Some of the fables attributed to Aesop have been
found on Egyptian papyri dating from one thousand
years before his time.)

strange bedfellows: people we are surprised
to find associating with one another

When candidates who have previously been on opposite sides of the political fence suddenly team up
and run on the same platform, we are wont to explain
it by saying that politics makes *strange bedfellows*. In
doing so, we are using a metaphor introduced by William Shakespeare in *The Tempest*, which was first performed in 1611.

Shakespeare's strange bedfellows were literally

that. Shipwrecked and stranded on an uncharted island, a jester named Trinculo came upon Caliban, a deformed native who lived on the island with his master, Prospero. Caliban was lying on the beach, wrapped in a cloak, and at first Trinculo mistook him for a fish that had been killed by a thunderbolt. When he realized Caliban was a human being and saw that the storm was worsening, he decided to take shelter inside the native's cloak, saying, ". . . there is no other shelter hereabout: misery acquaints a man with strange bed-fellows.''

Caliban, being fast asleep, made no protest, and the first of a long line of strange bedfellows came into being.

sulphite: *See* **bromide.**

superman/Superman: someone with greater-than-human powers

In the early 1930s, writer Jerome (Jerry) Siegel and artist Joe Schuster couldn't find a newspaper that would buy a comic strip about their newly created hero, Superman. In 1995 the portable Royal typewriter on which Siegel had tapped out Superman's first adventures went on sale for $65,000.

Siegel and Schuster first thought up the character of Superman during high school. But, when they took their strip to the newspapers, every editor they showed it to said the idea of a man of steel who comes to Earth from the planet Krypton to defend "truth, justice, and the American way" was just too fantastic to be accepted by their readers. It wasn't until they contacted the publishers of *Action Comics* that anyone took them seriously. "Superman" was one of the strips to appear in the first issue of *Action Comics*, which was published in June 1938, and its hero was an immediate success.

One year later Superman had his own comic book. For the next several decades comic book editor Morton Weisinger wrote the strip, embellishing on Superman's origins and powers in order to keep the plots lively and fresh.

In 1940 Superman began his radio career, with Clayton "Bud" Collyer providing the voice of the man from Krypton. From 1941 to 1943 there were seventeen short animated films made about Superman, and Collyer's voice was used in these as well. Toward the end of the 1940s, Superman's adventures began to be made into feature films. George Reeves starred in two of these and in the television series *The Adventures of Superman*, which aired from 1952 to 1957.

Throughout the 1960s and 1970s there continued to be an interest in the man of steel, with plays, television movies, and animated serials being produced every few years. Then, in 1978, Christopher Reeve starred in the feature film *Superman–The Movie* which sparked the imagination of a whole new generation. *Superman II* (1980) *Superman III* (1983) and *Superman IV–The Quest for Peace* also starred Reeve and perpetuated the new Superman cult in America.

Superman has been described as a combination of Robin Hood, Sherlock Holmes, Sir Galahad, and Hercules. As his alter ego, Clark Kent, he is shy, mild-mannered, and even bumbling. But in his role of hero his strength is boundless. Able to fly faster than a speeding bullet, able to stop a speeding locomotive in its tracks, able to leap tall buildings in a single bound: These are just a few of the feats that have made the name *Superman* synonymous with greater-than-human strength and power. When we call a person a *superman* (or a *superwoman*) we are implying that he or she is capable of much more than the average person, possesses greater mental and physical powers, and has much more stamina.

Interestingly, years before Superman was created by Siegel and Schuster, nineteenth-century German philosopher Friedrich Nietzsche invented the term *Übermensch,* which means *Superman*, and which he applied to a hypothetical human being of superior intellect and morals. In 1903 Nietzsche's idea of a superior being was popularized in England through George Bernard Shaw's play *Man and Superman*.

Svengali: one who exerts a sinister, controlling influence over another person

Readers who hear the name du Maurier are apt to think immediately of *Rebecca* and the other romantic

novels of Daphne du Maurier. As well-known and
prolific as she was, Daphne was not the only member
of her family to write novels, nor was she the one
who earned linguistic immortality as a result of her
literary works.

Daphne's grandfather, George du Maurier, only
wrote three books, but one of those—*Trilby*—enjoyed tremendous success and contributed two new
words to the English language.

Trilby, which appeared in 1894, tells the story of a
young artists' model, Trilby O'Ferrall, who is made
into a singing star by an older, disreputable man. The
man goes by the single name of Svengali, and du
Maurier's portrait of him is anything but flattering:

> . . . *a tall bony individual of any age between thirty
> and forty-five, of Jewish aspect, well-featured but sin-
> ister . . . very shabby and dirty . . . His thick, heavy,
> languid, lustreless black hair fell down behind his
> ears on to his shoulders. . . . He had bold, brilliant
> eyes, with long heavy lids, a thin, sallow face, and a
> beard of burnt-up black, which grew almost from un-
> der his eyelids; and over it his moustache, a shade
> lighter, fell in two long spiral twists.*

Du Maurier makes it clear from the outset that
Svengali is as repulsive morally as he is physically:
"Svengali walking up and down the earth seeking
whom he might cheat, betray, exploit, borrow money
from, make brutal fun of, bully if he dared . . . was
about as bad as they make 'em."

Svengali's only virtue is his love of music or, rather, of himself as a master of music. Du Maurier tells us that although Svengali's own voice resembles a raven's croak, he understands the human voice as perhaps no one has understood it before or since. The first time Trilby sings, everyone present is embarrassed for her, except Svengali: Only he recognizes the potential in her untutored voice.

The first indication du Maurier gives of Svengali's ability to control others comes when Trilby complains of a headache. Svengali claims he can cure her and tells her to look straight into his eyes. As he moves his fingers over her forehead and face, her eyes close and she stops moving. After a while he asks her if the headache is gone, and she answers that it has. Svengali tells an onlooker that she is not asleep, but she cannot open her eyes, speak, or stand up. When asked to do so, she is unable until Svengali says she is free. He then tells her that he will cure her whenever her pain returns, and she "shall see nothing, hear nothing, think of nothing but Svengali, Svengali, Svengali!"

Trilby's friend warns her about those who practice mesmerism, saying that once they get you into their power they make you do anything they want, including lying, stealing, and murdering. Terrified, Trilby refuses to allow Svengali to hypnotize her again, preferring to suffer the pain of her recurring headaches.

Eventually, however, Svengali wins out. When Trilby runs away from the man who loves her, be-

lieving he is too good for her, Svengali follows. He
marries her and makes her into the greatest singer of
modern times. Trilby's voice is "immense in its softness, richness, freshness . . . its intonation absolutely,
mathematically pure. . . . A woman archangel might
sing like that, or some enchanted princess out of a
fairy tale." And, when Svengali dies in the middle of
one of her concerts, Trilby can no longer sing. Shortly
after his death, she too dies, and her last words are
"Svengali, Svengali, Svengali."

Twenty years later, Svengali's friend, Gecko, explains the relationship that existed between Svengali
and Trilby:

There were two Trilbys. *There was the Trilby . . .
who could not sing one single note in tune. . . . But
all at once . . . with one wave of his hand over her—
with one look of his eye—with a word—Svengali
could turn her into the other Trilby, his Trilby—and
make her do whatever he liked. . . . She suddenly became an unconscious Trilby of marble, who could
produce wonderful sounds . . . and think his thoughts
and wish his wishes. . . .*

Trilby was a resounding success among readers and
was dramatized on the London stage a year after its
publication, with Beerbohm Tree as Svengali. Several
silent films were also made of the story. In 1931 John
Barrymore appeared as the villainous musician; in
1954 Donald Wolfit reprised the role; in 1983 Peter

O'Toole starred as a modern-day Svengali on television. It is quite telling that the title of these last three
versions of du Maurier's tale was not *Trilby*, but
Svengali. Although the names of the young singer and
her villainous mentor have both entered our language,
the branding of someone as a *Svengali*—a person who
exerts a sinister, controlling influence—is far more
common than is the use of the word *Trilby* to characterize someone who is easily controlled.

See also: **Trilby.**

syphilis: a virulent venereal disease

No one is sure where the virulent venereal disease we
now call *syphilis* originated. In South America, evidence of it has been found in some pre-Columbian
skeletons; however, it does not seem to have existed
in Europe until shortly after Columbus returned from
his first voyage to the New World. Scientists postulate
that the syphilis bacterium *(Treponema pallidum)*
flourished in fifteenth-century Europe, but local
strains were not transmitted sexually. It was the
American strain of *T. pallidum* that, when introduced
in Europe, began an epidemic of venereal disease.

When the French king Charles VIII mustered an
army to invade Naples in 1494, many of the Spaniards
who had sailed with Columbus offered the monarch
their services. Before dispersing and returning home
a year later, these mercenaries managed to spread the

disease they had contracted in the New World to
many camp followers and residents of Naples. During
the next fifteen years the disease spread like wildfire
through the known world, claiming at least ten million lives. Having contracted the disease in Naples,
the Frenchmen who brought it home called it the Ne-
apolitan sickness, while the Neapolitans—who
blamed the French army for introducing the malady
to their land—referred to it as the French sickness.

The first one to give the deadly disease a name was
Italian doctor, astronomer, and poet Girolamo Fracastoro. Fracastoro lived from 1483 to 1553 and wrote
in Latin, often using the Latinized form of his name:
Hieronymus Fracastorius. In 1530 he wrote a poetical
treatise, in three books, called *Syphilis sive Morbus
Gallicus (Syphilis or the French Disease)*. Book I expounds on the history and characteristics of the disease, as witnessed during its outbreak in Italy. In book
II Fracastoro tells the tale of Ilceo, a Syrian youth
who is stricken with the disease and cured by jour-
neying to the Underworld and bathing in a lake of
quicksilver. The central character of book III is a
shepherd of the New World named Syphilus. Angered
by Syphilus's refusal to worship him, the Sun god
inflicts the terrible disease on him. The disease then
takes his name, calling itself syphilis, spreads
throughout the New World, and is brought to Europe
by the returning Spanish conquistadors. At the end of
Fracastoro's poem, the gods take pity on mankind and
create the hyacus tree, which cures the disease.

Fracastoro's poetical work was followed by a scientific treatise, *De Contagione*, which was published in 1546 and which employed the word *syphilis* as a medical term. The Latin word became *sifilide* in Italian, *sifilis* in Spanish, and remained *syphilis* in French and English. Fracastoro's poem was first translated into English in 1686 by Nahum Tate as *Syphilis: or, a Poetical History of the French Disease*.

It wasn't until 1905 that syphilis's causative organism, a spirochete, was identified by German bacteriologists Fritz Schaudin and Erich Hoffman. Their discovery was followed, in 1907, by August Von Wassermann's development of a blood test to detect the venereal disease. The first cure for syphilis came, not from a tree, but from an arsenic compound called salvarsan, or 606, introduced by Paul Ehrlich in 1910. In 1931 it was found that salvarsan was more effective when administered in combination with bismuth, and this was the prescribed treatment for syphilis until 1943. At that time, some fifteen years after its discovery, penicillin was tried and found to be the most effective weapon in the war against syphilis: a war that had begun when the French invaded Naples five hundred years previously.

tar baby: a problem that cannot be solved and that seems to get worse with each action we take

Joel Chandler Harris was born in Georgia in 1848 and had a long career as a journalist. While on the staff of the *Atlanta Constitution* he created the character of Uncle Remus: a wise old Black man who entertained—and educated—the son of a plantation owner with his simple animal tales. One of the first of these, "The Tar-Baby Story," appeared in the *Atlanta Constitution* in 1879 and was included in Harris's book, *Uncle Remus, His Songs and His Sayings*, when it was published the following year.

Written in dialect, the story features two of Harris's best-known characters: Brer Rabbit and Brer Fox. Uncle Remus tells the little boy that, in one of his many attempts to outwit the rabbit, the fox "got 'im some tar, en mix it wid some turkentime, en fix up a contrapshun wat he call a Tar-Baby.'' In the book's illustrations the tar-baby is depicted as a doll, covered in tar and wearing a hat, that Brer Fox props up on the side of the road. He then hides in the bushes and waits for the rabbit to come along. Being a sociable creature, Brer Rabbit stops and greets the tar-baby. When his attempts to initiate a conversation fail, he thinks the tar-baby might be deaf and offers to holler louder. When that doesn't work, he concludes that the tar-baby is just stuck up, and he gets mad. He delivers a punch to the tar-baby's head, after which ''His fis' stuck, en he can't pull loose.'' Still unaware of the trick that the fox is playing on him, he tells the tar-baby that if it doesn't let go of him he's going to hit it again. He does, and his other fist sticks to it. Next he tries kicking it and with each kick he gets stuck again. Finally, he butts it with his head and all five of his appendages are held fast. It seems as though Brer Fox has finally got the rabbit where he wants him, and he comes out of the bushes, rolling on the ground with laughter. When the boy asks Uncle Remus if the fox ate the rabbit, Uncle Remus replies that maybe he did, maybe he didn't—that's as far as the story goes.

The story may not have gone far enough to satisfy the little boy's curiosity, but Harris's literary creation left a lasting impression on our language. Soon after the story's publication, the term *tar baby* became a synonym for a very sticky problem, one that cannot be solved. When faced with such a problem, we often try to take action to solve it but, like Brer Rabbit's kicks and punches, these only put us in a worse predicament.

During his lifetime, Joel Chandler Harris published a total of eight Uncle Remus books—two others were published after his death—as well as many other children's stories. He died in 1908, having devoted the last year of his life to the publication of *Uncle Remus's Magazine*.

Tarzan: a strong man

The idea of the child of an English nobleman being lost in Africa and brought up by apes, learning to speak their language and the language of other animals as well, is outlandish to say the least. It doesn't seem possible that such an implausible plot could ever be accepted, let alone lauded, by generations of readers. But it was: in the Tarzan series of Edgar Rice Burroughs.

Burroughs first introduced his unconventional hero in *All-Story* magazine in 1912. The first book in which Tarzan appeared was *Tarzan of the Apes*, published in 1914. Burroughs wrote a total of twenty-four Tarzan books; the last two in the series were published posthumously in 1964 and 1965.

Tarzan's real name was John Clayton, Lord Greystoke. Raised by great apes, he possessed tremendous strength, agility, and intelligence. He is the incarnation of natural man, his innate goodness unspoiled by civilization. The love of Tarzan's life was Jane Porter, the daughter whom Professor Archimedes Q. Porter brought with him to the jungles of Africa. Although the famous line "Me Tarzan, you Jane" is apocryphal, Jane did succumb to Tarzan's charms; they married and had a son who was named John, after his father.

Baby Jack Clayton first appeared in *The Beasts of Tarzan* (1916), in which he was kidnapped by an evil Russian. One year later, in *The Son of Tarzan*, he was a young man living in England who knew nothing of his birth or early years. Irresistibly drawn to Africa, he ran away and spent several years in the jungle with the great apes. They nicknamed him Korak, which in their language meant *killer.* Korak was eventually reunited with Tarzan and Jane and remained with them in Africa.

Tarzan of the Apes was made into a silent film of the same name in 1918, with strongman Elmo Lincoln as the hero. *Tarzan the Ape Man* (1932) was the first talkie version of Burroughs's story, and the first of twelve films that starred Olympic swimming champion Johnny Weissmuller as Tarzan and Maureen O'Sullivan as Jane. Other screen Tarzans included Buster Crabbe (also a swimmer), Herman Brix, Lex Barker, Gordon Scott, Jock Mahoney, Mike Henry, and Miles O'Keefe. *Greystoke: The Legend of Tarzan, Lord of the Apes* was released in 1984 and starred Christopher Lambert. Directed by Hugh Hudson, it has been hailed as the only film that did justice to Burroughs's conception of Tarzan.

Tarzan began his life as a comic-strip character in 1929. Cartoonist Hal Foster drew the first "Tarzan" newspaper strips from that year until 1937. Burne Hogarth then took over the strip, infusing it with a new vitality and depth that he continued to supply until retiring in 1950. Since then a series of artists have kept the character alive in newspaper strips and comic books.

On the radio, *Tarzan* was very much a family affair. Actor James H. Pierce, Edgar Rice Burroughs's son-in-law, played the hero for many years, while Burroughs's daughter Joan supplied the voice of Jane. Ron Ely took the part of the lord of the jungle in an American television series that ran from 1966 to 1969.

The name *Tarzan* is now a common epithet for a strong man. There is also a California town—Tarzana, which is near Los Angeles—that was named for the lord of the apes.

thespian: an actor; relating to the dramatic arts

The theater as we know it today originated in ancient Greece. The earliest plays were performed as part of religious festivals and observances. These evolved into the secular performances that the Greeks called tragedies and comedies, which reached their zenith with the works of Aristophanes, Aeschylus, Sophocles, and Euripides.

According to Aristotle, the first Greek plays were delivered entirely by a chorus, which sang or chanted their lyrics all together. There were no individual roles, nor was there any dialogue. But the plays of Thespis, a poet from the city-state of Icaria, changed the face of Greek drama forever.

Thespis lived during the sixth century B.C. An ancient chronicle lists him as the first playwright to win a prize for tragedy at the festival of Dionysius in 534 B.C. He is also said to be the first playwright who assigned specific parts to members of the chorus. He supposedly became the first actor, delivering a prologue and several monologues in his plays and exchanging dialogue with the leader of the chorus.

Nothing remains of Thespis's dramas today. The fragments of plays that have been attributed to him are most likely forgeries. Nor do we have any hard evidence on which to base the popular belief that he was the father of Greek tragedy. But the tradition was so widely accepted throughout ancient times that, to this day, an alternate name for an actor is a *thespian*, and we use the adjective *thespian* when referring to the dramatic arts.

Three Musketeers: three very close friends who are virtually inseparable

When we hear the name d'Artagnan, we immediately think of *The Three Musketeers*, the 1844 novel by Alexander Dumas the elder. What those who have not read Dumas's work are often unaware of is that d'Artagnan was not one of the original three musketeers.

The original members of the Fellowship of the Three Musketeers were Athos, Porthos, and Aramis, who, Dumas tells us, were three of the most renowned fighters of their time. The novel takes place in France in 1625, during the reign of Louis XIII. D'Artagnan is a young man from Gascony who arrives in Paris nearly penniless. He is determined to become one of the king's guards and proves himself by challenging each of the three musketeers to a duel. Impressed by his bravery, the three friends welcome him into their fellowship, becoming, in fact, the four musketeers.

The rest of the novel and Dumas's two sequels (*Twenty Years After* and *The Viscount of Bragelonne*) relate the exploits of the four friends between 1625 and 1665. *The Viscount of Bragelonne* is an extremely long work, which has often been published in several volumes. The best known of these is the *The Man in the Iron Mask*. Countless sequels to Dumas's work have been produced by other writers, and these and the original three novels have been made into many films.

Dumas's works were widely read in English translation, making the phrase *Three Musketeers* a popular way of referring to three friends who are so close they are virtually inseparable.

Dumas's four main characters were based on historical personages. Charles de Baatz d'Artagnan lived from 1623 to 1673, and Dumas based much of his fictional work on d'Artagnan's memoirs. His friends Athos, Porthos, and Aramis were also real-life figures.

(The) Three Stooges: three inept people

Slapstick comedy was the rage in the first few decades of the twentieth century. Mack Sennett and his Keystone Comedies, as well as dozens of vaudeville acts, capitalized on the American public's love of broad, physical humor. Seeing someone slip on a banana peel, fall out of a moving car, or get hit in the face with a pie was a sure-fire formula for success in the theater and on the screen.

One of the most successful of the slapstick comedy teams was that of The Three Stooges, whose films were popular from the 1930s through the 1950s and still continue to be shown on late-night television even in the 1990s.

The original Three Stooges began their career in vaudeville in the late 1920s, as part of comedian Ted Healy's act. They were Larry Fine and brothers Jerry and Moe Howard, who called themselves Larry,

Curly, and Moe on stage. They began performing alone in 1934 and the same year entered into their long association with Columbia Pictures. In the mid-1940s Curly became ill and was replaced in the act by his brother, Shemp Howard. When Shemp died in 1955, he was replaced in turn by Joe Besser.

The Three Stooges eventually made a total of 190 comedy shorts for Columbia. These were ten-to twenty-minute films that were part of most movie theaters' programs until the 1950s. By the end of the '50s, the popularity of television had forced Columbia and other film studios to cut back on production. The shorts—among them those of The Three Stooges—were first to be taken out of production. But, hoping to make a little money on the existing Three Stooges films, Columbia sold them to television. What followed amazed the studio heads, as well as the comedy trio.

The shorts were aired on television throughout America and attracted a whole new generation of fans. They became more popular than ever, and a huge market sprang up for Three Stooges memorabilia—watches, lunch boxes, comic books, coffee cups, etc. Columbia Pictures asked them to return to the studio in the 1960s to make a series of feature films.

When production began on the full-length films, another actor, Joe DeRita, took over the role of Curly from Joe Besser. The 1960s films still relied primarily on highly physical, slapstick humor, and they also reprised the earlier satire of the shorts. The Three

Stooges poked fun at everyone and everything: movies and movie stars, high society, political figures, etc.

Both the shorts and the feature films of The Three
Stooges have become so much a part of American
pop culture that we now routinely refer to any trio of
inept people as Larry, Curly, and Moe or *The Three
Stooges*.

tilt at windmills: fight imaginary foes; take
on idealistic, doomed causes

One of the most famous scenes in literature is that in
which Don Quixote attacks a group of windmills, believing them to be giants. Quixote, a middle-aged
country gentleman, has convinced himself he must
right the wrongs of the world. He got this notion from
reading so many romances of chivalry that "his brain
dried up and he lost his wits."

Mounted on a pitiful nag named Rocinante and accompanied by his "squire," a short, fat peasant
named Sancho Panza, Don Quixote declares himself
a knight errant dedicated to the service of his lady,
the beautiful Dulcinea del Toboso. In reality, Dulcinea is a young farm girl named Aldonza Lorenzo, but
in the mind of the besotted old gentleman she is every
bit as noble as Queen Guinevere.

As Don Quixote and Sancho approach a group of
thirty or forty windmills standing on a plain, Quixote
shouts:

*Look over there, friend Sancho Panza, where more
than thirty monstrous giants appear. I intend to do
battle with them and take all their lives. With their
spoils we will begin to get rich, for this is a fair war,
and it is a great service to God to wipe such a wicked
brood from the face of the earth.*

Sancho tries to reason with his lord, but Quixote
cannot be swayed from his purpose. Mounted on Rocinante, he rushes toward one of the "giants." The
wind picks up; the windmill's sails begin to turn; and
Quixote believes the giant is fighting back. "Though
you wield more arms than the giant Briareus, you
shall pay for it!" he shouts at the moving windmill.
Thrusting his lance into one of its sails, he is caught
on it. His lance is shattered, and Quixote and Rocinante are dragged across the plain.

Even after his ignominious defeat, Don Quixote refuses to believe that the windmills were anything but
giants. He is convinced that an evil enchanter named
Friston turned the giants into windmills in order to
"cheat me of the glory of conquering them."

When Cervantes's novel was translated into English, the above episode brought about the addition
of a new phrase to the English language. The verb *to
tilt* means to aim or thrust a lance while jousting or
to rush at. *To tilt at windmills* came to mean fight
imaginary foes or take on idealistic, doomed causes.
A variation of the expression is to fight with windmills.

Spanish author Miguel de Cervantes Saavedra published the first part of his masterpiece, *Don Quixote*, in 1605. It became an immediate success, and Cervantes continued working on part two until it was published in 1615. He died one year later, having completed what is often described as the first modern novel.

See also: **quixotic.**

Tobacco Road/tobacco road: a run-down, filthy place

At one time the American South was crisscrossed with paths that were made by rolling hogsheads of tobacco to market. It was on one of these long-abandoned tobacco roads, in Georgia, that Erskine Caldwell set his deeply disturbing story of poverty and hopelessness, which was published in 1932.

At the beginning of *Tobacco Road*, Caldwell describes the dwelling that is home to Jeeter Lester; his wife, Ada; his daughter, Ellie May; his son, Dude; and his aged mother.

> *The three-room house sat precariously on stacks of thin lime-rock chips that had been placed under the four corners. The stones had been laid one on top of the other, the beams spiked, and the house nailed together. . . . The centre of the building sagged between the sills; the front porch had sagged loose from the house . . . and the roof sagged in the centre. . . .*

Most of the shingles had rotted, and after every wind-
storm pieces of them were scattered in all directions
about the yard.... The house had never been
painted.

Jeeter talks about planting cotton, but he has no
money to buy seed and fertilizer, and no one will give
him credit. So the house continues to fall apart; the
yard is filled with debris; the family is hungry and in
rags. But as horrific as it is, the physical degeneration
of the Lesters is nothing compared to the state of their
morals. Caldwell's novel opens with the arrival of
Lov Bensey, the husband of the Lesters' twelve-year-
old daughter, Pearl. Bensey is carrying a sack of turnips that he bought for himself and Pearl and is
careful not to come too close to the family, lest one
of them steal the sack. He has come to ask Jeeter
Lester for advice about how to deal with Pearl, who
refuses to sleep with him—or even talk to him—and
cries all the time. He has kicked her, poured water
over her, thrown rocks and sticks at her, but she still
won't open her mouth. While Lov is talking to Jeeter
and guarding his turnips, Ellie May begins inching
toward her brother-in-law, making it apparent that she
is willing to do what Pearl will not. The two begin
copulating in the middle of the yard, and Jeeter grabs
the sack of turnips as Ellie May hangs on to Lov. Ada
and old Mother Lester brandish sticks to keep him
from getting up, as Jeeter runs into the woods with
his prize. Having eaten his fill, he gives some turnips
to his wife and children, then throws three of the
smallest to his mother.

As the novel continues, Caldwell paints an increasingly disturbing picture of the characters' inhumanity to one another. They have sunken to such a low state that they can hardly be said to belong to the human race anymore. Thus, when Mother Lester is run over by an automobile, she is left in the driveway to die. The same day that Pearl runs away from Lov, the Lesters send Ellie May to live with him, with instructions to bring them some of his food as soon as he goes to work. When the house burns down and Jeeter and Ada are killed, no one even sheds a tear. Ellie May watches in silence; Lov says Jeeter and Ada are better off dead; and Dude sifts through the rubble and thinks about planting cotton just as his father always thought about it—and never did.

Caldwell's description of life on Tobacco Road both shocked and fascinated the nation. A year after the novel was published, it was adapted for the stage by Jack Kirkland. The play was astonishingly successful, running in New York for seven and a half years. No sooner had the play closed than it was made into a film.

Between 1932 and 1941 a vast number of Americans either read *Tobacco Road* or saw it on stage or film. The story was so well known that *Tobacco Road* soon became a household word: a synonym for a filthy, run-down place where the residents were content to wallow like pigs—or like the Lesters.

(to grow like) Topsy: to flourish without any tending

One of the most memorable characters in Harriet Beecher Stowe's *Uncle Tom's Cabin* is a slave girl, eight or nine years of age, named Topsy. Topsy is purchased by Augustine St. Clare from a drunken, abusive couple who run a restaurant in New Orleans. St. Clare brings her home and asks his cousin to "give her a good orthodox New England bringing up, and see what it'll make of her." The sensible, pious Ophelia St. Clare takes on the challenge, but Topsy proves to be too much for even her to handle.

Miss Ophelia's first order of business is to get the child, who is dressed in filthy rags, cleaned up. She is filled with pity when she sees the welts and scars on Topsy's back. She asks the child how old she is, and is astonished to hear that Topsy has no idea. Nor does the child know where she was born or who her parents were: "Never was born . . . never had no father nor mother, nor nothin'. I was raised by a speculator, with lots of others. Old Aunt Sue used to take car on us."

One of St. Clare's other slaves explains to the woman from Vermont that it is common practice in the South for speculators to buy large numbers of Black children cheaply, when they are still infants, and raise them for the slave market. Miss Ophelia then asks Topsy if she knows who made her. Topsy doesn't have to think about her answer: "Nobody as I knows on," said the child, with a short laugh. The idea appeared to amuse her considerably; for her eyes twinkled, and she added, "I spect I growed. Don't think nobody never made me."

It was from this short scene that we got the expression *to grow like Topsy,* meaning to grow without being tended. However, Harriet Beecher Stowe would probably take exception to our adaptation of her phrase, which now carries the implication that someone or something that grows like Topsy flourishes without receiving any care.

Mrs. Stowe makes it plain that the little slave girl called Topsy may have survived her inhumane upbringing and learned to cope with the brutality around her, but neither Stowe nor anyone who believes that all men are born to be free would ever call that flourishing.

Trilby: a person who is easily controlled; a soft felt hat

It is said that a strong-willed person cannot be hypnotized. Conversely, someone who is open to suggestion and easily swayed by others is an ideal subject for a hypnotist. In his 1894 novel, *Trilby*, George du Maurier says of the title character: "She had a singularly impressionable nature, as was shown by her quick and ready susceptibility to Svengali's hypnotic influence."

Trilby O'Ferrall, a young artists' model, is so completely influenced by Svengali that he is able to make her a world-famous singer, despite the fact that she is completely tone deaf:

> *He had but to say "Dors!" and she suddenly became an unconscious Trilby of marble, who could produce wonderful sounds—just the sounds he wanted, and nothing else. . . . When Svengali's Trilby was singing . . . our Trilby had ceased to exist . . . our Trilby was fast asleep . . . in fact, our Trilby was dead. . . .*

Svengali, through hypnosis, is able to possess Trilby body and soul. Her life becomes so inextricably bound up with his that, when he suffers a fatal heart attack, not only does she lose her voice, but before long she follows him to the grave.

Trilby's complete loss of self made such an impression on du Maurier's readers and on theatergoers who saw the 1895 stage version of his novel that her name soon became a synonym for a person who is easily controlled.

Another meaning of the word *Trilby* comes from the above-mentioned stage play. Although no such headgear appears in du Maurier's narrative or illustrations, on the stage his heroine wore a soft felt hat with an indented crown, which was as malleable as she. The style became popular in England and such a hat is still called a *Trilby*.

See also: **Svengali.**

trip the light fantastic: dance

. . . me and Mamie O'Rourke
Tripped the light fantastic
On the sidewalks of New York.

Most of us are familiar with the expression *trip the light fantastic* from the above lyrics. They come from the popular song "The Sidewalks of New York" (also known as "East Side, West Side"), which was written in 1894. By that time, *trip the light fantastic* was a well-known expression meaning to dance—an expression that, believe it or not, was coined by English author John Milton.

Milton is best known for his 1667 masterpiece, *Paradise Lost*, and its 1671 sequel, *Paradise Regained*. He wrote many other dramatic poems on religious themes, such as *Samson Agonistes*, and a multitude of shorter poems in English and Latin.

One of his earliest poems was written in 1631 or 1632, during a two-year tour of Europe that followed his formal education. Its title—"L'Allegro"—means the cheerful or merry one, and it is a light, happy piece that bears little resemblance to Milton's later work. It is a celebration of youth, of joy, of song and dance:

Haste thee, Nymph, and bring with thee
Jest and youthful Jollity . . .
Sport that wrinkled care derides,

And laughter holding both his sides.
Come, and trip it as ye go
On the light fantastic toe.

Trojan horse: someone or something that subverts from within (a fifth column); a deceptive scheme

The story of the Trojan horse was told by Virgil in his *Aeneid*, which was left unfinished when the poet died in 19 B.C.

After laying siege to the city of Troy for ten long years, the Greek forces were on the point of packing up and sailing away when Odysseus devised a plan to end the war. First he stole Troy's Palladium—the sacred image of Athena that protected the city. Then he enlisted the aid of the goddess, who showed the Greek craftsmen how to construct a huge wooden horse with a hollow belly.

A number of armed Greeks hid inside the horse, and the rest of the Greek forces sailed off. When they saw their enemies in apparent retreat and found the horse in the deserted Greek camp, the Trojans were perplexed, to say the least. King Priam and others wanted to bring the wooden horse into the city, believing it to be sacred to Athena. The prophetess Cassandra and the Trojan priest Laocoön tried to dissuade their countrymen, but were ignored.

The Trojans rolled the horse into their citadel and

began celebrating the end of the war. Later, as they slept soundly in their beds, the armed warriors crept out of the horse's belly. A signal was given to the Greek ships that had been waiting, out of sight, off-shore, and the Greek forces returned. The infiltrators opened Troy's gates to let them in, and by morning Troy lay in ruins, its men dead, its women enslaved.

The Trojan horse has become a popular metaphor for a fifth column: infiltrators who subvert from within. The term is also applied, in a broader sense, to any scheme that is designed to deceive and mislead.

See also: **beware of Greeks bearing gifts.**

Tweedledum and Tweedledee: two nearly identical people

Two of the most memorable characters in Lewis Carroll's *Through the Looking-Glass* are Tweedledum and Tweedledee. They are so closely associated in our minds with Carroll's 1872 sequel to *Alice's Adventures in Wonderland*, and with Sir John Tenniel's illustrations, that it is almost impossible to believe they had existed—albeit in name only—for over one hundred years before Carroll wrote his famous children's stories.

The names Tweedledum and Tweedledee were, in fact, created by John Byrom, an English satirist who lived from 1692 to 1763. In his satiric poem "Feud between Handel and Bononcini,'' Byrom makes light of the ongoing quarrel between two schools of musicians, whose differences were really very slight:

> *Some say compared to Bononcini*
> *That mynheer Handel's but a ninny;*
> *Others aver that he to Handel*
> *Is scarcely fit to hold a candle.*
> *Strange all this difference should be*
> *'Twixt Tweedledum and Tweedledee.*

Given his propensity for silly-sounding names, it is not surprising that Lewis Carroll found inspiration in Byrom's poem. Using his particular genius for inventing nonsensical characters, he took the two most important traits of Byrom's musicians—their argumentative nature and the fact that they were almost indistinguishable from one another—and created a set of identical twins that share the same opinions yet quarrel constantly.

Alice meets the roly-poly pair while trying to find a way out of the woods. Tweedledum's favorite word is ''Nohow!'' and his brother responds to just about everything with ''Contrariwise!'' One minute the two are hugging each other and the next they are putting on makeshift armor and preparing for a duel because Tweedledee broke Tweedledum's rattle. Fortunately, a large crow flies overhead, frightening the twins away and postponing their battle.

Calling two people *Tweedledum and Tweedledee* is now a common way of saying they are nearly identical, either in looks or in opinions. How amazed John Byrom would be if he knew that, thanks to Lewis Carroll, two hundred years after he wrote his poem the names of his musicians have become household words!

Twilight Zone: a situation or state of mind in which everything seems somewhat strange

From 1959 to 1963 American television viewers could tune in each week to a program that specialized in the depiction of strange, otherworldly events. It was called the *Twilight Zone*, and its creator was writer and producer Rod Serling.

Serling wrote many of the scripts himself, and they dealt with such extraordinary things as time travel, visitors from outer space, and communication between the living and the dead. Serling's narration at the beginning and end of each tale emphasized the fact that just about anything can happen in the strange dimension called the Twilight Zone.

As a result, when things just don't seem to make sense or follow the rules as we know them, we are apt to make reference to Serling's show. People frequently say, ''I'm in the Twilight Zone,'' to indicate that they are perplexed by what is going on around them. Not only has the name of the program become synonymous with the strange and unexpected, but the program's eerie theme music is so well known that all one has to do is sing "doo-doo-doo-doo-doo-doo-doo-doo" and the allusion is understood.

Since the end of its first run in 1963, the series has continued in syndication. An archive at Ithaca College now houses films and scripts of Serling's television shows and movies, as well as other memorabilia. The college, where Serling once taught, even offers a course on his work. Rod Serling died in 1975, but after his death his widow found a screenplay and a story outline among his papers. The outline was turned into a script by another *Twilight Zone* writer, Richard Matheson, and both stories aired on television during 1994.

Type A/Type B: two contrasting personality types: the first is aggressive, competitive, and highly driven; the second is easygoing and relaxed

Who would think that a book in which two doctors published their research findings would become a best-seller and make a lasting contribution to the English language? That is just what happened when cardiologists Meyer Friedman and Roy Rosenman published *Type A Behavior and Your Heart* in 1972.

Based on their study of the character traits and temperaments of their patients, Doctors Friedman and Rosenman came to a surprising conclusion: Of the many factors that contribute to heart disease, the most

critical is a Type A personality. Their studies indicated that many individuals who were not overweight,
did not smoke, exercised regularly, had safe choles-
terol levels, and had no family history of heart trouble
still had heart attacks. The one thing these Type A
personality types—the majority of whom were men—
had in common was a competitive, aggressive nature.
They were driven individuals who became angry easily, had little patience, and suffered from *hurry sickness:* the need to rush through whatever they were
doing so they could get on to the next task. Waiting
in line at the supermarket or having to sit in a traffic
jam caused these people to suffer extreme stress. So,
too, did other people's mistakes or incompetence.

On the other hand, Friedman and Rosenman had
seen many overweight individuals who smoked,
rarely or never exercised, and had both high choles-
terol and a family history of heart disease. Yet they
had healthy hearts. Why? Because, according to the
doctors, they were Type Bs: individuals who were
laid back, patient, and noncompetitive. If they played
a game, it was for the fun of it, not to win. If they
were stuck in a traffic jam, they turned on the car
radio and sang along with the music. If they couldn't
finish a task in one day, they were entirely comfortable putting it away and taking it up again the next
day.

Type A and *Type B* have become common short-
hand terms for referring to people with one or the
other of these sets of traits. Since the publication of
Type A Behavior and Your Heart, many other studies

on the causes of heart disease have been released. None, however, has had the impact of that of Friedman and Rosenman, nor have any of the others left their mark on the English language.

ugly American: an ethnocentric American who treats those of other cultures as his inferiors

The term *ugly American* is used to describe a U.S. citizen who, while traveling abroad, shows a total disregard for the people and culture of other countries. *Ugly Americanism* is the boorish, arrogant, "We're better than you" attitude that Americans show when they insist on speaking English, refuse to eat native food, make fun of national costumes and customs, and compare everything to what they have back home.

This type of behavior was the subject of the bestselling novel, *The Ugly American*, by William J. Lederer and Eugene Burdick. Published in 1958, *The Ugly American* is a series of vignettes that deal with the actions and attitudes of Americans working and living in Southeast Asia. In the book's epilogue, the authors stress the fact that all of the characters in the novel are based on actual people that they knew in Southeast Asia.

Among these characters is Ambassador Sears, a man who got his job as a political favor and who had never heard of the country to which he was being posted. He knows nothing about the history, culture, or language of Sarkhan (a fictional country) and has no intention of learning about it. Then there is Joe Bing, a public information officer who tells potential recruits for the foreign service, "You'll have to work among foreigners, but we don't expect you to love 'em . . . I don't care where you go to work for Uncle Sammy, you'll be living with a gang of clean-cut Americans." Another ethnocentric boor is George Swift, a deputy chief of mission in Sarkhan who manages to insult the country's prince by neglecting to telephone him on an important matter, going out to buy liquor for an embassy reception instead.

Ironically, the character that the authors refer to as "the ugly American" is one of the few who doesn't treat the inhabitants of Southeast Asia with disdain. A retired engineer, Homer Atkins is a big, ugly man. But he is decent, honest, and wants only to help the Asians by introducing technology that will make their lives easier. His first attempt to do this, in Vietnam, is thwarted by a group of French, American, and Vietnamese bureaucrats. Atkins's commonsense proposals are anathema to them because they interfere with the political and financial arrangements that their various governments have agreed on.

Fortunately, Atkins is sent to Sarkhan, where he

and his wife quickly make friends by treating the natives as equals and learning their language. Unlike the Americans who are ugly in the figurative sense, Atkins does not try to cheat the Sarkhanese. He enlists the aid of an ugly Sarkhanese mechanic who helps him design a water pump to irrigate the crops growing on hillsides. Unlike the projects proposed by the bureaucrats, their invention is a huge success because it is simple and cheap and fills a need. The ugly American and the ugly Sarkhanese become partners in a pump factory, and the entire village benefits as a result.

ugly duckling: an ugly person, particularly a child; someone or something that initially seems homely or unpromising, then unexpectedly blossoms

Hans Christian Andersen was born in the slums of Odense, on the Danish island of Fyn. His father was a shoemaker, and his mother was an illiterate, superstitious woman. His grandfather was insane, and his grandmother was a pathological liar. He was a shy, lonely child who was happiest when playing alone. After his father died and his mother remarried, he was apprenticed in various trades, but he wasn't particularly good at any of them and was often the butt of the other apprentices' jokes.

In 1819, at the age of fourteen, Hans Andersen set

off for Copenhagen. His dream was to become famous in the theater, either as a performer or a playwright. He tried singing, but his voice changed and he was fired. The plays he wrote were rejected one after another. Finally, Jonas Collin, one of the directors of the Royal Theater, raised money to send the boy to school. Unfortunately, the headmaster of the school was a cruel man who constantly made jokes at Andersen's expense and made his life utterly miserable.

Andersen escaped into writing. His first major book was published in 1829, the same year that his first play was performed at the Royal Theater. From then until 1835, Andersen produced a variety of literary works, including travel sketches, poems, librettos, and plays. His most successful novel, *Improvisatoren*, was published in Denmark in 1835. Its translation into English and German ten years later marked the beginning of Andersen's international fame. Andersen continued writing novels and autobiographies until shortly before his death, but by then he had become famous for a completely different genre: children's stories.

Between 1835 and 1872 Hans Christian Andersen wrote 168 stories for children. Many of them have become classics, an unforgettable part of our childhood. "The Princess and the Pea," "The Little Mermaid," "The Tinderbox," "The Fir Tree," "The Snow Queen," and others are all about timeless human experiences and feelings. They deal with love and its loss, the search for happiness, the need to be accepted. Some, like "The Emperor's New Clothes," are satirical in nature.

But the tale into which Hans Christian Andersen put his whole heart and soul, and his own story, is that of "The Ugly Duckling." Who but a shy boy from the slums, an outcast among his peers, a clumsy fellow who was mocked by the other apprentices, could understand the feelings of a baby swan growing up surrounded by ducks? Gawky, awkward, bigger than all the others and lacking their soft down, the duckling that was hatched in the wrong nest endured the jokes and taunts of everyone—until he turned into a graceful swan. He is now the linguistic symbol of someone who begins life showing little promise, then blossoms into a real beauty or success.

During his first visit to England in 1847, Andersen was feted by many members of society and lionized by the most celebrated writers of the time. He spent five weeks at the home of Charles Dickens, where he was treated with great deference. In Denmark he was often a guest of the nobility. He courted many women, including the famous Swedish singer, Jenny Lind. The *ugly duckling* had truly become a swan.

See also: **emperor's new clothes.**

Uncle Tom: a Black person who is subservient to whites

A recent newspaper headline quoted U.S. Supreme Court Justice Clarence Thomas as saying, "I am not

an Uncle Tom.'' The denial was made in response to
questions from a group of Black journalists and other
African Americans, many of whom were angered by
Thomas's conservative views on such issues as affir-
mative action. By calling Thomas an *Uncle Tom*, or
accusing him of *Uncle Tomism*, they were voicing
their belief that he had sold out to the White estab-
lishment.

When she wrote *Uncle Tom's Cabin* in 1851 and
1852, Harriet Beecher Stowe couldn't possibly have
imagined how controversial her title character was to
become. She believed she was creating, in Uncle
Tom, the portrait of a brave, stoical man who was,
above all else, a good Christian. Like Jesus, he turned
the other cheek and forgave his persecutors, a true
martyr to his faith:

> . . . to live,—to wear on, day after day, of mean, bit-
> ter, low, harassing servitude . . . this long and wast-
> ing heart-martyrdom, this slow, daily bleeding away
> of the inward life, drop by drop, hour after hour,—
> this is the true searching test of what there may be
> in man or woman. When Tom stood face to face with
> his persecutor, and heard his threats, and thought in
> his very soul that his hour was come, his heart
> swelled bravely in him, and he thought he could bear
> torture and fire, bear anything with the vision of Je-
> sus and heaven just a step beyond. . . .

Tom is a slave from Kentucky who is forced to
leave his wife and children behind when he is sold.

He is bought by Augustine St. Clare, who brings him
to his home in Louisiana and treats him like one of
his own family. Tom is particularly attached to St.
Clare's daughter, Little Eva. After both Eva and her
father die, Tom is sold once again—this time to a
brutal master named Simon Legree. Legree hates Tom
from the start, a fact that Stowe explains as "the native antipathy of bad to good." Tom is made to endure constant humiliation and physical abuse at the
hands of Legree and his Black henchmen. Eventually,
when Tom refuses to reveal the whereabouts of two
female slaves who have run away, he is beaten so
severely that he dies.

Uncle Tom's Cabin was first published, in install-
ments, in the abolitionist journal the *National Era*.
Within one year after the work was published in book
form, it had sold over three-hundred thousand copies.
It was immediately adapted for the stage, and many
versions of the story (called Tom plays) were performed, the most successful being that of George L.
Aiken. The book was translated into several foreign
languages, as well, and was hailed around the world
as a chilling condemnation of slavery.

There is no doubt that *Uncle Tom's Cabin* was a
major force in galvanizing antislavery factions in the
North, and, as a result, was one of the catalysts that
began the Civil War. It is impossible to pinpoint ex-
actly when American Blacks began to view Uncle
Tom as a traitor to his race, but as early as 1885 the
Black poet Albery A. Whitman wrote, "All 'Uncle
Toms' and 'Topsies' ought to die. *Goody goodness* is

a sort of man worship: ignorance is its inspiration, fear its ministering spirit, and beggary its inheritance.'' In recent years James Baldwin published an essay entitled ''Everybody's Protest Novel,'' which condemned *Uncle Tom's Cabin* as ''a very bad novel ... [a work of] self-righteous, virtuous sentimentality.''

See also: **Simon Legree, (grow like) Topsy.**

Uriah Heep: someone who is insincerely humble and self-effacing

To many people, there is nothing more intolerable than a hypocrite. They can forgive many unpleasant character traits, as long as a person owns up to them. But it is hard to stand a person who constantly claims to be something he or she is not. Those are the sentiments that are inspired in the reader of Charles Dickens's classic novel, *David Copperfield*, when Uriah Heep is introduced.

Heep is an example of ''ambition and malice cloaked in false humility.'' He is very fond of telling others how '' 'umble'' he is, when he is anything but. Constantly scheming and thinking up ways to advance himself at the expense of others, Heep blackmails his employer, the kindly Mr. Wickfield. Fortunately, Wilkins Micawber discovers Heep's villainy and unmasks him in front of the world.

As repulsive as he is, Uriah Heep is an unforgettable character. Since the publication of *David Copperfield* in 1850, the name of Dickens's villain has come to be synonymous with insincerity and hypocrisy. When we call someone a *Uriah Heep*, we are saying, in no uncertain terms, that he or she wears an outward facade of humility and virtue to cover up an inner self that is corrupt and conniving.

See also: **micawberesque.**

Utopia/utopia: a perfect place

The word *Utopia* comes from the Greek *ou,* meaning *not* and *topos,* meaning *place.* Utopia is, therefore, no place—or at least no place on Earth.

But a place called Utopia existed in the mind of Sir Thomas More, and he described it in his 1516 work of the same name. Book I of *Utopia* describes the injustice and irrationality of English society in the sixteenth century. Book II shows how these ills have been remedied on a mythical island that More refers to as Utopia. There is no poverty, crime, or injustice in this perfect society. Why? Because Utopia is run according to the ideals of the English humanists, who extolled the power of reason over all else. More says that the Utopians:

> . . . *define virtue . . . [as] living according to Nature, and think that we are made by God for that end; they believe that a man then follows Nature when he pur-*

> *sues or avoids things according to the direction of reason. . . . Reason directs us to keep our minds as free from passion and as cheerful as we can, and that we should consider ourselves bound by the ties of good-nature and humanity to use our utmost endeavors to help forward the happiness of all other persons. . . .*

More's *Utopia* was written in Latin in 1516 and first translated into English in 1551. The generic term *utopia* has since been applied to all such idealized societies, including the one that was described in Plato's *Republic* in the fourth century B.C.

Other famous fictional utopias are described in Cicero's *De Republica*, St. Augustine's *De Civitate Dei*, Dante's *De Monarchia*, Sir Francis Bacon's *New Atlantis*, Friar Campabella's *Civitas Solis*, Samuel Butler's *Erewhon*, Edward Bellamy's *Looking Backward*, and several works of H. G. Wells, including *In the Days of the Comet, The World Set Free*, and *A Modern Utopia*.

There have also been many attempts by idealistic people to create actual utopias: communities where everyone would live and work in complete harmony, subjugating their own desires for the greater good. America alone saw the birth and death of more than 130 such settlements from the mid-seventeenth to the mid-nineteenth century. Among the longest-lived American utopias was Ephrata, which existed in Pennsylvania from 1732 to 1905. Also, several settlements were started by ''Father'' George Rapp and his followers, including: Harmony, in Indiana, which was founded in 1815 and sold ten years later to Robert Owen, whose secular-socialist community, New Harmony, only lasted two years; the Amana society, which lasted from 1714 until the 1930s, and whose name was taken over by some of its members when they opened an appliance company; and those of the Shakers, whose belief in celibacy caused them to die out. Two others were John Humphrey Noyes's Oneida Community and Charles Fourier's disciples' Brook Farm.

All these failed attempts to establish heaven on earth have caused the noun *utopia* and the adjective *utopian* to be applied to enterprises that are too idealistic ever to be successful. The fact that a perfect society has eluded human beings throughout history leads one to think that More's choice of a name for his ideal country was truly prophetic. Utopia, it seems, has never been any place and most likely will always remain no place.

Vanessa: a feminine name

In English, our names for females have come from many sources. Some, such as Rose and Iris, are the names of flowers. Others, including Ruby and Pearl, have been taken from gems. The months have also given us feminine names: April, May, and June. Some names, such as Helen and Diana, can be traced back to antiquity. But two English names share a unique origin: They were created by authors.

The name *Vanessa* did not exist until it was coined by Dean Jonathan Swift. For many years the English satirist and author of *Gulliver's Travels* corresponded with Esther Vanhomrigh, a good friend and quite possibly the love of his life. The pet name by which he addressed her in his letters was made up of the first syllable of her last name (Van) and a popular nickname for Esther (Essa). The new name, Vanessa, first became popular in England and is now a frequent choice of American parents for their female children. (Fortunately, the name with which Swift signed his letters never caught on for male children: He called himself Cadenus, an anagram of the Latin *Decanus,* which means *Dean.*)

Another name that was invented by an English author is Wendy. We do not know how he came up with it, only that J. M. Barrie coined it, in 1904, for the female lead in his play, *Peter Pan.* In the play, a little house is constructed for Wendy. With the great success of Barrie's work, many baby girls began to be named Wendy, and playhouses large enough for children to fit inside have since been referred to as Wendy houses. (British schoolchildren also use the name Wendy as a synonym for a sissy, but that use has not caught on in the U.S.)

Vanity Fair: the material world

The Pilgrim's Progress from This World to That Which Is to Come is an allegorical tale of man's search for salvation. It was written by John Bunyan in 1675 and published in 1678.

During his journey to the Celestial City (i.e., heaven), Christian, the hero of the tale, passes through several imaginary realms. All of these are symbolic of the obstacles that stand in the way of man's salvation, and they bear names such as the City of Destruction, the Slough of Despond, the Hill Difficulty, the House Beautiful, the Delectable Mountains, the Valley of Humiliation, Vanity Fair, the Doubting Castle, and the Enchanted Ground.

On the road Christian meets a fellow traveler named Faithful, and the two pilgrims continue their journey together. As they approach a town called Vanity, Evangelist appears and tells them that in the town they will be beset by enemies and one of them will be killed. He will be the fortunate one, because he will go directly to the Celestial City, while the surviving pilgrim will have to complete the treacherous journey alone.

At the town there is a fair that is open all year long. It is called Vanity Fair because all that is sold there is vanity. The fair was set up thousands of years before by Beelzebub, Apollyon, and Legion, and "at this fair are all such merchandise sold as houses, lands, trades, places, honours, preferments, titles, countries, kingdoms, lusts, pleasures; and delights of all sorts, as whores, bawds, wives, husbands, children, masters, servants, lives, blood, bodies, souls, silver, gold, pearls, precious stones, and what not."

Evangelist's prediction soon comes true, when Christian and Faithful refuse to purchase anything at the fair: ". . . they would put their fingers in their ears, and cry, 'Turn away mine eyes from beholding vanity,' and look upwards, signifying that their trade and traffic was in heaven." As a result, a disturbance breaks out and the pilgrims are arrested and tried. The judge is named Lord Hate-good, and the jury is made up of citizens of Vanity who bear such names as Mr.

Blindman, Mr. No-good, Mr. Malice, Mr. Liar, Mr. Cruelty, etc. Faithful makes the mistake of trying to defend his actions, and he is condemned to death. Faithful dies a horrible death: ". . . first they scourged him, then they buffeted him, then they lanced his flesh with knives; after that they stoned him with stones; then pricked him with their swords; and last of all they burned him to ashes at the stake." Faithful is taken up through the clouds to heaven, and eventually Christian escapes and continues on his way alone.

Since the publication of Bunyan's work, the term *Vanity Fair* has been used as a synonym for the material world and all the things that distract us on our quest for spirituality.

See also: **pilgrim's progress, slough of despond.**

(a) Walter Mitty: a quiet, retiring person who has a vivid fantasy life

A quiet, retiring person who takes refuge from the real world in fantasy is frequently called a *Walter Mitty* or said to be *Mittyish*. Such an individual's elaborate fantasies, in which he or she leads an exciting, often dangerous life, are described as *Mittyesque*. All these English words come from the name of James Thurber's fictional fantasizer, Walter Mitty.

Mitty is a henpecked husband who works as a magazine proofreader. He is shy and passive, the kind of person who never says "boo"—at least in his conscious moments. But day after day, as he sits proofreading sensational stories, he weaves extravagant fantasies in his mind. In all of these daydreams he is the hero: a daring sea captain, a pilot, an outlaw in the Old West, etc. A typical daydream has him fearlessly going to his death:

Then, with that faint fleeting smile playing about his lips, he faced the firing squad; erect and motionless, proud and disdainful, Walter Mitty, the undefeated, inscrutable to the last.

"The Secret Life of Walter Mitty" is perhaps the best-known of Thurber's many comic writings. First published in *The New Yorker* magazine in 1939, it was collected in the book, *My World—and Welcome to It* in 1942. The story was made into a film in 1947, with comic genius Danny Kaye playing the role of the chronic daydreamer.

Watson: *See* **Sherlock Holmes.**

wellerism/Wellerism: an expression of comparison made up of a well-known quotation followed by a facetious sequel

When Samuel Pickwick meets up with Sam Weller in Charles Dickens's *The Posthumous Papers of the Pickwick Club*, the latter is a bootblack at the White Hart Inn in London. He has a habit of peppering his speech with familiar sayings, onto which he tags facetious remarks. Perhaps the best-known of these sayings, which have come to be called *wellerisms*, is

" 'Everyone to his own taste,' said the old woman, as she kissed the cow."

Some of the others used by Sam in *The Pickwick Papers* are:

—*"What the devil do you want with me?"* as the man said when he saw the ghost.
—*"Out with it,"* as the father said to the child when he swallowed a farthing.
—*"There's nothing so refreshing as sleep,"* as the servant-girl said before she drank the egg-cupful of laudanum.

During their visit to the White Hart, Pickwick is so impressed with Sam's intelligence and personality that he asks him to act as his valet while he travels around England with three other members of the Pickwick Club. Sam is delighted at the prospect and, after being outfitted at Pickwick's expense, muses on his future:

I wonder whether I'm meant to be a footman, or a groom, or a gamekeeper, or a seedsman. I look like a sort of compo of every one on 'em. Never mind; there's change of air, plenty to see, and little to do; and all this suits my complaint uncommon; so long life to the Pickvicks, says I!

Wendy: *See* **Vanessa.**

(the) world is my oyster: endless opportunities are available to me

When someone says, *The world is my oyster*, that person is borrowing a metaphor from Shakespeare to boast about his or her chances for success. Just as an oyster can bring great riches if one finds a pearl inside it, there are endless opportunities in the world if one is talented, daring, or lucky enough to find and take advantage of them. The first fictional character who said, "The world's mine oyster," was neither talented nor lucky, but he was daring—and dishonest.

The main character in William Shakespeare's *The Merry Wives of Windsor* is Sir John Falstaff. The play, written in 1597, revolves around Falstaff's attempts to ingratiate himself with two married women in hopes of gaining access to their husbands' fortunes. When he arrives in Windsor, he is accompanied by several hangers-on who are as indigent and immoral as he. One of them, a loud braggart named Pistol, has a falling-out with Falstaff and leaves his service but returns later, asking to borrow some money.

When Falstaff says he will not lend him a penny, Pistol boasts, "Why, then the world's mine oyster, Which I with sword will open." In other words, he'll take what he wants, whenever he wants it, by force.

Shakespeare's metaphor has come down to us in slightly different form, the word *mine* having been replaced by *my,* but its meaning remains unchanged. And, while most of those who use it today do not have the same dishonorable intentions as Pistol, they do have their boastfulness in common with him.

(the) wreck of the Hesperus: a real mess

During the cold and stormy winter of 1838–1839, poet Henry Wadsworth Longfellow was living in Cambridge, Massachusetts, and teaching at Harvard. His journal for December 1838 includes the following entry:

> *News of shipwrecks horrible on the coast. Twenty bodies washed ashore at Gloucester, one lashed to a piece of wreck. There is a reef called Norman's Woe where many of these took place; among others the schooner Hesperus . . . I must write a ballad upon this . . .*

And that is exactly what Longfellow did, one year later. His diary for December 30, 1839, reads as follows:

> *. . . last evening . . . I sat till twelve o'clock by my fire, smoking, when suddenly it came into my mind to write The Ballad of the Schooner Hesperus; which I*

accordingly did. Then I went to bed, but could not
sleep. New thoughts were running in my mind, and I
got up to add them to the ballad. It was three by the
clock. I then went to bed and fell asleep. I feel
pleased with the ballad. It hardly cost me an effort.
It did not come into my mind by lines, but by stanzas.

The first stanza of Longfellow's haunting ballad
tells us, "It was the schooner Hesperus, / That sailed
the wintry sea; / And the skipper had taken his little
daughter, / To bear him company." The stanzas that
follow recount the beauty of the little girl and the
warning given to the skipper by an old sailor who
feared the weather was about to turn. The skipper
refused to listen to the sailor's warning, "And a
scornful laugh laughed he." But the skipper didn't
laugh for long; a nor'easter blew up, snow began to
fly, and the ship was buffeted by high winds and
rough seas. The skipper lashed his daughter to the
mast. He then tied himself to the helm, where he soon
froze to death. As the little girl prayed that she might
be saved, the ship rushed headlong toward the reef
called Norman's Woe. It smashed against the rocks;
the crew was swept "like icicles from her deck."

The horrific images of the poem's final stanzas
have been indelibly imprinted on the minds of generations of readers:

At daybreak, on the bleak sea-beach,
A fisherman stood aghast,

To see the form of a maiden fair,
Lashed close to a drifting mast.

The salt sea was frozen on her breast,
The salt tears in her eyes;
And he saw her hair, like the brown seaweed,
On the billows fall and rise.

Shortly after he wrote the ballad, Longfellow received a request for a poem from Parke Benjamin, editor of *The New World*. He sent "The Wreck of the Hesperus" to the newspaper and, after reading it, Benjamin replied: "Your ballad of the Wreck is grand. Enclosed a check for $25. The sum you mentioned for it. . . ."

In 1841, "The Wreck of the Hesperus" was republished in *Ballads and Other Poems*. Although Longfellow had enjoyed considerable literary success prior to this, his fame now swept the nation. He continued to write short poems for the next decade, but his longer works were written after he retired from teaching in 1854. *Evangeline, The Song of Hiawatha*, and *The Courtship of Miles Standish* are the full-length ballads for which he is best remembered. In 1863 he published *Tales of a Wayside Inn*. The first poem in that collection, "Paul Revere's Ride," soon became a national favorite.

During his lifetime Longfellow was the most popular poet in America. Hiawatha, Paul Revere, Evangeline, and the others may have been dead for decades or centuries, but they came back to life in Longfellow's poems. Entire families sat together in the evening, enthralled by these emotional tales, as Mother or Father read them aloud.

After Longfellow's death in 1882, it became fashionable in literary circles to denigrate his work. Critics lambasted his unrestrained romanticism and heavy-handed didacticism. But the snobbishness of the intelligentsia had little or no effect on the average American's admiration of Longfellow. Generations of American schoolchildren learned to recite "Under a spreading chestnut-tree / The village smithy stands. . . ."; "By the shores of Gitche-Goomee . . ."; and "This is the forest primeval. . . ."

When I was growing up in the 1950s, my mother never said the house was a mess: She always told us that it looked like *the wreck of the Hesperus*. We never knew where the saying came from, but we knew exactly what it meant—and we wasted no time getting things cleaned up.

yahoo: ruffian, uncouth person

In the course of his adventures, Lemuel Gulliver, the hero of *Gulliver's Travels*, arrives in the land of the Houyhnhnms. There he spies a band of strange animals, some standing in a field, some sitting in trees. "Their heads and breasts were covered with a thick hair, some frizzled and others lank; they had beards like goats, and a long ridge of hair down their backs and the fore-parts of their legs and feet; but the rest of their bodies were bare, so that I might see their skins, which were of a brown buff colour. They had no tails, nor any hair at all on their buttocks, except about the anus. . . . The hair of both sexes was of several colours, brown, red, black, and yellow. Upon the whole, I never beheld in all my travels so disagreeable an animal, or one against which I naturally conceived so strong an antipathy." Given Gulliver's reaction to these beasts, it is no wonder he is shocked and dismayed when he is taken for one of them by the Houyhnhnms.

The Houyhnhnms look just like horses but are, in fact, the rulers of this strange land. They are wise, gentle, and peace loving and have developed a society where reason rules. They speak a language similar to High Dutch or German. Gulliver learns from them that the beasts are called yahoos, and they are used by the Houyhnhnms as slaves and beasts of burden, much as humans use horses in our culture.

Gulliver is even more upset when he sees a yahoo up close: "My horror and astonishment are not to be described, when I observed in this abominable animal a perfect human figure . . . the same in every part of our bodies, except as to hairiness and color."

During Gulliver's stay in the land of Houyhnhnms he comes to identify with the yahoos more and more and to develop a deep sense of inferiority to the Houyhnhnms. The latter, although impressed by Gulliver's "teachableness, civility, and cleanliness," which they have never seen in a yahoo, still consider him to be one of the beasts. They explain to Gulliver that the yahoos are the most unteachable of beasts, that they are dirty, fight constantly among themselves, are greedy, and are given to drunkenness. In short, they possess all the worst traits of human beings.

After three years in the land of the Houyhnhnms, Gulliver is told that he must leave, and he is so upset that he falls into a faint. When he awakens he realizes that he no longer identifies with the human race: "When I thought of my family, my friends, my countrymen, or human race in general, I considered them as they really were, Yahoos in shape and disposition, perhaps a little more civilized, and qualified with the gift of speech, but making no other use of reason than to improve and multiply those vices whereof their brethren in this country had only the share that nature allotted them.''

Gulliver leaves the island with a heavy heart and returns to England a changed man. At the end of *Gulliver's Travels* he declares that after five years back home he has still not become accustomed to living among ''Yahoo-kind.'' He spends the majority of his time in his stable with the two horses he purchased upon his return.

Gulliver's Travels was written by Jonathan Swift in 1726 and has become a classic example of satire. Its popularity is attested to by the fact that several of the words Swift coined in the book have entered the English language. One of these is the word *yahoo,* which has come to mean a ruffian or an uncouth person, someone who is more beast than man.

See also: **lilliputian, brobdingnagian.**

yellow journalism/the Yellow Press: sensationalism in newspapers

With the invention of photoengraving in 1873, inexpensive newspaper illustration was made possible for the first time. American newspapers were soon engaged in a battle to see who could publish the most pictorial features and illustrations and, as a result, attain the highest circulation. They began sponsoring transatlantic races and expeditions all over the world, at the same time competing for reporters and artists to record these extraordinary events in words and pictures.

Two of the giants in the world of publishing were Wiliam Randolph Hearst and Joseph Pulitzer. On September 25, 1895, Hearst purchased the *New York Morning Journal*. The following year he announced the debut of a comic supplement to the newspaper. According to Hearst, the *American Humorist* was to be "eight pages of polychromatic effulgence that make the rainbow look like a lead pipe."

The centerpiece of the supplement was to be a new comic strip called *The Yellow Kid*. The strip would be drawn by Richard Felton Outcault, whom Hearst had lured away from Pulitzer's *New York World*. While working at the *World*, Outcault had created a strip called *Hogan's Alley*. Its protagonist was a worldly-wise street urchin called the Yellow Kid. (The Kid, who began life wearing a white nightgownlike garment, supposedly got his name when the foreman of the paper's color press room was looking for an area on which to test his tallow-drying process. He chose the Kid's white garment for his experiment, and from then on the nightgown was colored yellow in every edition.)

Hearst's raid on Pulitzer's personnel was the beginning of an intensive, often ruthless competition between the two men. Pulitzer hired another artist, George Luks, to create his own *Yellow Kid* strip for the *World*. The battle then escalated, with each newspaper trying to outdo the other's scare headlines, sensational articles, lavish illustrations, and, of course, comic features.

Disgusted by the tactics to which both sides stooped, a minority of responsible publishers and readers began calling this sensationalism of the news in order to sell papers *yellow journalism*, and its practitioners *the Yellow Press*. But the majority of the nation remained under the sway of the Yellow Press, as was demonstrated by the popular reaction to articles on the subject of Cuba's struggle for independence from Spain.

When the Cubans rebelled in 1895, Spain sent in troops under Captain General Valeriano Weyler y Nicolau. Thousands of Cubans, no matter what their political sentiments, were imprisoned in camps where the living conditions were deplorable, and many died. Pulitzer's *World* and Hearst's *Journal* were filled with graphic images of the suffering of the Cubans, and the result was a popular demand for the U.S. to intervene on the side of Cuba. In 1898 the *Journal* published a letter stolen from the Spanish minister in Washington, in which he referred to President McKinley as "weak and a popularity-hunter." The public were already inflamed by this incident when shortly after, on February 15, 1898, the U.S. battleship *Maine* was sunk in Havana harbor, killing 260 American seamen. Although it was never determined who was responsible for the explosion, the Yellow Press, particularly the *Journal*, set the blame squarely on Spain. "Remember the Maine, to hell with Spain!" became the rallying cry. On March 27 President McKinley issued an ultimatum to Spain, and on April 24 Spain declared war on the United States. There are many historians who are convinced that the ensuing Spanish-American War would never have occurred had it not been for the power of the Yellow Press.

The frenzied competition for readers finally died down, but we still use the term *yellow journalism* when we feel that the members of the news media are misrepresenting or distorting the facts in order to attract a greater share of readers, listeners, or viewers.

ABOUT THE AUTHOR

Dale Corey is a native of New York City who studied language and literature at New York University's Washington Square College and Graduate School of Arts and Science. Her first book, *From Achilles' Heel to Zeus's Shield*, was published in 1993 and is a lively, informative guide to more than 300 words and phrases that had their origins in mythology. She and her thirty-one cats now make their home in the foothills of the Adirondack Mountains.

BIBLIOGRAPHY

Anonymous. "Everyman" in *A Treasury of the Theatre, Vol. 1: World Drama From Aeschylus to Ostrovsky*. Gassner, John, ed. New York: Simon & Schuster, 1967.

Aesop. *Five Centuries of Illustrated Fables*. Selected by John J. McKendry. New York: The Metropolitan Museum of Art, 1964.

Alighieri, Dante. *The Divine Comedy of Dante Alighieri*. New York: The Modern Library, Random House, Inc., 1950.

Arabian Nights' Entertainments, The; or, The Thousand and One Nights. Translated from the Original Arabic, with notes explanatory of the text, by Edward William Lane. Philadelphia: David McKay, 1984.

Barrie, Sir James M. *The Plays of J. M. Barrie*. New York: Charles Scribner's Sons, 1956.

Baum, L. Frank. *The Annotated Wizard of Oz: The Wonderful Wizard of Oz by L. Frank Baum*. New York: Clarkson N. Potter, Inc., 1973.

Baum, L. Frank. *The Wizard of Oz*. New York: The Macmillan Company, 1962.

Benet's Reader's Encyclopedia, Third Edition. New York: HarperCollins, Inc., 1987.

Berkow, Robert, ed. *The Merck Manual of Diagnosis and Therapy*. Rahway: Merck Research Laboratories, 1992.

Boyce, Charles. *Shakespeare A to Z*. New York: Dell Publishing, 1990.

Brewer's Dictionary of Twentieth-Century Phrase and Fable. Boston: Houghton Mifflin Company, 1992.

Bunyan, John. *The Pilgrim's Progress*. New York: Great Illustrated Classics, Dodd, Mead & Company, 1968.

Byron, Lord George. *The Complete Poetical Works of Byron*. Boston: Cambridge Edition, Houghton Mifflin Company, 1933.

Caldwell, Erskine. *Tobacco Road*. New York: Grosset & Dunlap, 1932.

Carroll, Lewis. *Alice's Adventures in Wonderland & Through the Looking-Glass*. New York: The Macmillan Company, 1966.

Carson, Rachel. *Silent Spring*. Cambridge: The Riverside Press, 1962.

Casanova, Jacques. *The Memoirs of Jacques Casanova de Seingalt*. Trans. Arthur Machen. 6 vols. New York: G. P. Putnam's Sons, 1959–61.

Cervantes Saavedra, Miguel de. *The Adventures of Don Quixote*. Trans. J. M. Cohen. Baltimore: Penguin Books, 1968.

Cooper, James Fenimore. *The Last of the Mohicans: A Narrative of 1757*. Cleveland: The World Publishing Company, 1957.

Corliss, Richard. "Ringmaster and Clown." *Time* magazine, November 8, 1993.

Darwin, Charles. *The Origin of Species by Means of Natural Selection and The Descent of Man and Selection in Relation to Sex*. Chicago: Great Books of the Western World, Encyclopedia Britannica, Inc., 1952.

Defoe, Daniel. *Robinson Crusoe*. Garden City: Doubleday & Company, Inc., 1946.

Dibbley, Dale Corey. *From Achilles' Heel to Zeus's Shield*. New York: Ballantine Books, 1993.

Dickens, Charles. *Barnaby Rudge*. New York: Dodd, Mead & Company, 1944.

Dickens, Charles. *David Copperfield*. New York: Dodd, Mead & Company, 1943.

Dickens, Charles. *Little Dorrit*. London: Macmillan & Co., Ltd., 1953.

Dickens, Charles. *Martin Chuzzlewit*. London: Macmillan & Co. Ltd., 1954.

Dickens, Charles. *Oliver Twist*. New York: Books of Wonder, William Morrow and Company, 1994.

Dickens, Charles. *Our Mutual Friend*. New York: Dodd, Mead & Company, 1951.

Dickens, Charles. *The Posthumous Papers of the Pickwick Club*. New York: The Modern Library, Random House, Inc., 1943.

Dickens, Charles. *The Complete Works of Charles Dickens: Christmas Books, Great Expectations*. New York: The Kelmscott Society.

Doyle, Sir Arthur Conan. *The Complete Sherlock*

Holmes. Garden City: Doubleday & Company, Inc., 1960.

du Maurier, George. *Trilby*. New York: Everyman's Library, Dutton, 1969.

Dunn, Charles W., ed. *A Chaucer Reader: Selections from the Canterbury Tales*. New York: Harcourt, Brace & World, Inc., 1952.

Encyclopaedia Britannica. 24 vols. Chicago: Encyclopaedia Britannica, Inc., 1971.

Evans, Ivor H. *Brewer's Dictionary of Phrase and Fable, 14th Edition*. New York: HarperPerennial, 1991.

Farquhar, George. "The Beaux' Strategem" in *Twelve Famous Plays of the Restoration and Eighteenth Century*. New York: The Modern Library, Random House, Inc., 1933.

Flaubert, Gustave. *Madame Bovary*. New York: Random House, 1957.

Friedman, Meyer and Roy Rosenman. *Type A Behavior and Your Heart*. New York: Knopf, 1974.

Funk, Charles. *Thereby Hangs a Tale*. New York: Harper, 1950.

Goethe. *Faust Part I*. Baltimore: Penguin Books, 1962.

Gossett, Thomas F. *Uncle Tom's Cabin and American Culture*. Dallas: Southern Methodist University Press, 1985.

Hadas, Moses, ed. *The Complete Plays of Aristophanes*. New York: Bantam Books, 1962.

Hardwick, Michael and Mollie, comp. *The Charles*

Dickens Encyclopedia. New York: Charles Scribner's Sons, 1973.

Harris, Joel Chandler. *The Complete Tales of Uncle Remus*. New York: Houghton Mifflin, 1955.

Hawthorne, Hildegarde. *The Poet of Craigie House*. New York: D. Appleton-Century Company, 1936.

Heller, Joseph. *Catch-22*. New York: Simon & Schuster, 1961.

Hendrickson, Robert. *Human Words*. City: Chilton Book Company, 1972.

Henry, O. *The Complete Works of O. Henry*. 2 vols. Garden City: Doubleday & Company, Inc., 1953.

Hilton, James. *Lost Horizon*. New York: William Morrow & Company, 1957.

Hope, Laura Lee. *The Bobbsey Twins and the Talking Fox Mystery*. New York: Grosset & Dunlap, 1970.

Hope, Laura Lee. *The Mystery of the King's Puppet*. New York: Grosset & Dunlap, 1967.

Hope, Laura Lee. *The Bobbsey Twins of Lakeport*. New York: Grosset & Dunlap, 1960.

Huxley, Aldous. *Brave New World*. New York: Perennial Library, Harper & Row, 1989.

Irving, Washington. *Rip Van Winkle & The Legend of Sleepy Hollow*. Tarrytown: Sleepy Hollow Restorations, Inc., 1974.

Kafka, Franz. *The Trial*. New York: The Modern Library, Random House, Inc., 1956.

Keller, Charles, comp. *The Best of Rube Goldberg*. Englewood Cliffs: Prentice-Hall Inc., 1980.

Lang, Andrew. *Arabian Nights by Andrew Lang*. London: Longmans, Green and Co., 1951.

Langland, William. *The Vision of Piers Plowman*. New York: Sheed and Ward, 1945.

Lass, Abraham H., David Kiremidjian, and Ruth M. Goldstein. *The Facts on File Dictionary of Classical, Biblical, and Literary Allusions*. New York: Facts on File, 1987.

Lederer, William J. and Eugene Burdick. *The Ugly American*. New York: W. W. Norton & Company, Inc., 1958.

Lewis, Sinclair. *Babbitt*. New York: P. F. Collier & Son Corporation, 1922.

Longfellow, Henry Wadsworth, *The Poems of Longfellow*. New York: The Modern Library, Random House, Inc.

Machiavelli, Niccolo. "The Prince" in *Great Books of the Western World: Vol. 23*. Chicago: Encyclopaedia Britannica, Inc., 1952.

Macrone, Michael. *It's Greek to Me*. New York: HarperCollins, 1991.

Marlowe, Christopher. "Doctor Faustus" in *Four Great Elizabethan Plays*. New York: Bantam Books, 1960.

Melville, Herman. *Moby Dick*. New York: The Modern Library, Random House, Inc., 1950.

Metalious, Grace. *Peyton Place*.

More, Sir Thomas. *Utopia*. Ed. J. Churton Collins. London: Oxford University Press, 1964.

Morris, Desmond. *The Naked Ape*. New York: McGraw-Hill Book Company, 1967.

Mumford, Lewis. *The Story of Utopias*. New York: The Viking Press, Inc., 1962.

Murray, James A., et al., eds. *The Oxford English Dictionary: Being a Corrected Re-issue with an Introduction, Supplement, and Bibliography.* 13 vols. Oxford: Clarendon Press, 1961.

Nabokov, Vladimir. *Lolita.* New York: Berkley Medallion Books, 1971.

O'Sullivan, Judith. *The Great American Comic Strip: One Hundred Years of Cartoon Art.* Boston, Toronto, and London: A Bulfinch Press Book, Little, Brown and Company, 1990.

Opie, Iona and Peter. *The Classic Fairy Tales.* London: Oxford University Press, 1974.

Orwell, George. *Animal Farm.* New York: Signet Classic, Penguin Books.

Orwell, George. *1984.* New York: Signet Classic, Penguin Books.

Palgrave, F. T. *The Golden Treasury of the Best Songs & Lyrical Poems.* New York: The New American Library, 1961.

Peter, Dr. Laurence J. Raymond Hull. *The Peter Principle.* New York: William Morrow & Company, Inc., 1969.

Porter, Eleanor H. *Pollyanna.* The Colonial Press, C. H. Simonds & Co., 1913.

Pringle, David. *Imaginary People: A Who's Who of Modern Fictional Characters.* New York: World Almanac, 1987.

Rabelais, Francois. *The Portable Rabelais.* Trans. Samuel Putnam. New York: The Viking Press, 1946.

Remarque, Erich Maria. *All Quiet on the Western*

Front. New York: Little, Brown and Company, 1956.

Rowe, Nicholas. "The Fair Penitent" in *Plays of the Restoration and Eighteenth Century.* MacMillan, Douglas and Howard Mumford Jones, eds. New York: Henry Holt and Company, 1958.

Runyon, Damon. *Romance in the Roaring Forties and Other Stories.* New York: Beech Tree Books, William Morrow and Company, Inc., 1986.

Shakespeare, William. *The Complete Works.* Eds. Stanley Wells and Gary Taylor. New York: Clarendon Press, 1988.

Shelley, Mary. "Frankenstein; or, The Modern Prometheus" in *Three Gothic Novels.* Fairclough, Peter, ed. Harmondsworth: The Penguin English Library, Penguin Books, Ltd., 1970.

Sheridan, Robert. "The Rivals" in *Twelve Famous Plays of the Restoration and Eighteenth Century.* New York: The Modern Library, Random House, Inc., 1933.

Sheridan, Martin. *Classic Comics & their Creators: Life Stories of American Cartoonists from the Golden Age.* Arcadia: Post-Era Books, 1973.

Shivers, Alfred S., Ph.D. *The Life of Maxwell Anderson.* New York: Stein and Day, 1983.

Spenser, E. *The Faerie Queen.* 2 vols. London: Everyman's Library, 1962.

Stevenson, Robert Louis. *The Strange Case of Dr. Jekyll and Mr. Hyde and Other Famous Tales.* New York: Great Illustrated classics, Dodd, Mead & Company, 1961.

Stowe, Harriet Beecher. *Uncle Tom's Cabin*. New York: Signet Classic, Penguin Books, Inc., 1966.

Sundquist, Eric J., ed. *New Essays on Uncle Tom's Cabin*. Boston: Cambridge University Press, 1986.

Swasy, Alecia. *Soap Opera: The Inside Story of Procter & Gamble*. New York: Times Books, Random House, Inc., 1993.

Swift, Jonathan. *Gulliver's Travels*. New York: Washington Square Press, Inc., 1960.

Taylor, Deems. *A Pictorial History of the Movies*. New York: Simon & Schuster, 1943.

Tefertillar, Robert L. "Li'l Abner and Sadie Hawkins Day" in *Antiques & Collecting*, July, 1995. pp.42–44.

Thackeray, William Makepeace. *Vanity Fair: A Novel Without a Hero*. New York: Random House, Inc., 1958.

Toffler, Alvin. *Future Shock*. New York: Bantam Books, 1970.

Tomlin, E.W.F., ed. *Charles Dickens 1812–1870: A Centennial Volume*. New York: Simon & Schuster, 1969.

Toth, Emily. *Inside Peyton Place: The Life of Grace Metalious*. Garden City: Doubleday & Company, Inc., 1981.

Turgenev, Ivan. *Fathers and Sons*. New York: The New American Library of World Literature, Inc., 1961.

Voltaire. *Candide and Other Stories*. London: Oxford University Press, 1990.

Webber, Elizabeth and Feinsilber, Mike. *Grand Al-*

lusions: A Lively Guide to Those Expressions, Terms and References You Ought to Know But Might Not. Washington, D.C., Farragut Publishing Company, 1990.

Webster's Third New International Dictionary. 3 vols. Phillipine Islands: G. & C. Merriam Co., 1966.

White, David Manning and Abel, Robert H., eds. *The Funnies: An American Idiom.* London: The Free Press of Glencoe, Collier-Macmillan Ltd., 1963

Wilde, Oscar. *The Picture of Dorian Gray and Selected Stories.* New York: The New American Library of World Literature, Inc., 1962.

Word Mysteries & Histories. By the Editors of The American Heritage Dictionaries. Boston: Houghton Mifflin Company, 1986.